BY COLIN FLETCHER

The Complete Walker
The Man Who Walked Through Time
The Thousand-Mile Summer

THE COMPLETE WALKER

THE
Complete
WALKER

The joys and techniques
of hiking and backpacking

COLIN FLETCHER

illustrations by VANNA FRANKS

ALFRED · A · KNOPF

New York · 1971

This is a Borzoi Book

Published by Alfred A. Knopf, Inc.

Published November 22, 1968
Reprinted Nine Times
Eleventh Printing June 1971
Copyright © 1968 by Colin Fletcher

Library of Congress Catalog Card Number: 68–23956

Manufactured in the United States of America

ACKNOWLEDGMENTS

Several fibers woven into this book have been plucked from *The Thousand-Mile Summer,* published by Howell-North Books, Berkeley, California, and *The Man Who Walked Through Time,* published by Alfred A. Knopf. To protect readers of these earlier books from echo trouble, I have identified the rare passages in which I found it necessary to reuse any lengths of fabric.

A few strands also come from articles of mine that have appeared in *Field & Stream, Sports Afield, Reader's Digest,* and the San Francisco *Chronicle,* and I wish to thank their publishers for permission to rework the material.

C.F.

TO MY MOTHER
who understood that walking for fun
is no crazier than most things in life,
and who passed the information along.

Now shall I walk
Or shall I ride?
"Ride," Pleasure said;
"Walk," Joy replied.

       W. H. Davies

Contents

THE COMPLETE WALKER

WHY WALK?

Sanity is a madness put to good uses.
George Santayana

I had better admit right away that walking can in the end become an addiction, and that it is then as deadly in its fashion as heroin or television or the stock exchange. But even in this final stage it remains a quite delectable madness, very good for sanity, and I recommend it with passion.

A redeeming feature of the condition is that no matter how heavily you have been hooked you can still get your kicks from very small doses.

Ten minutes' drive from my apartment there is a long, grassy ridge from which you can look out over parkland and sprawling metropolis, over bay and ocean and distant mountains. I often walk along this ridge in order to think uncluttered thoughts or to feel with accuracy or to sweat away a hangover or to achieve some other worthy end, recognized or submerged. And I usually succeed—especially with the thinking. Up there, alone with the wind and the sky and the steep grassy slopes, I nearly always find after a while that I am beginning to think more clearly. Yet "think" does not

3

seem to be quite the right word. Sometimes, when it is a matter of making a choice, I do not believe I decide what to do so much as discover what I have decided. It is as if my mind, set free by space and solitude and oiled by the body's easy rhythm, swings open and releases thoughts it has already formulated. Sometimes, when I have been straining too hard to impose order on an urgent press of ideas, it seems only as if my mind has slowly relaxed; and then, all at once, there is room for the ideas to fall into place in a meaningful pattern.

Once in a while you can achieve this kind of release inside a city. Just the other day, when I had to leave my car at a garage for an hour's repair work, I spent the time strolling through an industrial area. I crossed a man-made wasteland, then walked up onto a little-used pedestrian bridge over a freeway. For a while I leaned on the concrete parapet and watched the lines of racing, pounding vehicles. From above they seemed self-propelled, automatic. And suddenly, standing there alone, I found myself looking down on the scene like a visitor from another planet, curiously detached and newly instructed.

But no one who has begun to acquire the walking habit can restrict himself for very long to cities, or even to their parks. First he explores open spaces out beyond the asphalt. Then, perhaps, he moves on to car camping and makes long all-day treks, out and away. But in due course he is almost sure to start dreaming of the truly wild places, far from any road. And at this point he is in danger of coming up against a mental block.

Even in these mercifully emancipated decades, many people still seem quite seriously alarmed at the prospect of sleeping away from officially consecrated campsites, with no more equipment than they can carry on their backs. When pressed, they babble about snakes or bears or even, by God, bandits. But the real barrier, I'm sure, is the unknown.

I only came to comprehend the reality of this barrier quite recently. To be more exact, I re-comprehended it. I was taking a four-day walk over some coastal hills. (I was taking it, as a matter of fact, in order to sort out ideas and directions for this book.) One warm and cloudless afternoon I was resting at a bend in the trail—

there was a little triangular patch of shade, I remember, under a rocky bluff—when some unexpected tilt of my mind re-exposed a scene that I had completely forgotten.

For all the vividness of the vital features, it is a curiously indistinct scene. I am not at all clear when it happened, except that it must have been more than ten years ago. I do not even remember for sure whether it happened in Africa or in North America. But the salient contours stand out boldly. I had come to some natural boundary. It may have been the end of a trail or road, or the fringes of a forest or the rim of a cliff, I no longer know which. But I do know that I felt I had gone as far as a man could go. So I just stood there looking out beyond the edge of the world. Except for a wall of thick, dark undergrowth, I am no longer sure what I saw, but I know it was wild, wild, impossible country. It still looms huge and black and mysterious in the vaults of my memory.

All at once, quite without warning, two men emerged from that impossible country. They carried packs on their backs, and they were weatherbeaten and distilled to bone and muscle. But what I remember best of all is that they were happy and whole. Whole and secure and content.

I talked to them, quite briefly and in considerable awe. They had been back deep into the wilderness, they said, away from civilization for a week. "Pretty inaccessible, some of it," admitted one of them. "But there's a lot of beautiful country in there—some of the finest I've ever seen." And then they walked away and I was left, still awestruck, looking out once more into the huge, black, mysterious wilderness.

The awe that I felt that day still hangs in my memory. But my present self dismisses it. I know better. For many times in recent years I have emerged from wild country, happy and whole and secure and content, and have found myself face to face with astonished people who had obviously felt that they were already at the edge of the world. And I know, now I have come to consider the matter, that what I have seen on their faces is exactly what those two men must have seen on mine, many years ago on the edge of that other wilderness. And I know now that the awe is quite unwarranted.

There is nothing very difficult about going into such places. All you need is the right equipment, a reasonable competence in using it, a tolerable degree of physical fitness, and a clear understanding of your own limitations. Beyond that, all you have to do is overcome the fear of the unknown.*

Once you have overcome the fear of the unknown and thereby surmounted your sleeping-out-in-the-wilderness block, you are free. Free to go out, when the world will let you slip away, into the wildest places you dare explore. Free to walk from dawn to dusk and then again from dawn to dusk, with no harsh interruptions, among the quiet and soothing cathedrals of a virgin forest. Or free to struggle for a week, if that is what you want at that particular time, toward a peak that has captured your imagination. Or free, if your needs or fancies of the moment run that way, to follow a wild river to its source, fishing as you go, or not fishing. Free, once you have grasped the significance of this other reality, to immerse yourself for two months in the timeless silence of a huge desert canyon—and to discover in the end why the silence is not timeless after all.

But long before the madness has taught you this kind of sanity you have learned many simple and valuable things.

You start to learn them from the very beginning. First, the comforting constants. The rhythm of boots and walking staff, and their different inflections on sand and on soil and on rock. The creak of leather harness as small knapsack or heavy pack settles back into

---

* You will see that I tend to write of walking as if it is something that must be done alone. Most people prefer company, and by all reasonable standards they are right. For efficiency and comfort and the rewards of sharing, and above all for safety, a walking party, like a political party, should consist of at least two or three members.

But I like to walk alone. And therefore, when I am being honest, that is how I tend to write. It does not matter, though: if you choose, sensibly, to travel in twos or threes or twenties, just about everything I have to say still applies. You miss something, that's all. You never quite learn for instance that one of the riches a wilderness has to offer is prolonged and absolute silence.

There is one notable exception to my rule. When you and your companion are newly in love, the two of you walk with minds interwoven, and the bond enriches everything you see. And that is the best walking of all.

place after a halt. And the satisfactions of a taut, controlled body. Then there are the small, amplified pleasures. In everyday life, taking off your socks is an unnoticed chore; peeling them off after a long day's walk is sheer delight. At home, a fly is something that makes you wonder how it got into the house; when you are lying sprawled out on a sandbar beside a remote river you can recognize a fly as something to be studied and learned from—another filament in the intricate web of the world. Or it may be a matter of mere money: five days beyond the last stain of man, you open the precious little package of blister-cushioning felt pads that is marked "45¢" and discover, tucked away inside, a forgotten and singularly useless five-dollar bill. Yet two days later you may find your appetite suddenly sharp for civilized comforts that a week earlier had grown flat and stale. Quite recently, toward the end of a week's exploration of a remote headwater basin, I found my heart melting at the thought of hot buttered toast for breakfast. And once, in the final week of a summer-long walk, I even found myself recalling with nostalgia the eternal city hunt for parking.

But long before such unexpected hankerings arise, your mind as well as your body has been honed. You have re-remembered that happiness has something to do with simplicity. And so, by slow degrees, you regain a sense of harmony with everything you move through—rock and soil, plant and tree and cactus, spider and fly and rattlesnake and coyote, drop of rain and racing cloud shadow. (You have long ago outgrown the crass assumption that the world was made for man.) After a while you find that you are gathering together the whole untidy but glorious mishmash of sights and sounds and smells and touches and tastes and emotions that tumble through your recent memory. Then you begin to connect these ciphers, one with the other. And once you begin to connect, only to connect, nothing can stop you—not even those rare moments of blackness (when all, all is vanity) that can come even in the wilderness.

When you get back at last from the simple things to the complexities of the outside world, you find that you are once more eager to grapple with them. For a while you even detect a meaning behind all the complexity. And that of course is the way it has to be. We are creatures of our time; we cannot escape it. The simple life is not a substitute, only a corrective.

For a while, I said, you detect new meanings. For a little while. That is where the hell comes in. In due course the hot buttered toast tastes like damp sawdust again and the parking hassle is once more driving you crazy and the concrete jabs at your eyes and the din and the dirt sicken you, and all at once you realize that there is no sense to be discovered, anywhere, in all the frantic scurryings of the city. And you know there is only one thing to do. You are helplessly trapped. Hooked. Because you know now that you have to go back to the simple things.

You struggle, briefly. But as soon as the world will let you slip away, or a little sooner, you go. You go in misery, with delight, full of confidence. For you know that you will immerse yourself in the harmonies—and will return to see the meanings.

That is why, on balance, I can recommend walking with passion. It is an altogether delectable addiction. Sometimes nowadays I find myself wondering what in God's name I would have done with my life if I had failed to fall an early victim.

Naturally, not everyone understands.

At a cocktail party some time ago, a smooth and hyper-satisfied young man boasted to me that he had just completed a round-the-world sightseeing tour in seventy-nine days. In one jet-streamed breath he scuttled from St. Peter's, Rome, via the Pyramids, to a Cambodian jungle temple. "That's the way to travel," he said. "You see everything important."

When I suggested that the way to see important things was to walk, he almost dropped his martini.

Walking can even provoke an active opposition lobby. For many years now I have been told with some regularity that by walking out and away I am "escaping from reality." I admit that the question puts me on the defensive. Why, I ask myself (and sometimes my accusers as well) are people so ready to assume that chilled champagne is more "real" than water drawn from an ice-cold mountain creek? Or a dusty sidewalk than a carpet of desert dandelions? Or a Boeing 707 than a flight of graceful white pelicans soaring in unison against the sunrise? Why, in other words, do people assume that the acts and emotions and values that stem from city life are more real than those that arise from the beauty and the silence and the solitude of wilderness?

A couple of years ago the thing touched bottom: I was gently accused of escapism during a TV interview about a book I had written on a length-of-California walk. Frankly, I fail to see how going for a six-month, thousand-mile walk through deserts and mountains can be judged less real than spending six months working eight hours a day, five days a week, in order to earn enough money to be able to come back to a comfortable home in the evening and sit in front of a TV screen and watch the two-dimensional image of some guy talking about a book he has written on a six-month, thousand-mile walk through deserts and mountains.

As I said, I get put on the defensive. The last thing I want to do is to knock champagne and sidewalks and Boeing 707's. Especially champagne. These things distinguish us from the other animals. But they can also limit our perspectives. And I suggest that they—and all the stimulating complexities of modern life—begin to make more sense, to take on surer meaning, when they are viewed in perspective against the more certain and more lasting reality from which they have evolved—from the underpinning reality, that is, of mountain water and desert flowers and soaring white birds at sunrise.

Here endeth the lesson.

But perhaps you are an unbeliever and need proof—a no-nonsense, show-me-some-practical-results kind of proof.

I can tell you now that I have had an unholy awful time with this introductory chapter. I wrote it a dozen times, over a period of several months, and a dozen times it utterly refused to say what I wanted it to say. In the end I drove an hour out of town, parked the car on a dirt road, heaved the pack onto my back, walked for another hour, and then camped on the flat, grassy summit of a hill that I know quite well. That was two evenings ago. I am still there. In front of me the long grass is billowing like the sea. Far beyond it and far below sprawls the city. It is very gray. But here on my hilltop there is only the grass and the wind and the sky.

From time to time since I climbed up here I have strolled around my domain. Once, I went down a few hundred feet with the pack on my back and filled all four canteens at a spring. But mostly I have sat up here in the shade of my poncho awning. I have looked at the billowing grass. I have looked beyond it at the sprawling gray city and have listened to the roar from a freeway that feeds it. I have consulted with a number of hawks, mice, beetles, and trees. And this morning—after two nights and one day of bitter, bitter struggle and many, many words—I suddenly relaxed and began to write. I do not say that I am yet satisfied with what I have written. But I think it will do. And I guess that if you have come this far you must think so too.

Words of warning

I am down off my hilltop now, but before we move on to consider the ways and means of walking I must point out two pitfalls that you should bear in mind—always—or as always as you can manage.

First, make sure the ways and means remain just that. They will always be threatening to take over. They will tend, particularly at the start of a trip, to imprison your thoughts on a treadmill of trivial worries: "Is that a blister forming on my right heel?"; "If the storm breaks, will that little tarp really keep me dry all night?"; "My God, is the water going to last out?" And any sudden small problem is liable to inflate without warning and fill the horizons of your tight little world. It all sounds very silly, I know; but anyone who has traveled on foot, especially alone, will recognize the syndrome. I should like to report that experience cures such nonsense. Unfortunately, it doesn't. It helps; it helps a lot. But I still find, especially on long trips with a sharp physical challenge that I need at least a few days of "shakedown cruise." On a two-month journey I made some time ago through Grand Canyon, it took me all of two weeks to break free.

Whether you like it or not, the trivia are always there. And never underrate them; either you subdue them or they subdue you. A single blister can blacken the most shining day. And if you are miles from anywhere, soaked through and shivering and with no confidence in your ability to contrive a warm, dry shelter for the night, you will be deaf to the music of raindrops drumming against your poncho and blind to the beauty of clouds swirling around sawtooth peaks.

The important thing, then, about running your tight little outdoor economy is that it must not run you. You must learn to deal with the practical details so efficiently that they become second nature. Then, after the unavoidable shakedown period, you leave yourself free to get on with the important things—watching cloud shadows race across a mountainside or passing the time of day with a hummingbird or discovering that a grasshopper eats grass like spaghetti or sitting on a peak and thinking of nothing at all except perhaps that it is a wonderful thing to sit on a peak and think of nothing at all.*

The second pitfall is more subtly camouflaged. Naturally, your opinions on equipment and technique must never fossilize into dogma: your mind must remain wide open to the possibilities of better gear and to new and easier ways of doing things. You try to strike a balance, of course—to operate efficiently and yet to remember, always, that the practical details are only a means to an end. But I am not altogether convinced that after years and years of it—when you have at last succeeded in mastering most of the business and people have begun to call you an expert and someone may even ask you to write a book on the subject—I am not at all sure that it is then possible to avoid the sobering discovery that you have become, ex officio, a very tolerably accomplished fuddy-duddy.

---

* It would probably be a good thing if you reread this paragraph at least once—and tried to remember it later on. This is essentially a "know-how" book, but we must never lose sight of the fact that what matters in the end is the "feel-how" of walking.

HOUSE ON YOUR BACK

Ground Plan

As long as you restrict your walking to one-day hikes, you are un-likely to face any very ponderous problems of equipment or tech-nique. Everything you need can be stuffed into pockets or if neces-sary into a convenient little pouch slung from waist or shoulders. And if something should get left behind, why, home is always wait-ing at the end of the day's road. But as soon as you start sleeping out you simply have to carry some kind of

A house on your back.

Obviously, there is an appreciable difference between the kind of house you need to carry for a soft, summer weekend in the woods and for a month or more in wild mountain country. But it is extremely convenient and entirely possible to devise a standard structure that you can modify to suit a broad range of conditions. In this book I shall describe in detail the fairly full-scale edifice, very simply modifiable, that I have evolved over a considerable number of years. If some of the architecture seems too elaborate for your purposes, all you have to do is simplify.

Similarly, I shall discuss most techniques as they apply to trips of at least a weekend. Often I will talk in terms of more ambitious journeys. Again, if my suggestions seem too elaborate for what you have in mind, just simplify.

I make no apologies for writing a highly subjective book—a book that will give many experienced walkers a whole slew of satisfying chances to snort with disagreement. For backpacking is a highly subjective business. What matters to me is what suits me; and what matters to you is what suits you. So when I describe what I have found best, try to remember that I am really saying that there are no truly objective criteria, and the important thing in the end is not what I or some other so-called expert happens to use or do, but what *you* find best. Even prejudice has its place: a technique or piece of equipment that you have devised yourself is much more satisfying to use than an "import"—and in your hands it may well prove more efficient. The most a book can do, then, is to suggest guidelines.*

Guidelines are all I can offer for another reason too. Backpacking is at the moment in a stimulating if mildly confusing state of evolution—or perhaps I mean revolution—in both design and materials. Plastics in particular seem to change with every tide. And, at least on the West Coast of the United States, a new retail outlet seems to spring up every other month. This is a healthy development. We have a wider choice, and the competition compels makers to produce better merchandise. I understand that such a state of affairs is known as capitalism.

All this means that some of my solemn advice will soon be outmoded. But it does not matter. Although I shall often be describing specific items, the essence will lie not so much in the items themselves as in the governing principles—in the vital factors an intelligent backpacker should keep his eyes skinned for.

---

* Frankly, my advice to those genuinely interested in walking has always been to forget the books and to get out and get on with it, and I'm not at all sure a piece of me doesn't stand by that advice now.

Custom suggests that I avoid trade names. But only by discussing brands and models can I adequately indicate the details. And if I recommend one brand of soup over another it is because I find it suits my needs better, not because, for crying out loud, I adore Mr. Maggi and deplore Mr. Knorr.

It should be borne in mind, though, that geography often plays a part in my own choices. You will find that a lot of my equipment is made by Trailwise of Berkeley, California. Now I consider their products to be excellent. But the fact remains that I live a dozen blocks from the Ski Hut, makers of Trailwise equipment. And the fact is obviously relevant. If you live in Centralia, Illinois, your druthers may be different. But the fact also remains that Ski Hut-Trailwise are the makers-retailers who perhaps offer the fullest range of backpacking equipment—though one must not forget Gerry Mountain Sports, with headquarters in Denver, Colorado; the Alpine Hut, centered in Seattle, Washington; or Holubar of Boulder, Colorado. All these firms maintain countrywide mail-order services. So do many firms that are primarily or exclusively retailers. Of these, Recreational Equipment Incorporated—a cooperative enterprise of Seattle, Washington, that sells many items at highly competitive prices—offers a range as full as the Ski Hut's. Other catalogues with a wide selection come from Eastern Mountain Sports of Boston, Sport Chalet of La Canada, California, and The Smilie Company of San Francisco. Many others firms carry a fairly full range of equipment, and some of these specialize in certain products and have established themselves as close to undisputed leaders in their field of specialization. Two names that spring to mind are A. I. Kelty of Glendale, California, for packs and L. L. Bean of Freeport, Maine, for "Maine Hunting Boots" (see page 29). When it comes to tents and down clothing and sleeping bags, no one offers finer workmanship than the new and fast-growing firms of Sierra Designs (Point Richmond, California) and Alp Sport (Boulder, Colorado). A new and possibly pregnant addition is Frostline Outdoor Equipment, also of Boulder, who offer premarked do-it-yourself kits of what is apparently good-quality lightweight equipment: tents, sleeping bags, and down-filled and other clothing.

Appendix II (page 329) is a list of retailers throughout the United States and Canada who specialize or deal exclusively in backpacking equipment and maintain countrywide mail-order services. The list is as complete and current as I can make it. But I repeat that the whole field is in a state of flux. Every month brings new expansions, reorganizations, and mergers—or at least rumors of them. So please treat my list as a guide, not a gospel.

When planning the house on your back, the weightiest matter is

Weight.

The rules are simple:
1. If you need something, take it.
2. Pare away relentlessly at the weight of every item.

In paring away you will find that if you look after the ounces the pounds will look after themselves. Any good sports store that specializes in backpacking equipment will list in its catalogue the weight of each article to the nearest ounce, and will also keep an accurate arm scale handy. When shopping in other stores I often take along a postal scale and weigh every item like gold dust. I still like to remember the bewilderment of one sales damsel when I produced my scale and insisted on comparing the weights of two rival pairs of jockey shorts.

I find that the paring process never ends. At home, such foods as raisins that come in cardboard containers get repacked in plastic bags. At the start of a trip, margins and unneeded areas are trimmed off maps. And when I'm laboring along under a knee-buckling load I'm never really happy until I've eliminated the last eliminable fraction of an ounce. Once or twice, in really phrenetic moments, I've even found myself tearing the labels off tea bags.

Unfortunately it seems impossible to predict just what your load will be for a given trip. No matter how carefully you plan, you have to wait for an answer until you hoist the fully-furnished pack onto your back on the first day. The only thing you can be sure of is that it will weigh more than you had hoped. If you want a meaningful figure, don't rely on the way the pack feels; get it onto a trustworthy scale. And memorize the reading. When it comes to talking about the loads they carry, lamentably few backpackers seem to restrict themselves to confirmed, objective, unembroidered fact.

Men (or women),* such as Himalayan Sherpas, who have toted huge loads all their lives, can carry almost their own weight all day long. And even a halfway-fit, fully citified man can pack very heavy loads for short distances, such as canoe portages. Again, people whom I trust implicitly talk of having to carry eighty or one hundred pounds or even more on slow and painful approach marches of five or ten miles at the start of mountain-climbing expeditions. But this kind of toil is hardly walking, in our sense. The heaviest load the average man can carry with efficiency and enjoyment for a long day's walking seems to vary within rather wide limits, but a rough guide would be "up to one third of body weight." Naturally, this figure assumes an efficient pack frame and a reasonably fit and practiced body. Practiced, mark you. The only way of getting used to heavy loads is to pack heavy loads.

One of the few occasions on which I have weighed my pack, operationally stocked, was at the start of the two-month journey I made through Grand Canyon. Then, with a week's food supply and two gallons of water, the pack turned the scale at 66½ pounds. At the time I weighed 194 rather flabby pounds (twenty more than I did at the end) and the load felt appallingly heavy. But the start is always the worst of it. Each day you use up not only food but also such items as stove fuel and toilet paper. And beyond each refill point the water diminishes steadily, hour by hour. By the end of my first week in Grand Canyon, when I took an airdrop of food beside a big rainpocket in the rock, my pack must have weighed less than thirty pounds. And that made a tremendous difference.

It always does. People often say, "I guess you get so used to the pack that after a while it doesn't worry you any more." But only when the load falls below forty pounds can I sometimes forget it. At fifty I can't. At sixty it always feels desperately heavy. At 66½ it just

* Everything I have to say in this book about men applies equally to women. Well, almost everything. And almost equally.

about takes the joy out of walking. And short sidetrips with no load on my back are always like running into the sea after a hot and bothersome day in the city.

Cost

The only really satisfactory way to approach the price problem is to ignore it. Good equipment always seems expensive, but whenever you find yourself in a store scowling at a price tag, try to remember that out in the wilds, where money becomes utterly meaningless, the failure of a single item can easily ruin a trip. It may even endanger your life.

"Ignore the cost" is easier said than done, of course (though I should like to add, at the risk of sounding smug, that I am perfectly content to drive to the mountains in my reliable nineteen-year-old Plymouth but would not think of walking away from it with any equipment in my pack that fell short of the best available). In the end, naturally, everyone has to establish his own standards, with due consideration for other responsibilities. But when it comes to such critical items as sleeping bags the only safe rule is to buy the best you can afford—and then another grade better.

I have indicated in this book a price for almost every article I mention. Generally speaking, the figures represent a fairly high West Coast average for 1968.

Renting

If you live near a good camp-equipment store you may be able to rent certain items, such as packs and tents (and perhaps ice axes and crampons—though when you start using such gear you're perilously close to the limit of what can reasonably be called "walking"). It is possible, but unlikely, that you will also be able to rent boots and sleeping bags.

Renting is well worth consideration if you want a tent, say, for only one week in the year. It is also a useful way of testing equipment. It makes every kind of sense to rent for a trial run a tent or pack of a kind you are thinking of buying outright. Sample rental rates: Two-man tent: $5 a weekend; $18 for two weeks. Pack: $3 a weekend; $9 for two weeks.

It would probably be a good thing to take a brief look, here, at the general considerations to be borne in mind when deciding on

EQUIPMENT FOR A SPECIFIC TRIP.

Most decisions about what to take and what to leave behind will depend on the answers you get in the early stages of planning when you ask yourself "Where?" and "When?" and

"For how long?"

The length of the trip makes rather less difference than many people imagine. The amount of food you can carry is what mostly determines how long you can operate without some kind of outside help, and even on long journeys I normally plan once-a-week replenishments. Occasionally I travel self-contained for ten days, and I suppose I could if necessary stretch it to two weeks. But even on my rather Spartan menu I would have to carry more than thirty pounds in food alone, and with all the other gear that normally has to come along—not to mention water in some kinds of country—that would mean a prohibitively heavy load. (For replenishment methods—by outposts of civilization, caches, airdrops, etc.—see pages 285–94.)

As far as equipment is concerned, then, even a very long journey boils down in essentials to a string of one- or two-week trips. Besides replenishable items, all you have to decide is whether you'll be aching too badly before the end for a few extra comforts. A paperback book, a toothbrush, and even camp footwear may be luxuries on a weekend outing, but I imagine that most people would think twice about going out for two weeks without them.

What does make a difference is that the longer the trip the greater the uncertainties about weather; but here we begin to ease over into

"Where?" and "When?"

The two questions are essentially inseparable. Terrain, considered apart from its weather, makes surprisingly little difference to what you need carry. The prospect of sleeping on rock or of crossing a big river may prompt you to take an air mattress, as opposed to an Ensolite pad for snow, or nothing at all for sand (see pages 169–76). In cliff country you may elect to take along a climbing rope, even when on your own (page 254). Glaciers or hard snow may suggest crampons. But that is about all. And snow and ice, in any case, come very close to being "weather."

In the end it is weather that governs most of the decisions about clothing and shelter. And weather is not simply a matter of asking "where?" and answering "desert," "rainforest," or "alpine meadows." You must immediately ask "when?" And from the answer you must be able to draw accurate conclusions.

In almost any kind of country, the gulf between June and January is so obvious that your planning allows for it automatically. But the difference between, say, September and October is not always so clear—and it may matter a lot. The most convenient source of accurate information that I know is the series of booklets issued by the U.S. Weather Bureau under the title *Climatic Survey of the United States—Supplement for 1931 through 1952*. Each booklet covers one state (exceptions: one booklet each for New England, Maryland–Delaware, and Puerto Rico–Virgin Islands). For every weather station with records for more than five years, the summaries list monthly figures for total precipitation, snowfall, and temperature (mean, mean maximum, mean minimum, highest, and lowest). Where records exist prior to 1931, averages are given. An index locates each station on a sketch map and gives its latitude and longitude and elevation. These booklets are available, at prices ranging from twenty to seventy cents according to the state or region, from the Superintendent of Documents, U.S. Government Printing Office, Washington, D.C. 20402.

Recently, a new and similar series has appeared, for the years 1951–60. I have not yet seen any of the new booklets, but coverage is apparently the same, except that the West Indies are now included in the Puerto Rico–Virgin Isles section. Costs are now twenty-five cents to $1.

In Canada, the equivalent is a series of mimeographed sheets, two for each province, titled "Precipitation Normals for British Columbia" (or wherever) and "Temperature Normals for British Columbia" (or, again, wherever) (ten cents per sheet). Unfortunately, the temperature sheets give only the monthly and annual normals of mean daily maximum, mean daily minimum, and mean daily temperatures. Highest and lowest readings are omitted—and they are vital. No map is included either, nor even the stations' latitude and longitude. But all this information, plus a mountain more, is given for much of the country in two sizable booklets called *The Climate of Central Canada* and *The Climate of British Columbia and the Yukon Territory.* ($1.30 each.) All these publications are obtainable, remittance payable with order, from The Director, Meteorological Branch, Department of Transport, 315 Bloor Street West, Toronto 5, Ontario.

Monthly figures can never tell the whole story, but these booklets (or at least the U.S. ones, which I use regularly) can be a great help in planning a trip. In deciding what night shelter you need, it may be critical to know that the lowland valley you intend to wander through averages only 0.10 inches of rain in September (twenty-year high: 0.95 inches), but 1.40 inches in October (high: 6.04 inches). And decisions about what sleeping bag and clothing to take on a mountain trip will come more easily once you know that a weather station 8,390 feet above sea level on the eastern escarpment of the 14,000-foot range you want to explore has over the past thirty years averaged a mean daily minimum of 39°F. in September (record low 19°) but 31° in October (low, 9°); by applying the rough but fairly serviceable rule that "temperature falls three degrees for every 1,000-foot elevation increase," you can make an educated guess at how cold the nights are going to be up near the peaks. Remember, though, that weather is much more than just temperature. See page 183.

A wise precaution before any trip that will last a weekend or longer is to check on the five-day forecast for the area. The weather-man at my nearest international airport is always amiable, often right. A similar public service is available in many areas. Look in the telephone book under "U.S. Government, Department of Commerce, Weather Bureau, Public Weather Service."

But the finest insurance of all is to have the right friends. Or, to be more exact, the right friend. I have one who is not only a geographer with a passion for weather lore but a walking computer programed with weather statistics for all the western United States and half the rest of the world. I phone him before I go anywhere. "The Palisades in early September?" he says. "Even close to the peaks you shouldn't get night temperatures much below twenty. And you could hardly choose a time of year with less danger of a storm. The first heavy ones don't usually hit until early November, though in 1959 they had a bad one in mid-September. Keep an eye on the wind, that's all. If you get a strong or moderate wind from the south, be on the lookout for trouble." By the time he has finished, I am all primed and ready to go.

Unless you have the only infallible memory on record, you ought to have a couple of copies of a

Check list of gear.

It should be a full list, covering all kinds of trips, in all kinds of terrain, at all times of year. On any particular occasion, you just ignore what you don't want to take along.

Eventually, everyone should evolve his own list. But many local and national hiking organizations (see Appendix III) are happy to supply beginners with suggestions. So are some commercial firms, such as Kelty Packs and Camp Trails of Phoenix, Arizona (see Appendix II)—but don't be misled by some of the skimpier lists into imagining that you can really get away in comfort and safety with ultra-light loads. Appendix I of this book (page 325) is a very full list that might be a useful starter. But as soon as experience permits, draft your own list.

I'm afraid I have no advice to offer on what to do when you lose your list—especially if, as will very likely happen, you simply can't lay hands on the spare copy you filed away in an infallibly safe place.

There is one question that seems to haunt almost all inexperienced hikers when they are planning a trip:

"How far can I expect to walk in a day?"

For most kinds of walking, the question is wrongly put. Except along flat, straight roads, miles are just about meaningless. Hours are what count.

Naturally, there is a connection—of sorts. I have only once checked my speed with any accuracy, and that was more or less by accident. It was during my summer-long walk up California. One afternoon I followed the Atchison, Topeka and Santa Fe for nine arrow-like miles into the desert town of Needles. It so happened that I began at a mileage post and I checked the time and jotted it down on my map. I traveled at my normal speed, and I recall no difficulty about stepping on ties (as so often happens when you follow a railroad track), so it must have been straightforward walking on a well-banked grade. I took a ten-minute halt at the end of the first hour; and exactly one hour and fifty-five minutes after starting I passed the six-mile mark. I would guess that this three-miles-per-roughly-fifty-minutes-of-actual-walking is about my norm on a good level surface with a pack that weighs, as mine probably did that day, around forty pounds. In other words, seven hours of *actual walking* are roughly the equivalent of a twenty-mile day on the flat, under easy walking conditions.

But cross-country you will rarely come close to twenty genuine miles in seven hours. Even on good trails, two miles an hour is probably good going. Over really rough country the average can fall below half a mile. The nonsense that hikers commonly talk about mountain miles walked in one day is only equaled, I think, by the drivel they talk about loads.

But if you now ask the amended question, "How many hours

can I expect to walk in a day?" it remains difficult to give a straight-forward answer. The thing is seamed with variables. On any given day—provided you are well rested and not concerned with how you will feel next morning—you can, if you are fit and very powerfully motivated, probably keep going most of the twenty-four. But what really matters in most cases is what you are likely to keep up, fully laden, day after day. Even a rough estimate of this figure demands not so much a grasp of arithmetic as an understanding of human frailty. I have published elsewhere a table representing a typical day's walking on the desert half of my California trip—a day on which, beset with all the normal and quite fascinating temptations of walking, I pushed tolerably hard, though not even close to my limit. Mildly amended to fit more general conditions, the table may help to explain the difficulties of computation:

	Hours	Minutes
Walking, including ten-minute halts every hour	7	
Extension of half the ten-minute halts to twenty minutes because of sights, sounds, smells, ruminations, and inertia		30
Compulsive dallying for photography and general admiration of the passing scene—4²⁄₇ minutes in every hour		30
Photography, once a day, of a difficult and utterly irresistible object (this will seem a gross overestimate to non-photographers, an absurd underestimate to the initiated)	1	
Conversations with mountain men, desert rats, eager beavers, or even bighorn sheep	1	
Cooking and eating four meals, including tea	3	30
Camp chores		30
Orthodox business of wilderness traveler: rapt contemplation of nature and/or navel		30
Evaporated time, quite unaccountable for		30
Sleep, including catnaps	8	59
Reading, fishing, additional rest, elevated thinking, unmentionable items, and general sloth		1
Total	24	

Always, before you walk out into any kind of country, whether for a few hours or for several weeks,

Let some responsible person know where you're going and when you'll be back.

This registration should be automatic. It is not merely a question of your own safety. If you do not return, someone will eventually come out to look for you; and if they have nothing to go on except the place your car was parked and perhaps the vague recollections of someone you happened to chat with, they will waste a great deal of time searching in useless places. And men may expose themselves to quite unnecessary dangers—on the ground and in the air.

In national or state parks and forests, leave full information with a ranger. In other places, cast about until you find someone that strikes you as thoroughly reliable (your life may depend on his reliability). If possible, leave a map marked with your proposed route. Above all, state a date and hour by which you will return—or will emerge elsewhere and immediately check back by phone. Let it be clearly understood that if you have not reported back by the time specified, then you are in trouble. In fixing the deadline, allow yourself a little leeway. And, once you've fixed it, make hell-and-high-water sure you meet it. I repeat: make hell-and-high-water sure you meet it.

Foundations

The foundations of the house on your back are your feet and their footwear, and the cornerstone is a good pair of

BOOTS.

One pair of boots should be enough to fill anyone's normal walking needs. But they must be carefully chosen.

First, they must be stout enough to protect and support your feet with the heaviest load you expect to carry. Your feet are used to supporting your full bodyweight, and provided you do not add much to it they will, once hardened by practice, carry you comfortably over long distances even on thin soles and uppers. Soles for this unladen kind of walking, though they must be stouter than those of city shoes, need be no more than $\frac{5}{16}$ inch thick. The uppers can be thin leather or even suede. For my money, the uppers should protect and support the ankles, but there are some walkers who go in for oxfords. Quite a number, including a few backpackers, somehow manage to cover long distances in basketball or even tennis shoes. They're welcome.

As soon as you carry a pack and so add appreciably to the burden on your feet, they need extra protection and support. Remember that you may be increasing their normal load by a third. For cushioning effect as well as for durability and traction, by far the most popular soles today are heavily lugged rubber-and-synthetic compound types such as the Vibram and Commando. The $\frac{1}{2}$-inch thickness is probably best for general use. (This measurement is of the sole itself, with lugs; it does not include the softer mid-sole embodied in most good hiking boots, which helps the cushioning effect.) If you expect to do any rock climbing or to operate a great deal in snow, thicker

26

soles might be an advantage—for rigidity in rock climbing, insulation on snow.

Uppers must be stout enough to support foot muscles that are being strained by an abnormal load, and to afford adequate protection. But they must be pliant enough to allow feet to bulge outward slightly when under a heavy load. They must also be very close to waterproof (when properly treated—see page 33), but must allow your feet to "breathe."

There is no substitute for good leather. Uppers with the rough side of the leather turned outward—called "roughouts"—resist abrasion very well but do not waterproof satisfactorily. Uppers with the smooth side outward tend to scuff easily, especially in the cheaper grades, but waterproof well. Virtually all really high-quality boots have smooth-side-out uppers. The only advantage of suede boots is cheapness.

The fewer seams in the uppers, the more rugged the boot—and the more expensive. A many-seamed boot will probably stand up all right if you keep to trails. If you do much cross-country work, especially on talus, it probably won't.

A thin leather lining will increase a boot's warmth and may possibly reduce friction. A thin padding such as foam rubber between uppers and lining will make the boots very easy to break in and comfortable and warm to wear. It will also give extra protection. But there is some danger that in deserts and other fiery places it may make them uncomfortably hot.

In extreme cases, terrain may affect your choice. Jagged volcanic rock or steep talus will soon knock hell out of thin or poor quality material, both soles and uppers. And tough going like that can also bruise poorly protected feet. So if you expect to cross a lot of really rough country it may be as well to increase stoutness and/or quality a notch all around.

But extra stoutness means extra weight, and that can be critical. It is all too easy to pare away at the ounces that go into your pack and to overlook the boots. Yet the successful 1953 Mount Everest Expedition came to the conclusion that in terms of physical effort one pound on the feet is equivalent to five pounds on the back. As usual, then, you have to compromise. But remember that although it is obviously stupid to wear unnecessarily heavy boots, choosing too light a pair is asking for trouble.

Many people consider that ankle boots—six or seven inches high—are too low. But it seems to me that, except in heavy brush country, tall boots do not add enough protection to warrant the extra weight. They are hotter, too—though that means "warmer" in cold weather. They also tend to restrict your calf muscles.

The requirements I have outlined do not really restrict you much. The equipment catalogues list and illustrate such an array of boots that just looking at them gives me mental indigestion.

I am presently using a pair of medium-weight mountaineering and climbing boots made by the Italian firm of Pivetta and sold in the United States under the name "Eiger." The black leather uppers are seven inches high and support and protect my ankles very adequately. There is only one seam—on the inner side of each boot. The lower part of the heel—a point at which seams are liable to split— is solid leather. The boots have a hard toe and strong heel counter. Lacing is through eyelets. The thin leather lining is padded with foam rubber. The ½-inch Vibram Montagna sole ends flush with the uppers and therefore remains reasonably rigid at the edges, even when worn thin—an important advantage for rock climbing (at least, I think so; some people feel just the opposite). My size 10 Eigers weighed five pounds, twelve ounces when new. Cost: $32.50.

Now I don't want to suggest that these boots are necessarily "the best" on the market, whatever that might mean. Like most people, I have actually tried very few different kinds. And I came to these by the orthodox route: a combination of chance and whim and experience and personal prejudice, mitigated by a salesman's advice. But I've used my Eigers for five years now, in daytime shade temperatures ranging from 20°F. to over 100°F., on snow and sand, in places as different as Grand Canyon and Kilimanjaro. And I'm satisfied. I have yet to come across a pair of boots that looked as though they would prove better for all-around use.

My only possible complaint is that the foam padding perhaps makes them rather hot for desert use; but I do not really have a yardstick by which to measure this factor. The padding certainly makes for greater comfort and for warmth in snow and reduces both the time and trauma involved in breaking in a new pair.

Naturally, special conditions may call for special boots.

In rain forest such as occurs in coastal British Columbia and on the Olympic Peninsula, where your only route is often along slippery fallen tree trunks, and undergrowth is always snatching at your legs, the only satisfactory footwear is a pair of calked knee boots.

A summer in the muskeg-and-lake country of Canada's Northwest Territories taught me that in such places you need a stout and roomy pair of leather-topped rubber boots (worn with thick insoles and two pairs of socks). The Maine Hunting Shoe made by L. L. Bean of Freeport, Maine, is the standard, though there are others. The generic name for the breed is "Shoepac." Ten-inch boots are probably the most popular, but they come in all heights from six to sixteen inches. I understand that boots of this type are admirable for much eastern wilderness—the sort of flat, soggy terrain in which old tote roads skirt or even run through spruce and cedar swamps. They're especially good when hiking is largely a means to camping or hunting or fishing, and a day's backpacking may amount to no more than five miles and is unlikely to exceed twelve. In recent years Shoepacs have tended to give way to rubber boots heavily insulated with fiber glass or some similar material. They're often called "Korean" or "Mickey Mouse" boots.

In really cold weather—especially at high altitudes—it may be necessary to wear extra-thick boots (a size or two larger than usual, to accommodate more sock). You may even need overboots. But here we are coming close to the fringe of "just plain walking."

Insoles

Many boots—and especially those with hand-stitched soles (because the stitching may protrude and chafe your feet)—need insoles. In emergencies I have used cardboard cut-outs from cereal boxes (they last about six hours), regular foam-rubber insoles of the kind you can pick up at a drug store (intolerably hot), and makeshift devices fashioned from asbestos gasket sheeting bought at a wayside garage (effective, though they tend to curl). But the best material is plain leather. It is probably an advantage to glue the insoles in. If they are left loose, though, you can transfer an old pair, already well molded to the contours of your soles, into a new pair of boots and so cut down appreciably the grief of breaking them in.

Laces and lacing

Braided nylon laces are extremely strong. I have never had one break on me. They do not rot, absorb water, dry out stiff, or become brittle in extreme cold. Unlike leather laces, they are never eaten by mice or their allies. They usually come in red too, and are therefore pretty unlosable. I know of no other lace with all these advantages. The only drawback to nylon, and it's a very mild one, is its tendency to slip out of the top eyelets when your boots are unlaced.

I used to follow tradition and carry a spare pair of laces, but long ago decided to rely on a length of my ubiquitous ⅛-inch nylon cord (page 264).

Some people prefer lacing hooks to eyelets. Hooks are an advantage in weather so cold that you have to lace your boots with gloves on (which is why they're used on ski boots). But they can be a snagging hazard in brush country, and I am always aware—perhaps overaware—of the danger of breakage.

Laces should not be drawn too tight in the lower eyelets or hooks: the pressure can block the necessary wiggle-freedom of your toes and may even constrict circulation. But on the vertical part of the boot the laces must be tight enough to prevent your foot from sliding forward under the kind of pressure you generate when walking downhill.

Fitting new boots

Think of yourself as trying to put a glove on your foot. But do not picture a skin-tight glove. What you need is a boot that fits snugly at the broadest part of the foot (the trick is deciding exactly what "snugly" means, and in the end you have to make your own decision, based on experience) but which leaves one finger's width of free room in front of the toes. You check this toe space by unlacing the boot, standing up without a pack, and pressing forward until your toes meet the end of the boot. If you can just slide a forefinger down into the gap left at the heel, that part of the fit is about right. With the boot laced, you should be able to wriggle your toes fairly freely (the shape of the toe cap is important; for most feet, the broader and squarer the better). But it is vital that, with the boot laced tightly up the vertical part, there is as little movement as possible at the heel, upward or sideways. The difficulty is that new boots are relatively stiff, and that with wear all boots mold themselves to the shape of your feet. You simply have to guess how much change will take place —how much the sides will "give," and how well that stiff-feeling heel will conform to the contours of your particular foot. Cheaper boots tend to alter more than good-quality ones, especially if they are unlined; buy them a little on the tight side. I find that with my Pivettas—presumably because of their lining and foam padding and high-quality leather—a good fit in the store seems to mean a good fit on the mountain.

Do not, by the way, pay too much attention to sizes. Base your decision on the feel of the boot. If the size is not the same as last time, it doesn't matter a damn. Different boots marked as the same size may vary appreciably.

If you feel confident that the salesman knows what he is talking about, lean heavily on his advice. Even if you hike like crazy, all year round, you buy new boots only once every few years, and you tend to forget the rules. But the salesman is at it all day and every day. Frankly, I found when I came to write this section that I really couldn't quite remember what I looked for. So I talked to a salesman I trusted and have gratefully incorporated most of his testament. All I can say about the way I've managed to apply the rules in the past is that I've never been dissatisfied with any hiking boots I've bought. Mind you, it may take me an hour to select the pair I want.

Breaking in new boots

All new boots need slow and careful breaking in. Until some of the stiffness has gone and insoles and uppers have begun to conform to the contours of your feet, they are almost sure to be uncomfortable. And they'll be great at generating blisters. I have heard people advise: "Just put your new boots on and soak them in water for a while and then go out and walk. You'll never have any trouble." It sounds pretty drastic treatment to me, and I have never tried it. (But one experienced mountaineer I know, who had always felt as I do about the soaking theory, once tried it out as a crash program and found that it worked. Perhaps it's relevant, though, that he says he hasn't repeated it). All I do is take short, easy walks, with little or no load at first, and gradually increase load and distance. At the very beginning, even wearing the boots around the house helps. Naturally, they should be well waxed as soon as you buy them (page 33).

For a major backpacking expedition—the kind that threatens to wear out a pair of shoes—you obviously have to start with new ones. After all, you wouldn't set out on a transcontinental road rally with worn tires. For such expeditions, breaking in your new boots can become a problem. The theory is simple: the boots will take care of themselves during those practice hikes you plan to take for several weeks beforehand in slowly increasing doses that will painlessly harden your feet and muscles. But I have found that in practice the press of administrative arrangements just before the start rises to such a frantic peak that there is no time for any practice hikes worthy of the name. So you start with flabby muscles, soft feet—and stiff boots. And this is no laughing matter. It is not simply that sore feet soon take the joy out of walking. They can make walking impossible. Just before my Grand Canyon trip, while putting out a food cache and at the same time trying rather belatedly to harden my feet and soften a new pair of boots, I attempted too much in a single day, generated a blister, developed an infected heel, and had to postpone the start for a week. Fortunately, I had planned an easy first week's shakedown cruise. But even with an old pair of insoles in the boots, my feet barely carried me through the second critical and much harder week of the trip. I offer no solution to this kind of problem (which can also crop up on shorter journeys), but I suggest that you at least make every effort to allow time for a gentle shakedown cruise at the beginning. As we have seen (page 10) there is an even more important reason for such an arrangement. See also page 43.

Care of boots

Leather uppers must always be kept well oiled or waxed. For many years I used Kiwi neutral wax, but found that my boots tended to dry out too fast on long journeys, even though I applied an average of one 2½-ounce tin a week. Recently I switched to Sno-Seal, an old and well-tried preparation. It seems to keep the leather supple for very much longer. Whenever your boots show any sign of drying out, simply clean and dry them and apply Sno-Seal over direct heat (at home, a burner of the stove; in the wilds, a campfire—or a cooking stove, if you have fuel to spare). The heat quickly liquefies the Sno-Seal. Rub it well into the leather, particularly at joints and seams, with fingers or a rag.

If your boots get thoroughly wet, dry them slowly. Packing loosely with newspaper or toilet paper helps absorb internal moisture. Never put wet boots close to a fire: the soles may curl up and the leather lose some of its life. Someone recently gave me a pair of cunning devices for preventing wet soles from curling. Called "stretchers," they're made of light alloy and plastic-covered cord, and are designed to apply tension that counteracts the tendency of drying soles to curl toward their uppers.

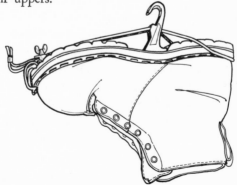

I haven't used my stretchers yet, but although I do not plan to carry them in my pack they promise to come in useful at home.

SOCKS

On almost every count—resilience, sweat absorption, insulation, and general comfort—wool is the material. But nylon reinforcement—10 per cent throughout, and/or up to 40 per cent at heels and toes—increases durability without detracting appreciably from the other qualities. The best sock thickness depends on whether you tend to suffer from hot feet, cold feet, tender feet, or none of these afflictions. In theory it would seem obvious to put on a thicker pair of socks in cold weather. But if your boots fit perfectly with the socks you normally wear they will pinch with a thicker pair. You are left with two alternatives: buying a second pair of boots, or getting by with the usual socks. (If conditions are severe enough to justify overboots, you probably need two pairs of thick socks and big boots anyway.) Some people wear only one pair of socks at a time, others find that two pairs—the thinner ones inside—help reduce friction between feet and boots.

I wear a single pair of medium weight Aspen socks, made by Adler. They're 85 per cent wool with 15 per cent nylon reinforcement throughout and 39 per cent nylon-reinforced heels and toes. (Weight, 4 ounces; $1.50 per pair; three for $4.) These socks are labeled "shrink resistant," and to my surprise they are. Their eleven-inch tops are long enough to turn down over ankle boots when I'm wearing shorts (which is almost always) and an ordinary rubber band keeps stones and dirt from falling down between socks and ankle. I buy my socks in a hue so shocking-red that I could hardly walk away from camp and leave a pair hanging out to dry or just lying around. Red is the photography color too: a small splash of it can crystallize an otherwise amorphous subject. And the more bright colors in your clothing, the greater the chances of your being seen— from land or air—in case of accident.

These Aspen socks now come only in white, and I've not yet

been able to find a red equivalent. Nor have I yet tried out a new sock called Wick Dry (4½ ounces; $2.95). It has two layers. The inner layer of moisture-repellent orlon and nylon is reputed to "wick" perspiration to the outer layer of moisture-absorbing yarn (10 per cent cotton), where it evaporates. Some experienced hikers have reported favorably, but I confess to skepticism.

I carry three pairs of socks at a time. The two spare pairs go into an instantly accessible pocket on the outside of the pack flap. In hot weather I often change socks every hour and tie the sweat-drenched pair on top of the pack to dry. A three-foot length of nylon cord knotted to the upper crossbar of the packframe secures the tops of these socks with a clove hitch (see illustration, page 53); and tucking the socks under the pack's closure strings prevents them from slipping off to one side. (Well, usually prevents.) In cooler country I may wear the same socks all day, or almost all day, but any dirty pairs hang purifying on top of the pack. If a dirty pair has to go inside the flap pocket for any reason (such as rain or snatching tree branches or recently washed socks that monopolize the outside drier) I segregate them hygienically in a plastic bag.

A pair of socks no doubt lasts longer for some people than for others. In the six months and thousand-plus map-miles of my California trip (many more on the ground) I wore out nine pairs.

Care of socks

Like all woolen articles, socks must be carefully washed. Some backpackers carry packages of Woolite, specially made for washing wool in cold water. But you eliminate one item and do almost as good a job if you use soap, which probably goes along in your toilet gear anyway. Avoid detergent; it removes vital oils from the wool. Whatever you use, rinse the socks thoroughly. If no washing agent is available, plain rinsing out of dirty socks, even in cold water, can be surprisingly effective.

Strictly speaking, socks should be dried away from the sun and lying flat rather than hanging, but I often break both rules without paying any apparent penalty. I find, in any case, that drying out socks on top of the pack as I walk is often the only way I get to dry them out at all. (Warning: wet socks are heavy, and when spread out to dry on a rock will stay put in moderate winds; but as they dry out, so the tendency to flight increases. Solution: always hobble them with rocks, full canteens, or what have you.)

Try to wash your socks fairly often. In hot weather that may mean once a day. Dirty socks insulate poorly, absorb little sweat, and because the wool is no longer soft and resilient can quickly cause abrasions.

The only time I wore a hole in a sock while out and away, I patched it with a small foam-rubber disk cut from a sheet of "moleskin" (see page 46). The repair turned out to be astonishingly effective.

Camp footwear

Wearing boots around camp is usually a nuisance, can often be uncomfortable, and may even amount to a serious inefficiency. (Toward the end of my first week's real traveling in Grand Canyon my feet became so sore that I rested a day and a half beside a spring. Because I had moccasins, which slip off and on very easily, I was able to expose my feet almost continually to the air and never to the painful pressures of boots. If I had had to wear the boots for the many small chores that always need doing around camp, I am sure my feet would not have recovered as quickly as they did.)

Unless you feel confident that conditions will allow you to go barefoot in camp—and they almost never will—the only answer is to carry lightweight campwear.

I have found nothing to equal moccasins with an external composition sole about a quarter of an inch thick. The sole adds little weight but it keeps out thorns and blunts the cutting—and bruising—edge of almost any stone. My present pair weighs 15½ ounces. They cost $6.95, and with occasional applications of Sno-Seal should last for years. I nearly always take them along.

If the weight problem becomes acute, consider unsoled moccasins (average, 9 ounces; $7). But in stony country don't expect too much from the unprotected underleather. The pair I carried in Grand Canyon just about lasted out the two months.

When your feet are really sore, even camp moccasins can feel uncomfortable, particularly if they're new. One solution: pad toes and heels with toilet paper.

Down booties

See page 206.

AIDS AND ATTACHMENTS

Walking staff

Although the vast majority of walkers never even think of using a walking staff, I unhesitatingly include it among the foundations of the house that travels on my back. I take my staff along almost as automatically as I take my pack. For many years now it has been a third leg to me—and much more besides.

On smooth surfaces the staff helps maintain an easy rhythm to my walking and gives me something to lean on when I stop to stand and stare. Over rough going of any kind, from tussocky grass to pockety rock, and also in a high wind, it converts me when I am heavily laden from an insecure biped into a confident triped. It does the same only more so when I have to scramble across a chasm or a big boulder or a mildly obstructive stretch of rock and keep reaching out sideways for a balancing aid or backwards for that little extra push up and over. And it does the same thing, even more critically and consistently, when I cross a steep, loose slope of talus or gravel or dirt, or wade a fast-flowing creek, or cross it on a log. In marshland or on precarious rock or snow, and in failing light or darkness anywhere, it tests doubtful footing ahead. It reconnoiters bushes or crevices that I suspect might harbor a rattlesnake. It often acts as the indispensable upright needed to rig up a shelter from rain or sun with fly sheet (page 153) or ground sheet or poncho (pages 161 and 162). Occasionally, held down by a couple of heavy stones, it serves as ground anchor for the windward side of such a shelter (illustration, page 162). It has performed successfully as a fishing rod. It has acted as a marked measuring stick to be checked later, when a rule is available, for the exact length of fish, rattlesnakes, and other dead animals. It forms a rough but very ready monopod for steadying binoculars if my hands are shaking from exertion, or for a camera if I need to shoot with a shutter speed slower than $\frac{1}{60}$ second. And day in and day out, at almost every halt, it props up my pack and gives me a soft and stable backrest (page 65). (As I am lazy enough to believe that being able to relax against a soft backrest for even a ten-minute halt is no minor matter, I am almost inclined to regard this function of my staff as one of its most vital.) Finally—though I had never really thought about it until this minute—the staff probably gives me a false but subconsciously comforting feeling that I am not after all completely defenseless against attack by such enemies as snakes, bears, and men.

My staff is nothing much to look at: a $4\frac{1}{2}$-foot length of ordinary stout bamboo* (average diameter $1\frac{3}{8}$ inches—just right for a firm but comfortable grip). After years of use, small cracks have developed up and down its whole length, some of them quite threatening. Mostly, they stop when they come to a knot mark, and the general structure remains sound. But each end-section has split so severely that, left to itself, it would flap like an empty banana skin, and I have bandaged the wounds with several rings of rip-stop tape (page 260). The staff is ten years old now, and I suppose I cannot reasonably expect it to last more than another decade or two, but I must confess that when I look at its weatherbeaten surface, and especially at the brown patina that has formed around the second knot, where my hand usually grips, I feel sad at this thought. In

---

* I don't know what kind of bamboo it is, but the man who gave it to me— near the start of my California walk, beside the Colorado River—said he had cut it on his own property near Los Angeles.

When I told him that I wanted the bamboo to replace a yucca staff I had broken in killing a rattlesnake he said, "Well, I hope you get a rattler with it. One of them killed my brother." But one of the few things the staff has never done is to kill a rattlesnake—at first because I did not want to risk breaking it or getting venom on it; and quite soon because, growing up, I came to realize that there is no reason except fear for killing rattlesnakes that live in places where they are unlikely to meet people (page 295).

other words, I have come to regard my staff with a warm affection. I suppose some people would call it a soggy sentimentality.

One small but constantly recurring matter: you cannot conveniently lift a pack onto your back while holding a staff. Where possible, lean the staff against something before you lift the pack, so that once you're loaded up you can easily take hold of it. But even in open places there is no need to waste the not inconsiderable energy expended in bending down with a heavy load on your back: just hook one foot under the staff, lift it with your instep, and take hold of it when the top angles up within reach of your hand. With practice, you'll probably find yourself flipping the staff up with your foot and catching it at its apogee. You'll soon get used to laying the staff ready for this maneuver on a low bush or stone or across a depression in the ground before you hoist up the pack, so that afterward you can slide a toe under it. If you forget the precaution and can't get a toe under, simply roll the staff up onto your instep with the other foot. It sounds gymnastic but is really very simple.

There are, I admit, times when a long staff like mine becomes a nuisance.

One is during river crossings in really fast water, when it could tangle dangerously with your legs as you go through rapids. In calm water it's easy enough to pull the staff safely along behind on a length of nylon cord (illustration, page 275). When a fast-water situation was plainly going to arise on a recent trip, I left my regular staff behind and on the first day cut a four-foot section from the stem of a dead agave, or century plant. With the thicker end carefully rounded it made a very serviceable third leg. During river crossings it tucked conveniently out of the way in the bindings of my packframe, protruding only very slightly at the top (page 278). The odd thing was that by the end of two weeks I was feeling for this little staff the same kind of affection that I lavish on my regular one—so much so that when it broke on the next-to-last day and I had to cut a fresh length of agave, I stuffed the scarred, foot-long stub into my pack and carried it all the way home. I guess "soggy sentimentality" is about right.

A staff is also a nuisance, even a hazard, if you have to do any climbing that demands the use of two unencumbered hands. Occasionally, on short and unexpected pitches, I've pulled the staff up after me on a nylon cord, or lowered it ahead. If you know you're likely to face some rock climbing, it may be worth leaving your regular staff behind and cutting a temporary one that can be discarded and replaced (climbing was a contributory reason for my doing just that on the recent fast-water trip). If you expect to do very much climbing, there are two solutions. Either do without a staff of any kind; or take along an

Ice ax.

Even if you use the ax little if at all for ice work, it will serve as a reasonably efficient staff, even in its pack-prop role. And while you are climbing you can tie it out of the way on your pack. An ice ax (about 2¼ pounds, $16) is, incidentally, a splendid instrument for extracting stubborn tent pegs from packed snow (page 149).

When walking, hold the ax by the head, pointed part of the head forward, so that in case of a fall the danger to you is reduced. A rubber tip-protector can be used on hard surfaces, and definitely should be used when the ax is in the car or at home.

The technical use of an ice ax does not, of course, fall within the scope of a walking book.

Two other walking aids that lie close to the fringes of walking deserve brief mention:

Crampons.

Although crampons are essentially ironmongery for climbers, they are sometimes worth carrying if you expect to cross ice or hard snow. And not only steep snow. A flat snowfield that has weathered hard is quite likely to have developed basins and ridges and even savage pinnacles that in naked boots create considerable and potentially dangerous obstacles. And not long ago I discovered by accident, when I climbed out onto the lip of an ice-covered gully on Mount Shasta, that when you are carrying a heavy load crampons can transform a sloping slab of very soft rock from a nasty barrier into a cakewalk.

For beginners, ten-point crampons are said to be best (21 ounces; $13.95). Twelve-pointers, with a pair of spikes protruding forward, can easily trip unwary users. When you buy crampons or rent them (at, say, $1.50 a weekend or $7 for two weeks) take great care that they fit your boots exactly, for both width and length. A loose pair can be extremely dangerous. Make sure too that you learn how to strap them on properly. I will not try to describe the correct method here: it is quite a complicated thing to verbalize but very simple to learn from a salesman.

Snowshoes

My experience is meager, but I have learned that snowshoes permit you to move over the very surface of snow into which your booted legs plunge knee deep—and that immediately after a storm they will allow you to travel (sweating hard, but sinking in less than a foot at each step) across snow into which you would otherwise go on sinking forever if God had not arranged that human legs eventually converge. I have also learned that if you have an old hamstring injury, snowshoeing may let you in for some nagging discomfort. Also that, short of a shovel, there is nothing like a snowshoe for digging out your tent during and after a storm.

When I first inquired about the technique of snowshoeing, several people said, "Oh, you just put them on and go." And that seems to be just about right. The vitally important thing is not to splay your feet out. At the very start, keep looking down to see how close together you can slide your feet without entrapping one snowshoe under the other; or, after a little practice, how far forward you must step in order to get away with lifting the edge of one shoe *just* over the edge of the other at the bulging widest part. Soon you find yourself moving along without thinking about how to put your feet down. Naturally, the closer the movement comes to normal walking, the less tiring it is.

Without a pack, the thing soon becomes simple. But if you are backpacking the chances are that the pack—what with a stout tent and warm clothing and big sleeping bag—will be hippopotamic; and although snowshoes make movement possible under conditions that would otherwise bog you down, you should be prepared for the discovery that snowshoeing can be a pretty laborious, not to say boring, business. But it has its moments. In really deep, soft, new snow you may get the disturbing notion that if you lose your balance and fall with that huge load on your back you will "drown."

At one end of the snowshoe spectrum lie little tear-shaped "bearpaws" (average thirteen inches by thirty inches, weight six pounds), too awkwardly wide for normal cross-country use but apparently valuable around cabins or in thick brush where maneuverability is vital. At the other end come prodigious structures five feet long and more that look as if they would support an elephant on detergent foam. The only kind I have used were "trail shoes" measuring ten inches by fifty-six inches and weighing six pounds. On them I was able to move comfortably over deep snow with a crust too weak to support my boots; and to move rather laboriously through a storm that had already dropped more than four feet of powder-soft snow. This, incidentally, was when I found out about the drowning threat. It was pretty hard work with a heavy pack anyway, and my solution was to break trail unladen, backtrack, and then pack forward over an easy, trampled trail. I can imagine experienced snowshoers extracting considerable amusement from this admission. But at least I emerged undunked.

When not in use, snowshoes can in reasonably open terrain be tied horizontally on your pack. Laying them across the top of the open pack and just pulling tight on the flap is often the simplest way. Where trees or brush are likely to snag the protruding ends, strap the shoes vertically.

Standard hickory-and-leather-thong snowshoes need occasional revarnishing. (Spray varnishes are now available.) An alternative to buying your own (around $30) and having to maintain them is to rent a pair (say, $3 a weekend, $10 for two weeks) and let the store look after the varnishing.

At least one snowshoe with nylon thongs is now on the market, and I hear whispers of aluminum frames. And yesterday I actually saw, for the first time, a pair of plastic snowshoes, no less! (Cold temperature, high impact polyprene; 29 by 12 inches; 2½ pounds and $15 per pair. Makers: Sportsmen Products, Inc. [see Appendix II]). I understand that they're proving quite popular.

The way to move across snow country is to ski. But on skis you are no longer walking.

CARE OF FEET

Some people seem to have naturally tough feet. But if you are like me you know that it pays to take stringent precautions before and during any walk much longer than you are currently used to, or with a load much heavier than you have very recently carried. If you do not yet understand the value of such precautions, then you've never generated a big, joy-killing blister with many miles still to go.

Getting your feet ready

This vital task is best achieved by practice—by taking time out beforehand to work up slowly from a few gentle miles, unladen (if you are in really bad shape), to a long day's slog with a load as big as you mean to carry. But somehow (see page 32), you rarely seem to have the time to take out, and even more rarely the determination to take it. The only substitute I know, and it's a poor one, is to toughen up the skin (soles, toes, and heels particularly) by regular applications of rubbing alcohol for a week or so beforehand. If you put the alcohol bottle beside your toothbrush, it is not too difficult to remember this simple half-minute chore, morning and night. It helps too, if you cannot get out for any serious walking, to wear your boots—especially new ones—as much as you can for a week or so beforehand, even if only around the house.

On the march

The important thing is to begin easily. Men—and whole families—who backpack into the bush for once-a-year vacations all too often find the whole week or fortnight ruined at the very beginning by too much ambition and too little discretion. Their feet never quite recover from the pounding of the first day or two. A gentle shakedown cruise (see pages 10 and 32)—a day or a week, depending on the total length of the trip—can make all the difference. On my thousand-mile California walk, although I began with stiff new boots and soft city feet, I suffered only one blister—a minor affair generated by an ill-advised insole experiment. But I took great care in the first week and averaged barely seven miles a day, over very easy going. In Grand Canyon my feet fared less well. But I began with a barely cured infected heel, and because of it had worn nothing but moccasins for almost two weeks. If it had not been for two days of easy ambling at the start and a further four days of taking it fairly easy, I should probably have been crippled before I got fully started.

It's essential that you continue to take precautions until your feet are quite comfortably lasting out the longest day and the heaviest load—even with steady downhill work, which gives feet a much more brutal hammering than they get on the level or uphill. I rarely seem to reach this point for at least a week or two. Until then I go on applying rubbing alcohol. For years I have carried about five ounces of it in a flat, plastic bottle, but recently I bought a squeeze-type plastic bottle of two-ounce capacity that ejects a thin spray, and it seems to be much more economical than the open-mouthed bottle, which tends to pour very untidily. The bottle travels, immediately accessible, in an outside pocket of the pack (page 272). Normally I rub my feet with a little alcohol morning and night, and in hot weather or when my feet are really sore I may do so several times a day. I also carry a three-ounce can of foot powder, in the same pocket of the pack. I always sprinkle the insides of my socks with it in the morning, and often do so again several times during the day.

Many experienced hikers deplore all this messing around. "Unless something is seriously wrong," I heard one advise a beginner not long ago, "keep your boots on until you stop for the day. You'll have far less trouble with your feet that way." And no doubt such advice is sound enough for some people. I go to the other extreme. In hot weather I often take my boots off at each halt and let the air get at the perspiring feet. When my feet are really sore I anoint them with alcohol and powder at almost every hourly halt. If water is available, I may even wash them at each halt (an act a lot of people regard as skin-softening idiocy) and change socks, repowdering the pair that has been drying out on top of my pack.

I find that such treatment works well. And it seems to make theoretical sense too. Heat is the cause of all blisters. Locally, the heat comes from the friction of a rucked sock or an ill-fitting boot. But it seems reasonable to suppose that the overall temperature of your feet makes a big difference. I certainly find deserts the hardest places on feet. And it is not really surprising: few people realize how hot the ground underfoot can be. In Grand Canyon I repeatedly checked air and ground temperatures. With air temperature about 85° I would get a ground reading on unshaded rock (and that meant just about any rock) of around 115° or 120°. On unshaded sand the mercury would go well past the last gradation of 120°. When air temperature climbed over 90° I had to be careful where I left the thermometer, for fear the mercury would blow off the top.*

Remedial treatment

If, in spite of all your care, your feet need doctoring, start it early. The moment you feel what may be the beginnings of a blister, do something about it.

---

* An article by A. Court in the *Geographical Review* (1949, No. 2, pages 214–20) gives these figures for extreme conditions in American deserts: air at five feet, 125°F.; at one foot, 150°; at one inch, 165°; at ground, 180°.

This kind of heat layering is by no means confined to deserts. See, for example, page 259.

Interesting temperatures recorded during World War II at a naval research center in Imperial Valley, California, on a day when the official air temperature touched 120°F., include 145° in the gasoline in a fifty-gallon drum left in the sun, 155° in the vapor above the gasoline, and 190° on the seat of a jeep.

First remove any obvious and rectifiable local irritant, such as a fragment of stone or a rucked sock. Then cover the tender place. Cover it even if you can see nothing more than a faint redness. Cover it, in fact, if you can see nothing at all. Being a "hero" is being a bloody fool. The covering may only be needed for a few hours; if you take it off at night and let the air get at the skin you may not even need to replace it next morning. But if you do nothing at the first warning you may find yourself inside the hour with a blister that will last a week.

For covering, a piece of surgical tape or a Band-aid will do, provided its adhesive surface is efficient enough to prevent rucking —a requirement not always met when the trouble is on your toes. By far the best patches I know are those cut from "moleskins" (one-ounce package, 45 cents). These oddly miraculous devices, available in most drug stores, are nothing more than sheets of thin white felt, adhesive on one side. They stick to skin like glue, even after your feet get wet. In fact, it is sometimes quite a business peeling the thin protective layer of plastic off new patches. (The makers leave a helpful projecting band of this layer and advise you to remove the plastic before cutting patches to the required shape. But in order to preserve the adhesive qualities—which can be rather easily damaged by handling—I shape the patch first with a pair of scissors, carefully beveling all edges, then lever up one corner of the plastic with the scissors' point, and peel it off.) But mere adhesion does not begin to explain the extraordinary efficiency of moleskins. I suppose their secret has something to do with the resilience and sideways-sliding quality of the felt. Anyway, I know for a fact and with gratitude that they can stop embryonic friction trouble dead; can stifle the pain from any surface blister and often keep it from getting worse; and can even, apparently from mere cushioning, deaden the worst pain from those deep, dismal, often invisible blisters that occasionally form under heel or ball of foot.

Moleskins are made in foam rubber as well as felt, but I mistrust this kind. Rubber, I imagine, must hold the heat. My moleskins travel in my "office" (page 256), and conveniently protect both scissors and signaling mirror (page 249).

If you generate a blister in spite of all your care—or because you were not careful enough—and if it is either very deep or is not yet very bulbous, the best treatment is probably just to cover it. But if the blister is close to the surface and has already inflated you will need to burst it before you can walk with comfort. Pierce it with a needle, from the side, down near the base of the balloon, so that all the liquid can drain away. Cauterize the needle first in a flame. (I carry several needles, primarily for repair work, in my waterproof matchsafe [page 261].) If you have got to keep walking and if the loose skin of the balloon does not ruck up when deflated, it is probably best to leave the skin in place and cover it, and to cut it away only when the skin beneath has had time to harden. But if you can rest long enough for the under skin to harden—which it does more quickly if exposed to the air—or if the deflated outer skin puckers so badly that it seems likely to cause further damage as you walk, remove it by scissoring carefully around the edges of the blister. Take care to keep the exposed area clean. And leave no dead skin likely to cause new chafing. If you must keep walking, and apply a moleskin or other adhesive cover, use a thin fragment of gauze to prevent the cover from sticking directly to the exposed and tender skin. A sprinkling of foot powder helps reduce friction further, and so does an antiseptic of some kind that will not only lubricate but also reduce the danger of infection.

But never forget that a blister is a sign of failure. The efficient way to deal with foot trouble is to avoid it. Practice. Pre-harden. On the march, and especially in the early days of a trip, attend assiduously to preventive measures. And nip tribulations in the bud. Alternatively, arrange to be born with tough feet.

THE FOUNDATIONS IN ACTION

A book on walking should no doubt have something to say about the simple, basic, physical act of walking.

On the most fundamental level, advice is probably useless. Anyone old enough to read has almost certainly grown too set in the way he puts one foot in front of the other to alter it materially without devoting a great deal of time and determination to the task. Unless, of course, there is something correctably wrong with his feet.

On the other hand, it is very easy to improve by a little conscious thought what I regard as the most important single element in the physical act of walking: rhythm. An easy, unbroken rhythm can carry you along hour after hour almost without your being aware that you are putting one foot in front of the other. At the end of a really long day you will be aware of the act all right, but as long as you maintain a steady rhythm very little of your mind need be concerned with it. And your muscles will complain far less than if you have walked all day in a series of jerky and semi-coordinated movements, sometimes pushing close to your limit, sometimes meandering.

With experience you fall into your own rhythmic pace quite automatically. (At least, mostly you do. There will still be days when you have to fight for it, and not always with total success.) But when you first take up real walking you may have to think deliberately about establishing a stride and a speed that feel comfortable. And both stride and speed may be rather different with and without a load.

You will almost certainly have to concentrate at first on the important matter of not disrupting the rhythm unless absolutely necessary. This means stepping short for a stride when you come to some minor obstacle such as a narrow ditch, or even marking time with one foot. I cannot emphasize this unbroken rhythm business too strongly.

Of course, rhythm is not always a simple matter of constant stride and speed. In fact it remains so only as long as you walk on a smooth and level surface. The moment you meet rough going underfoot or start up or down a gradient you have to modify stride or speed or both.

Climbing a gentle slope means nothing more than a mild shortening of stride, though leaning forward slightly may help too. But long before a mountainside gets so steep that you start reaching out for handholds, stride becomes a meaningless word. Now, you put your feet down almost side by side at one step, a foot or more apart at the next, depending on the immediate local gradients and footholds. Even the rate at which you move one leg past the other—slowly and deliberately and almost laboriously, though not quite—may vary in response to changes in the general gradient. But the old rhythm persists. I am not sure where the relationships lie. It is not—though I have sometimes thought so—that you continue to expend the same amount of energy. Steep climbing takes more out of you, always (page 85). But the fact remains that although you must change gear in an almost literal sense at the bottom and top of a steep hill you can maintain the deeper continuity of the old rhythm. The pulse is still there, somewhere, if you know where to feel for it.

Downhill walking, though less sweaty than climbing, is less easy than it ought to be. In theory you merely relinquish the potential energy you gained with such labor as you climbed; but in practice you do no such thing. At every step you expend a great deal of effort in holding yourself back—and this effort too demands a deliberate change of gear. If the gradient is at all severe you reduce both stride and speed by as much as you think necessary to prevent yourself from hammering hell out of knees and ankles and feet (especially feet). Again, though, you find with practice that it is possible to maintain the essence of the old rhythm.

You may also have to apply a conscious effort to maintaining your rhythmic pace when you come to certain kinds of rough going —soft sand or gravel that drags at your feet like molasses; talus that slides away from under your feet like a treadmill; rough rock or tussocky grassland that soon disrupts an even stride; or prolonged sidehill work that puts an abnormal strain on foot and leg muscles and may also present something of a problem in balance.

Walking after dark, especially on pitch-black, moonless nights, can also destroy your customary rhythm. If you have been walking in daylight and simply keep going, little trouble seems to arise. But if you get up in the middle of the night and hike out into darkness you may have a surprise in store. As I have written in *The Thousand-Mile Summer,* the only time I traveled at night on my California walk was in Death Valley. The first night inside the Valley I had no sleeping bag, and I failed quite dismally to stay asleep (page 184). At three thirty I got up from the gully in which I had camped and headed north into the darkness. There was no moon. From the start I found myself walking in a curious and disturbing state of detachment. The paleness that was the dirt road refused to stay in positive contact with my feet, and I struggled along with laborious, unrhythmic steps. All around hovered hints of immense open spaces and distant, unconvincing slopes. Time had lost real meaning back in the gully; now it lacked even boundaries. When dawn gave the landscape a tenuous reality at last, I was still two hours away from my next cache. In those endless two hours I completely failed to reestablish my usual rhythmic pace.

Next night I was on the move by nine thirty. This time, bright moonlight made the physical world something real and conquerable. I could plant my feet firmly and confidently on the solid white road. But soon after eleven o'clock, the moon set. The world narrowed to hints of colossal open space, to a blur that achieved reality only through jabbing at my feet. Distance degenerated into marks on the map. Time was the creeping progress of watch hands. All through the long and cold and dismal night that followed I had to struggle to hold some semblance of my usual daytime rhythm. I succeeded only marginally. But I succeeded, oddly enough, far better than on the previous night.

A delicate sense of balance is vital to good walking. And it's not just a matter of being able to cross steep slopes without tightening up. Your body should always be poised and relaxed so that you put down your feet, whatever their size and whatever your load, with something close to daintiness. Before I walked through Grand Canyon I met the one man who seemed to know much about hiking away from trails in its remote corners. Trying to get some idea of whether I would be able to cope with the rough, steep country that he crossed with such apparent ease, I asked him to tell me, honestly, if he were a good climber. "No," he said, "definitely not. I'd say I was a very mediocre climber indeed. But in the Canyon it's mostly walking you know, even though it can be pretty tricky walking at times." He smiled. "I guess you could say, come to think of it, that maybe I don't dislodge quite as many stones as the next guy." And I knew then that he was a good walker.

One of the surest ways to tell an experienced walker from a beginner is the speed at which he starts walking. The beginner tends to tear away in the morning as if he meant to break every record in sight. By contrast, your experienced man seems to amble. But before long, and certainly by evening, their positions have reversed. The beginner is dragging. The expert, still swinging along at the same easy pace, is now the one who looks as though he has records in mind. One friend of mine, a real expert, says, "If you can't carry on a conversation, you're going too fast."

The trap to avoid at all costs, if you want to enjoy yourself, is spurious heroism—the delusion that your prowess as a walker rests on how dauntlessly you "pick 'em up and lay 'em down." It's a sadly common syndrome.

The actual speed at which you walk is a personal and idiosyncratic matter. Settle for whatever seems to suit you best. It is really a question of finding out what you can keep up, more or less effortlessly, hour after hour after hour. The terrain and the load make a lot of difference, but mileage figures are next door to meaningless (see page 23).

The halts you choose to take are a matter of personal preference, but frequent and irregular halts are a sure sign of an inexperienced hiker. Unladen, it may be a good thing to keep going hour after hour without disturbing your rhythm. But if you're carrying a sizable pack you will almost certainly find that, no matter how fit you are, you need to get the weight off your back for a short spell about once an hour. I halt every hour with fairly mechanical regularity, modifying slightly to suit terrain. I like to get to the top of a hill before I stop, for example; and I often halt a few minutes early or late to take advantage of convenient shade or water. In theory, I rest for ten minutes. When I have a map, I mark the halting place and pencil in the exact time I stopped. I am no longer sure why I began doing this, but I do so now because I know only too well that it is horribly easy to let a halt drift on for fifteen, twenty, or even thirty minutes, and the penciled figures on the map act as a reminder and a spur. They also help me to judge how I am progressing across a given kind of country, and make it much easier to estimate how far I should be able to travel in the next hour or afternoon or day or week.

At each halt I take off the pack and prop it against a rock or a tree or my staff and lean against it with my back comfortably between the protruding outside pockets (see page 65). I try to relax completely. Sometimes, warding off the attractions of scenery, animals, and the map, I succeed. I may even doze off for a few minutes. Getting started again may demand quite an effort, especially toward the end of a long day; but within a few paces I slip back into the old regular rhythm. With luck I will hold it, unbroken, for another fifty minutes.

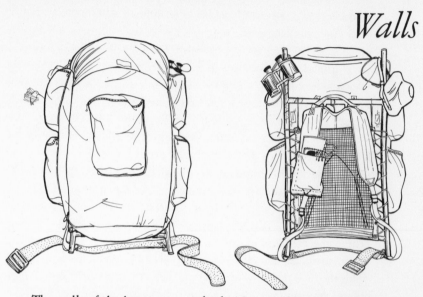

The walls of the house on your back (the outside walls, that is —the shell that contains and protects everything else) are your packframe and packbag; and there is no item of equipment, except perhaps a bad pair of boots, that's so certain to ruin a walking trip as an inadequate or ill-fitting

PACKFRAME.

On one-day trips, the kind of small pack you carry, if you carry one at all, does not really need a frame. And for light-load weekends a tolerably comfortable solution may be a Bergans-type rucksack with a small frame that puts most of the weight on the shoulder straps but transfers some of it to a band bearing against your hips. Such packs are lightweight and reasonably inexpensive. What's more, the soft and somewhat amorphous bags do not tend to catch too often in thick brush; and (a critical matter for climbers) they do not push you unexpectedly away from steep rock or ice. But rucksacks are not designed for heavy loads. The limit of real comfort for most people is probably around thirty-five pounds. Beyond that, and perhaps well below it, you need a pack with a rigid frame.

For many years, the only rigid type available was the Yukon or Trapper Nelson packboard with a straight wooden frame and wrap-around cloth or canvas that distributed the load efficiently over your whole back. But these packboards were heavy and cumbersome. And the wrap-around material, fitting snugly the whole length of your back, was abominably hot, even in temperate climates.

Today, by far the most widely used frame is the contoured aluminum type (see illustration, page 53).

These welded frames have all the advantages of the old packboards and few of their disadvantages. The tubular aluminum structure is rigid and extremely light. Contrary to appearances, it is remarkably strong. The two uprights curve in a very gentle "S" that echoes the contours of your waist, back, shoulders, and neck. The frame therefore sits close to your body throughout its length and holds the load far forward, where it exerts the least possible leverage against your muscles. But the construction leaves plenty of air space between load and back for ventilation. And the outward-curving lower ends never bear on your rump in the uncomfortable way that a straight frame can. These aluminum frames, like the old Trapper Nelson, are versatile. You can take off the packbag if you want to and tie on a slaughtered deer, or a five-gallon can containing a cache of food or water. With one of the several kiddie seats now on the market you can convert the frame into a rickshaw for junior.

An integral part of a modern rigid packframe—an item without which its effectiveness is halved—is the broad waistbelt. We'll discuss it presently (page 56).

There are certain disadvantages to tubular packframes—though they are marginal compared with the advantages. In dense brush, the ends of the frame tend to catch in branches and creepers. And when you're climbing the frame may bear unexpectedly on solid rock or ice and throw you dangerously off balance. But it is worth noting that most high-altitude climbing expeditions—for which load-carrying is as vital as actual climbing—now use tubular frames.

Holbein and Unsoeld did so on their technically difficult final assault up the West Ridge of Everest.

There are many good tubular aluminum packframes on the market. The best known, at least in the western U.S., is probably the Kelty. The Trailwise is very similar. And I have heard good words spoken about a less expensive grade of frame, The Cruiser, made by Camp Trails of Phoenix, Arizona. I suspect that the choice most people make between these frames and several others is governed by the familiar compound of chance, prejudice, and mildly informed opinion. Unless you are a congenital experimenter, you are unlikely to have put more than one or at the most two frames to really exhaustive tests.

A great deal of chance, a little prejudice, and almost no informed opinion led me to choose a Trailwise No. 502 frame (see illustration, page 53). But I have had it ten years now and it has done me proud. It has withstood three long trips totaling about twelve months. Every year it comes on a couple of week- or two-week-long wilderness trips and perhaps half a dozen two- to four-day jaunts. In addition I carry it on a considerable number of afternoon walks—partly to help keep me in backpacking shape, but often so that I can take along lunch and a typewriter. The fully loaded pack has withstood without a murmur an untold number of heavings into and draggings out of my station wagon, and many journeys in the luggage compartments of taxis, buses, and airliners. I don't think I treat the frame particularly brutally but I take no very great care of it, and it is still in perfect condition. It has never, in fact, given me a moment's trouble.

The bare frame weighs 1¼ pounds. Complete with back supports, yoke, and waistbelt (but no packbag), it weighs two pounds, ten ounces, costs $29.75. These Trailwise frames come in three sizes: small, regular, and large.

Back supports

There is much more to a packframe than aluminum tubing. First, some form of tightly stretched support or supports must hold the frame away from your back.

Now when the weather is even mildly warm I like to walk stripped to the waist; and where weather and privacy are both right (as often happened in Grand Canyon) I like to strip to hat, socks, and boots. So for many years I have used as back supports two woven nylon bands, each 4½ inches wide. One rested against my shoulder blades. The other, which did the real work, fitted across my hips. In the eight-inch gap between them air circulated freely, and when I walked bareback or even with a thin shirt the ventilation made a crucial difference to keeping cool. The only difficulty was that with loads of more than about 40 pounds the lower band began to press uncomfortably and sometimes even rucked.

This double-band arrangement is still standard on many good packs. But Trailwise have now replaced it with a single nylon mesh support, seventeen inches high, that greatly improves weight distribution. For some time I resisted the change because I felt that, in spite of the open mesh, the long support would prevent adequate ventilation. The material also felt very harsh to have pressing against your bare back. But I tried out the new support on a recent trip in temperatures well over 100°F. and found that my fears on both counts were quite unjustified.

The shoulder yoke, or harness

The yoke I use is three inches wide and is padded with ⅜-inch Ensolite (light foam plastic). The yoke used to be an extremely important fitting on any pack: in spite of contouring and efficient back supports, most of the weight bore down on your shoulders. But some years ago there appeared on the popular market a simple but revolutionary item:

The wide waistbelt.

The uninitiated never quite believe that a two-inch web belt with friction buckle, weighing a total of 5½ ounces, has revolutionized backpacking. A non-walking friend once slipped my pack on when it held about fifty-five pounds and was appalled at the dead weight on his shoulders. I told him to fasten the waistbelt. "Why," he said when he had done so, "it practically takes the sting out of the load!" It does too. The belt removes almost all the weight from the shoulders and puts it on your hips.

That is where it belongs. The human backbone has evolved from a system designed primarily for horizontal use, with the weight taken at fixed end-points. Our newfangled upright stance has therefore assured us a rich legacy of back trouble. Old-type packs put most of the load on your shoulders and imposed fierce vertical pressure on the easily damaged spine. They also put a heavy strain on the muscles of shoulders, neck, and back, hastening fatigue. A waistbelt removes this pressure and strain and transfers the weight to the simple, strong, and well-muscled structure of hips and legs. It also lowers your center of gravity—a material help in many situations.

Always wear the waistbelt tight. First, pull it firmly. Then hoist the pack higher on your back and tighten again. Now take a deep breath and pull even harder. If the belt almost hurts, it's about right.

At first you may find that the tight belt, taking almost the whole weight of the pack, tends to constrict your hip muscles. It may even cause mild cramp pains. But persevere. In a day or two the muscles will accept their new work. And the ease with which you now find yourself carrying the load will soon make you forget any temporary discomfort. If you want to, you can ease the strain from time to time by loosening the belt and returning the load to the shoulders. At least, I understand that that is the theory. I find that in practice I almost never do so.

Many waistbelts are now made of nylon. Provided you wear thick pants, they are good. But if you ever walk without pants or wearing only a swim suit or some such thin garment, the nylon will cut you. A softer belt of woven cotton or some such fabric does the trick.*

The belt I use completely encircles the waist. I am told that sidestraps from the base of the frame fail to do the job adequately.

* I have recently returned from a two-week desert trip on which I used a new Ensolite-padded Trailwise pack belt that is covered with nylon fabric (5½ ounces; $5.95). Excellent.

On the question of weight distribution in the pack when you are using a waistbelt, I am at present in a state of mild indecision. It was always said, and I think rightly, that with the old shoulder-load packs you should keep the weight as high as possible, as well as close to the body. Some makers maintain that, even with a waistbelt, high loading is still an advantage. So they design packbags that come only three-quarters way down the packframe and leave a space underneath for strapping your sleeping bag (which weighs precious little) in its stuff bag. I have made a few rough and ready experiments by moving twenty pounds of full canteens to points as high and as low as they would fit in my otherwise normally loaded packbag. Frankly, I remain unconvinced that there was much, if any, difference in the feel of the two loads. But I see that Kelty recommends fixing the three-quarter-length packbag in the high-load position for normal hiking, and suggest that the sleeping bag might go on top and the packbag be moved down to the lower part of the frame for activities that require greater stability, such as skiing, difficult climbing, or crossing rugged terrain.

Maybe I'm too conservative, but I remain skeptical about the practical value of the three-quarters-bag-with-sleeping-bag-underneath system. It's not only that I have yet to be convinced about any great load advantage; I dislike the loss of valuable space, and I wonder about the sleeping bag, even when it's protected by a stuff bag. No backpacker's sleeping bag is a robust article, and it is the one piece of equipment you just have to keep dry. Yet it seems to me that every time you put your pack down, the sleeping bag receives the maximum quota of both wear and moisture. Stuff bags may be protective and waterproof when new, but I wonder how long they remain so under this kind of treatment. Yet, to judge by the catalogues, the three-quarter-length pack has caught on.

There is no doubt at all about the value of keeping a load close to your back. At one stage of the California walk I got into the habit of tying my sleeping bag on the back of the pack. When rain forced me to stuff it inside again one day, I was amazed at the improvement in the way the pack rode. As far as possible, I now stow heavy articles close to the packframe, or at least keep them away from the back of the bag (see page 270). And the contouring of the frame, combined with the pull of the waistbelt, holds the load as close to my back as is consistent with adequate ventilation.

Tumpline

A tumpline is an adjustable band that runs around your forehead and attaches to the packframe, usually to its sides, and helps take some of the strain of heavy loads off back and shoulders. I have never used one, but a friend of mine who does so occasionally says they are an appreciable help, especially on steep upgrades. Unfortunately, he says, you cannot really use them effectively until your neck muscles have grown accustomed to the unfamiliar back strain.

Tumplines should apparently be attached to packframes as low down as possible. At a pinch they can, in an emergency, be used alone for quite heavy loads. The women in parts of Africa use them that way all the time for huge loads.

End-buttons

Small plastic buttons that plug the four open ends of the tubular frame are now standard fittings on my Trailwise pack. You need them. Open ends at the bottom pick up samples of any soft ground that you put the pack down on; and when you walk on again the samples neatly decant, if you are wearing shorts, into waiting sock tops. The buttons also protect the interior of car and home.

A spare button travels in my "Odds and Ends Can" (page 267).

I have made two minor modifications to my packframe:

Binocular bump-pad

My binoculars normally travel slung on a short cord over the projecting top of the frame, at my left shoulder (see page 230). At every step they bump, very gently, against the frame. For years I accepted the slight metallic sound without thinking about it. Then, one summer when I was out with a party in the Washington Cascades, a young fellow who had been following close behind me for several days said, "You know, I can't understand how you tolerate the rattle of those binoculars just behind your ear. Even walking several feet back of you like this, it nearly drives me crazy." After that, of course, it began to drive me crazy too, so I finally stuck a thick wrap of air mattress patching fabric around the frame's upright and crossbar, just where the binoculars bump. Now I am happily back to not noticing the muffled sound. I imagine fewer animals are scared out of my view too. Naturally, the pad needs a patch from time to time, when it wears through.

For further notes on carriage of binoculars see page 230.

Office-on-the-yoke

Because I so often walk without a shirt and therefore without a front pocket, I have had a five- by six-inch pocket sewn onto the front of my yoke strap, roughly where the shirt pocket comes. Into it go notebook and map, and sunglasses when not in use. Pen, pencil, camel-hair lens brush (page 233), and metal-cased thermometer (page 259) clip onto the front of it. I cannot imagine how I ever got along without such a pocket. Mine is made of ordinary blue-jean material, but anything stout will do.

For which side to put your office, see page 64.

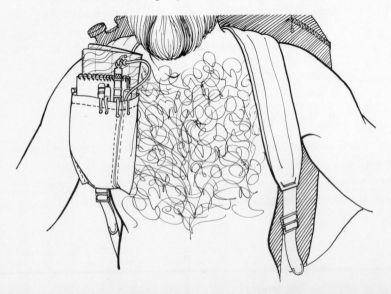

PACKBAG

Any good packbag is big, tough, as close to waterproof as you can make it, and multi-pocketed.

Generally speaking, the bigger the better. A cavernous sack weighs only an ounce or two more than a middle-class job, and it will accept just about everything you can carry, even on winter snow trips, when the bulk problem looms largest.

The fabric of the bag must be tough enough to withstand the sudden grabbing onslaughts of the sharpest rock outcrop and the most viciously pointed branch. It must not crack in extreme cold, as some synthetics do. And the bottom must resist constant scuffing.

"Water-repellent" is a term that fills me with distrust. Like "hi-fi" and "psychosomatic," it can mean almost anything or almost nothing. But your packbag must at the very least repel water. The ideal bag is waterproof, but even waterproof fabrics that stand up to hard wear do not insure a waterproof bag, as all untreated seams leak through the stitching holes. The seams can be waterproofed, but it is a tedious job that must be done by hand and I know no makers who do it. In downpour country—and also if you may have to swim across a river (see page 276)—you should certainly do it yourself with one of the specially made brush-on solutions suitable for the fabric of your particular bag. You might be wise to do it anyway. If you mean to do a good job—and no other kind is worth considering—do not expect to get through with it under an hour or two. Frankly, I am not yet convinced that any waterproofing job, no matter how carefully done, stays totally waterproof for very long. Not, at least, for river crossings.

It is hardly possible to have too many outside pockets on your packbag. In them you put all the things you are continually wanting. Also items you may need in an emergency, such as a first-aid kit, and a stack of small articles that you could never lay hands on if they languished at the bottom of the main sack. For suggestions, see page 272.

The bag itself must be anchored to the frame like a super-limpet.

Down the years I have used a number of different Trailwise packbags. The designs have steadily improved. The latest—called the 72L (L for large)—seems to me to be a highly efficient unit, close to ideal (see illustration, page 53).

The bag is about as big as they come: ten inches deep by fourteen inches wide by twenty-five inches high; but it weighs only one pound, seven ounces ($21.50—and worth every penny). It is made of very tough heavy-duty nylon duck, coated on the inside with waterproof Urethene that I am told does not crack under extreme cold. It is held to the frame at ten points: strong aluminum eyebolts screw into the frame and secure the bag by grommets let into continuous flaps that run down each side of the bag. The eyebolt arrangement does not look particularly reliable, but in ten years' rough use I have never had one pull out. The countersunk female units into which the bolts screw may work loose in time, but they are easily replaced. (Easily replaced at the store, that is. I've never tried it in the field.)

The bag has six large outside pockets: two on each side, one in the center, and a flat patch-type one on the flap. There is a single inside pocket—patch-type, open at the top—on the frame side of the bag. All outer pockets have nylon zippers, which run more smoothly than metal ones and do not so easily become iced up. They will fuse if you somehow succeed in dropping a hot coal on them; but on balance they seem an improvement over metal.

The bag is sold with a rigid aluminum bracket that holds the mouth squarely open, for easier loading. I've removed my bracket—partly because it prevents me from reaching back and down into the lower fastnesses of the bag when the pack is propped up behind me; partly because the bracket ruins the emptied pack as a backrest (see page 65); but mainly because I recently had to waterproof the bag thoroughly for a series of white-water river crossings (page 277), and the bracket, which fastens onto the packframe, has to pass through two open slits in the bag, nine inches below its top. By discarding the bracket I also saved two ounces.

My only complaint about this bag is that in its present form the two nylon cords that hold the flap closed fasten to eyelets at the bottom of the bag. So to close the pack you not only have to expend unnecessary energy bending or kneeling down but may also have to fiddle about in grass, brush, mud, or snow. But it shouldn't be too difficult to fix an upward extension from the eyelets, and by the time you read this maybe I'll have convinced Trailwise that they should do something about it.

For ten years now, the only backpacking rig I have owned has been this combination of the same old aluminum frame and one of the series of packbags. I suppose such a house is really too elaborate for short trips, but it has proved so comfortable and efficient, and I handle it now with so little thought, that it never occurs to me to turn to something else, even for an overnight jaunt.

The complete rig—packframe and accessories, bag, and waist-belt—weighs four pounds even, costs $51.25. Mine is the large size. The regular size weighs three pounds, twelve ounces; small, three pounds, ten ounces.

The equivalent packbag in three-quarter size (leaving room for your sleeping bag at the bottom of the frame) is one inch less deep, six inches shorter, has only one pocket on each side, and weighs and costs one ounce and $3 less.

THE WALLS IN ACTION

Packing

It is too early to consider ways of stowing gear into your house: we have not yet discussed the furniture. See page 270.

Getting the pack onto your back

You carry out this operation in the field many times each day, and the total energy consumed is considerable. At the end of an exhausting day it might even be crucial. So it pays to give the matter some thought.

The easiest way to load is to use a loading platform—a con-

venient rockledge or bank or fallen tree trunk—and just slip your
arms through the yoke straps.

Failing a loading platform—and rest assured that you will almost always fail—you can sit down, enyoke, and then stand up with
an easy if inelegant sidle. With a back-breaking load this is about
the only possible method. I believe it is the one the time-and-motion
sages agree is the least expensive in energy.

For light loads (under thirty pounds, say) I find that the
simplest method is to hoist the pack up into position with an easy
swinging motion, one hand gripping the yoke and the other the top
of the packframe. I now have a small nylon hand-strap on the upper
crossbar of my packframe—see illustration, page 53—and it certainly helps this lifting business. The strap is standard on new Trailwise frames. Swing the pack up from whichever side comes naturally;
but if you use an office-on-the-yoke (see page 60) make sure you
have it stitched on the yoke strap that slips onto your shoulders first.
On the other side it will infallibly foul things up.

The question remains: "At what stage should I switch from the
easy-swing-up to the sit-and-enyoke method?" My own answer is:
"Not until somewhere around sixty-five pounds, and not even then
for sure." I find that by swinging the pack up onto a raised upper
leg first, and then onto the shoulders without ever quite stopping,
you use surprisingly little energy. Yet one experienced friend of mine
sits-and-enyokes with a load as low as forty pounds. To find out what
suits you, experiment.

THE WALLS AS NON-WALLS

Your more or less empty pack may from time to time act as
windbreak on one side of a tent or bivouac, as ground insulation for
your feet when they protrude out beyond a three-quarter length air
mattress or pad (pages 172 and 175), or even as a pillow.

But for my money by far the most important auxiliary use is

The pack as backrest.

If you prop the full pack at an angle and lean against it so that your back comes between the side and center pockets, it makes a very comfortable chair back. When the bag has been emptied or part-emptied, prop the frame at right angles to your axis and lean back on it either direct or with the luxury padding of an air mattress (page 171).

When you can, simply prop the pack against a tree or a rock. But if, like me, you believe in resting on the smoothest and softest piece of ground in sight, there will nine times out of ten be no such convenience. So mostly you use your staff as the prop. It soon becomes almost automatic, the moment you halt—even for a ten-minute rest—to look for a rock or a crevice or a tree or even just a clump of grass to wedge the butt of the staff against. Failing all these —and here again you will fail regularly—just angle-prod the staff down into the soil until it holds firmly, with or without an assist from a stone, and then jam the top of the staff between the yoke and the top crossbar of the pack, hard up against the bag. (The new nylon handstrap on my pack holds it perfectly.) Fine-adjust the angle of the packframe, and you are ready to rest. It sounds rather complicated, I know, but after a while the whole operation takes about four seconds—and virtually no conscious thought.

Kitchen

FOOD

There is an altogether delightful simplicity about the idea of just walking out and away and living off the land, and the system's allure is stiffened by obvious practical advantages: no heavy food in your pack; constant variety; fresh, vitamin-rich products at every plucking. It seems as if you could hardly ask for a more perfect fusion of romance and efficiency.

Forget it. Above all, forget the efficiency. There are no doubt a few places in which certain temperaments could live off the land and still find time to do one or two other things as well, but my advice is to leave the happy dreams to those who have never tried it.

That does not mean ignoring what the land drops into your lap. I often supplement my regular rations with trout, and occasionally with mushrooms or watercress or a few wild strawberries. And not long ago I came close to eating my first rattlesnake steak (page 297). But in most cases and places, the time and energy you would have to expend in shooting, snaring, catching, or otherwise gathering in a day's food and then preparing it is simply better applied elsewhere. (See, though, Rattlesnakes, page 298.) Remember too that a gun and its ammunition outweigh several days' rations.

An emergency is a different matter. And a deliberate attempt to live off the land may be well worth it for the spiritual effect of sheer primitive simplicity. But for normal walking, when one of your objects is to get somewhere, I recommend unequivocally that you carry everything you expect to need.

66

In choosing what foods to take, consider:

1. Nutritional values, especially stick-to-guttability
2. Weight
3. Ease of preparation
4. Palatability
5. Packaging (with a special thought for litter)
6. Cost.

On every count except cost, dehydrated food is the only answer.*
Less than 2¼ pounds of it can satisfy your nutritional needs for a
highly energetic day. Meals are childishly simple to prepare. And
although a steaming mess of pemmican and dehydrated potatoes
is hardly the kind of dish you would want to find on the table at
home, I assure you that at the end of a twenty-mile hike it tastes
better than a porterhouse steak does at home. Many modern dehydrated foods are packaged in strong, ultra-light, almost moistureproof envelopes made of some material such as polyethylene that
can be burned after use.

Dehydrated food, properly processed and packaged, is stable.
Its flavor does not become haylike. And provided the water content
remains below 5 per cent neither bacteria nor mold will grow on it
and insects will not eat it. It is not perfect, of course. It is damnably
expensive, makes you fart like a bull, and demands a certain quota of
tender loving care to make it consistently palatable. But if you are
carrying any considerable number of days' rations it is in my opinion
the only practical solution.

When it comes to the detailed problem of how much and what
kinds of food to carry, there are two possible approaches:

Trial and Error, in which you follow personal preferences and are

* By dehydrated I mean freeze-dried as well as vacuum-processed, though a
distinction is sometimes drawn. Freeze-dried products are more expensive but
tend to taste better. I find that I rarely use them because they're often intolerably
fussy to prepare.

guided only by rules of thumb; and
The Scientific Nutritional Method, in which you calculate in calories
and try to balance the carbohydrate-protein-fat intake against
your energy output.

TRIAL AND ERROR

The advantage of this approach is that, although it involves a
lot of built-in chance, your answers begin with a bias toward your
individual requirements and evolve along the same axis. This is
important, physiologically and psychologically. Each individual's
alimentary system works in its own idiosyncratic way. And different
men have very different philosophies of outdoor eating. Some like
to make a meal out of making a meal. At the other extreme lie those
who, like me, were born British and therefore, as far as food goes,
barbaric.*

I began, years ago, with the trial and error method, and in the
course of time I developed a well-tested backpacking menu, entirely
adequate for barbarians. Naturally, the details continue to change.
They also vary a good deal in the face of different conditions. But
for a seven-day period—the normal basis on which I plan (see page
19)—my current standard food list reads:

	Net Weight		Cost	Based on Price of:
	lbs.	*oz.*		
Special dry cereal mixture	2	0	$2.10	$0.92/14 oz.
3 Pkgs dehydrated fruit				
(4 oz.)	0	12	1.40	.70/6 oz.
6 Energy bars	0	9	2.94	1.47/3 *bars*
Beef jerky	0	4	1.50	1.50/4 oz.

* Hell has been described as a place in which the politicians are French, the
policemen German, and the cooks British.

	Net Weight		Cost	Based on Price of:
	lbs.	oz.		
8 Pkgs dried soup	1	4	2.88	.36 ea.
1 Pkg instant gravy powder	0	1	.12	.24/2 pkgs.
7 Meat bars	1	5	10.15	1.45 ea.
5 Pkgs dehydrated beans (4 oz.)	1	4	.81	.65/16 oz.
2 Pkgs dehydrated potatoes (4 oz.)	0	8	.87	.65/6 oz.
1 Pkg dehydrated mixed vegetables (4 oz.)	0	4	.65	.97/6 oz.
Herbs and spices	0	1	.10	Various
Powdered nonfat milk	1	6	.75	1.09/2 lbs.
Granulated sugar	1	8	.18	.59/5 lbs.
1 Bar semisweet chocolate	0	8	.46	.46 ea.
3½ Bars Kendal Mint Cake candy (6 oz.)	1	5	1.40	.40 ea.
Dry raisins	1	0	.42	.39/15 oz.
30 Tea bags	0	3	.37	.59/48
2 Pkgs fruit drink mix	0	6	.25	.25/2 pkgs.
Margarine	0	4	.09	.35/lb.
Salt	0	3	.03	.25/24 oz.
Salt tablets (about 40)	0	1	.25	.59/100
Emergency ration: 1 meat bar	0	3	1.45	1.45 ea.
Totals	15 lbs.	3 oz.	$29.17	
Daily average	2 lbs.	2½ oz.	$4.17	

(For simplicity's sake I have not attempted to introduce gross weights, but with today's efficient packaging I doubt if there is a difference of more than an ounce between daily gross and net totals.)

I often amend this standard, basic list to suit time and place —for example, by substituting other items (see below) for the meat-and-vegetable dinner. Sometimes I take no margarine, though in trout country I may carry an extra four ounces for frying.*

The basic menu presently reads:

Breakfast: (*Immediately after waking, often in darkness, nearly always in a hurry, and therefore kept very simple.*) Four ounces cereal with milk; *or* one package fruit, often with cereal and/or chocolate. A stick or two of beef jerky; *or* half an energy bar. Six or seven cups of tea—with milk and copious sugar. During a recent two-week trip I boosted the breakfast protein by eating about half the dinner meat bar, raw. It worked well: I never actually gagged, and the effect seemed to last through the morning.

Lunch: One package soup. A half or whole energy bar, and/or a little beef jerky. Occasionally, tea.

Britannic afternoon tea: Tea.

Dinner: (*Late, often after dark.*) "Stew": 1 meat bar; 1 package beans or potatoes; about ½ ounce mixed vegetables; gravy; herbs and spices.

---

* Not long ago, on a three-day mountain trip, I took only the following food:

	lbs.	oz.
10 Meat bars	1	14
1 Tiny package herbs and dried onions	0	0
2 Ounces beef jerky	0	2
7 Bars Kendal Mint Cake	2	10
2 Energy bars	0	3
1 Pkg. fruit drink mix	0	3
9 Tea bags	0	1
Powdered milk	0	3
Sugar	0	8
Three-day total	5	12
Daily average	1	14⅔

I left behind my cooking pots, stove, and white gas (see pages 100 and 106), thereby saving three pounds, two ounces. Instead, I took along an ordinary medium-size tin can, made two holes near the rim, and threaded through a baling-wire handle. In this can I boiled—on a small wood fire—the water I needed for tea and, usually, for making gruel out of the meat bar at night. Otherwise, I just bit off and chewed whatever I wanted.

The experiment definitely succeeded. I was never hungry, walked well, found no "meal" objectionable, and reveled in the light load.

The practical details of how to prepare these meals will have to wait (page 123) until after we have taken a look at the furnishings of our kitchen.

I repeat that I have listed only my *basic* menu. Fancier eaters can compose endless variations on its simple theme. I often ignore the score myself. A soup lunch, for example, assumes that I can stop to cook; when time presses I may just eat a half or whole meat bar —perhaps with some mintcake or an energy bar—and save the soup for dinner.

You must buy backpacking food quite differently and much more carefully than the food you use at home. Compare all weights, of course, and packaging. Read the cooking instructions and choose the simplest, always. Ignore cost, to the limit of purse and temperament. Above all, make sure that each item will give you a maximum of either quick energy or stick-to-guttability. In other words, forget the "zesty richness" and "tangy flavor" and other alluring horse-radish printed on the packages; what you want to know is how much better this particular item is going to make you feel when you're tired and hungry, and how long it will go on making you feel better. Advice on this score is useful only up to a point: what really matters, remember, is how the food suits *you*. And the only way to decide that is to experiment.

After several years of trial and error with a whole slew of foods, I have reached these current conclusions about the uses and brands of each item (items treated in same order as in list on pages 68–9):

Dry cereal mixture: I have quite recently "discovered" two excellent and very similar Swiss cereal-fruit-and-nut mixtures, FINI and FAMILIA. Both are very sweet. Both contain a high proportion of oats. FINI includes a little dried skim milk. Neither needs cooking. Both claim to be "the Original Swiss Bircher Muesli"—made from organically grown produce and based on the health foods recommended by a Dr. Bircher-Benner who in 1895 founded "a new medical school, based on dietetics." All I know is that they taste good and stick to your gut. I use them not only for breakfast, regularly, and lunch, occasionally, but also for filling odd corners of emptiness as and when they become insistent—particularly for a quick snack when, as sometimes happens, I run short of energy toward the end of a hard day.

Ordinary unembellished dry cereal such as corn flakes is fine for odd-corner-filling and to help out a fruit breakfast or light lunch, but it's hardly enough by itself to launch you on a long day's walking. I no longer carry it. But All Bran can be useful in the first days of a trip if, because of the suddenly changed way of life, your bowels need prompting.

Dehydrated fruit (which averages one eighth the weight of the unprocessed product) was for years my standard four-ounce breakfast. I still use it fairly often, either alone or with a little cereal and/or chocolate. It needs no cooking: just soak overnight. I ring the changes on apple, apricot, date, peach, pear, and fruit cocktail. The Trailwise brand I use now comes in six-ounce polyethylene bags. But for long trips you can buy it in bulk tins (average 2½ pounds), and then package four-ounce portions in small polycel heat-seal bags by pressing along the open edge with a warm iron. It's a simple operation that saves money and permits fancy mixtures. My favorite: apple and date.

Fruit is also a useful snack, nibbled straight out of the bag at any time of day or night.

Beef jerky (those same thin brown strips, very tasty, that the barman sells you) not only beefs up breakfast but does it simply. You can even suck it while you're striking camp or when on the move. It makes an excellent odd-corner snack, any time of day. It is heavily salted though, and may make you thirsty. Each pound of it is equivalent to 3½ pounds of fresh beef. At least, so the makers claim.

You can if you like drop a few pieces of jerky into the lunchtime soup or evening stew. But don't expect it to rehydrate; during the curing process it has, unlike most dehydrated food, been heated past the point at which tissue structure is irreversibly damaged, and no amount of soaking will soften its leathery soul.

Energy bars. Not long ago I bought on impulse, exactly as the store intended I should, some prominently displayed bars called

Nu-V. The label claimed that each highly concentrated 1½-ounce bar contained 200 calories, in the optimum carbohydrate-fat-protein ratio (see page 80). The ingredients list ran to thirty-six improbable items, including safflower oil, honey, yeast, papaya, watercress, riboflavin, and enough other vitamins to sink a dietary conference ($1.47 for a three-bar, 4½-ounce package).*

The boost these expensive little bars give me certainly seems to last. They taste good, too, to my ultra-sweet tooth, whether as part of a meal or as nibble food. I often use them now as an alternate breakfast booster, instead of beef jerky. It so happened that during the first trip I carried them I suffered from mild mountain sickness for the first time in my life, and for several days they were the only food I could consistently face. I could have done with five times my one-a-day ration. Perhaps that is why I am now enamored of them, at least temporarily.†

Alternative breakfasts: Some people—perhaps most—demand a cooked breakfast. There are plenty of dried-egg preparations on

---

* I have just learned that Nu-V bars are no longer being made. But I shall let them stand in these pages—and only in part because they're built into several calculations in this chapter. They seemed to me to fill a need, and no doubt something similar will emerge.

† At high altitudes, anyone's appetite is liable to falter. In particular, you may revolt against the very thought of fats and proteins. The elevation at which such awkward things happen varies widely from person to person, even from trip to trip. It may start as low as eight or nine thousand feet. It's apparently rather likely to happen above, say, seventeen thousand. Slow acclimation helps but does not necessarily cure. All you can really do is take along a fair variety of foods and hope there's always something in your pack that appeals to you. Sweet things are probably the best bet, but the range of sudden demands is unpredictable. Frank Smythe, struggling on and up, alone, toward the summit of Mount Everest, longed for frankfurters and sauerkraut; Hillary, high on Cho Oyu the year before he climbed Everest, for pineapple cubes. I had always thought these reports a bit farfetched. But on a recent trip I found myself feeling, at a mere 14,000 feet, the same craving for pineapple. Such vagaries of appetite are the results of a particular kind of stress. A soldier may face a similar situation, and the U.S. Army Food Service recognizes the palatability problem that can arise under combat stress. They have a saying: "It doesn't matter how many calories you give a man if he won't eat."

In the mountains, the trick is to guess right—short of pineapple cubes— and still keep the menu short. It's as simple as that. And as difficult.

the market now, plain or in fancy omelettes, but none of them exactly sends me—not, at least, when Fletcher-cooked. And above all there is the time-and-trouble factor. For rest days I often try to catch fish the evening before and fry them for breakfast.

Some people regularly carry ham or bacon for breakfast. Others take such freeze-dry concoctions as Ranch Style and Campsite Breakfasts, alluringly subtitled "scrambled eggs, sausage patties, and hash brown potatoes." Read the instructions before you buy them.

Soups: I am always a little surprised that I go to the trouble of cooking soup for lunch. But even in the desert I go on doing it, almost every day there is enough time. Hot food seems to recharge me best.

The Swiss soup powders now generally available in foil packets seem by far the best. I choose Maggi over Knorr because it is simpler to prepare. There is almost no stirring or fancy work, and at the end of a long, long morning that makes a monumental difference. Herbs improve any soup. So does a dab of margarine.

I used to switch soup flavors around just to suit my taste. For a long time, though, I have suspected that the flavors differed in food value, and quite recently I've discovered that they most certainly do (see footnote, pages 82–3).

Gravy masculates the evening stew. For variety I alternate between instant gravy powder and the eighth package of soup on my food list (usually oxtail or mushroom).

Meat bars: Pemmican—from a Cree word meaning "fat meat" —is made by pounding dried lean meat into a paste with fat and preserving it in the form of cakes or bars. The cakes sometimes include raisins, sugar, and even suet. The object is to concentrate as much nutrition as possible into a convenient form that will keep almost indefinitely.

The word "pemmican" recently seems to have slunk out of favor, but the bars still flourish. One reason most makers no longer call them pemmican may be the connotation of hardship. Also, perhaps, because a regular diet of the old, strong-flavored pemmican grew horribly monotonous. (It's a sound general principle—liable to avert considerable suffering—that if some items of your diet are frequently repeated you should try for bland-tasting versions.)

The meat bar I now use is almost tasteless, so by using a variety of vegetables, gravies, and herbs or spices I can make it the nutritional foundation of every day's big meal and yet still dine off a different dish each night of the week. Well, vaguely different, anyway.

The easily crumbled bar is austerely labeled "Wilson's Certified Meat Food Product," and contains nothing but dehydrated beef and pork, beef fat, and salt. But don't let the austerity put you off. This is a highly efficient source of fat and protein. One three-ounce bar is said to be the equivalent of one pound of fresh meat. It has become the base for six out of every seven backpacking dinners I eat.

Chewed for lunch—straight out of its foil wrapping, like a half-peeled banana—the stuff is about as interesting as a midday TV program. But it satisfies. And the satisfaction lasts.

I have recently tried it out for breakfast (see page 70).

Nowadays I carry an eighth meat bar as my emergency ration (see page 78).

Vegetables. As the main vegetable in my dinner stew I mostly use four ounces of precooked beans, with diced potatoes as a change perhaps twice a week. About an ounce of mixed vegetables helps leaven the taste. Good alternatives are tomato, cabbage, onion flakes, and diced carrots. A bad alternative is flaked spinach—as savagely tasteless as sawdust. Trailwise vegetables do not now come in the four-ounce packages that I find most convenient, but it is simple and also thrifty to buy them in the larger sizes (up to 16 ounces) and divide by eye in the field. Or you can reapportion at home and iron-seal in polycel bags to suit your own requirements (see page 72).

Herbs and spices can go a long way toward making a dull and repetitive diet both interesting and varied. I carry very small bags of ground cumin seed, oregano, thyme, and an "Italian" herb mixture. Also dried onion flakes.

Alternatives to basic dinner. I know that many people could not face my "stew" every day, and even I like an occasional change. Most packaged "main dishes" for backpacking need far too much care lavished on the cooking for my taste, but if you enjoy juggling four different ingredients through a maze of stirrings and simmerings (not to mention "patting with a paper towel") then you can have yourself a ball with some of Armour's or Wilson's freeze-dry concoctions, such as Pork Chop or Beef Steak Dinners. The only dinners I have found that approach the simplicity of my all-purpose stew are Seidel Trail Packets (especially chili beans in sauce and spaghetti with tomato sauce). With all dinners, ignore such printed fiction as "Serves four." If you need the kind of evening meal I do, allow a total of at least seven or eight ounces.

Milk. Powdered whole milk, though it contains valuable fat, dissolves slowly and imperfectly. I use Carnation Non Fat—because it is the quickest-dissolving kind I have tried, and because you can buy it in boxes containing ten little envelopes, each 3.2 ounces net, and the contents of one envelope exactly fill my plastic milk-squirter (page 103) and with care last exactly one day.

Granulated sugar. The simplest quick-energy food. Use with everything.

Semisweet chocolate, used mostly for cooking, melts less easily than the ordinary kind. Still, it melts. In deserts, avoid. Elsewhere, it's a fine filler of odd corners, and a piquant change.

Mintcake candy. At hourly halts—except, sometimes, the first of the day—I give myself a quick-energy boost by sucking a piece or two of an English product, "Wilson's Celebrated Original Kendal Mint Cake—A Lakeland Sweetmeat." This candy is popular with mountaineering and caving expeditions. It comes in six-ounce bars, contains $6/7$ sugar and $1/7$ glucose, tastes good in both white and brown variants, and does not seem to induce thirst. I allow myself half a bar a day. But I eat none on stay-in-camp days and very little on easy days, and save as much as I can spare for days when I'm pushing hard.

Raisins. An every-halt booster that I eat with the mintcake. Some people, I know, quickly get tired of raisins. I am inclined to do so, but find that I go on using them. To avoid goo-coated fingers, buy the dry type, always.

Tea bags naturally form the backbone of any British-type menu.

Fruit drink mix. A pleasant quick-energy supply. Valuable in killing the taste of alkaline or otherwise unpalatable water: makes even the Colorado River quite drinkable. Wyler's fruit-ades, complete with sugar, come in convenient three-ounce foil packages that make one quart. Flavors: orange and lemonade (the two best); pineapple-grapefruit (pleasant); strawberry, raspberry, cherry, and grape (also-rans). Ratings are my own, but seem to be widely shared.

Margarine (rather than butter, because it keeps) improves almost any cooked dish. In trout country I sometimes carry an extra four ounces for frying.

Salt and salt tablets. When you sweat you lose salt, and unless you replace it you may suffer from heat exhaustion. So use it more lavishly on food than you would at home, especially in low humidity when sweat dries quickly and you often fail to realize how much liquid you have lost. Only experience will tell you whether you also need tablets. Individual requirements vary widely. A Death Valley Ranger once told me, "When it reaches 110°F. I take one tablet a day. I need that one, but my stomach won't accept more. Yet there's a guy at Park HQ who has to take twenty a day. If he doesn't he ends up in the hospital."

Salt deficiency may cause mild or acute exhaustion, or produce other, highly variable, symptoms. I've only once been sure I was suffering from it. As I approached Death Valley on my California walk, in temperatures around 100°, my leg muscles began to ache and my head to flutter. Several hours passed before it occurred to me that the trouble might be salt. Soon after I swallowed a few tablets, legs and head returned to normal. From then on, in really hot weather, I took eight tablets a day. Now, I always carry enough for at least a four-a-day dosage. Some people need more, some less. If in doubt, overdose yourself. That Death Valley Ranger told me he suspected too much salt might cause a mild skin rash. He may be right; but if so it's a price worth paying. Extra table salt will do instead of tablets, but tablets are very convenient—and more likely to get taken. Buy them in any drug store. Most brands now include some sugar as an energy boost.

Emergency ration. It is probably wise to carry a small emergency ration of some sort, just in case of trouble. Its nature depends on what you expect to do if things go wrong. If you are always going to be able to get out to civilization within one day, some quick-acting high-energy food may be best. Horlick's rum fudge bars (seven ounces, 826 calories), specially developed for expeditionary use, are effective—and delicious. Mostly, though, I now carry an extra Wilson's meat food product bar (three ounces, 513 calories). Almost all fat and protein, it releases energy more slowly than the fudge and would therefore be more effective if my aim were merely to keep alive—as would be the case if I were injured.

Morale boosting: goodies. If you have been living on dehydrated food for days or weeks or months you will not hesitate, given half a chance, to call in at a cafe (as I could occasionally on the California walk) and order a red-blooded steak. Even under more Spartan conditions you may be able to engineer a change of pace. I do not mean only such delicacies as small trout so fresh that it's a problem to keep them from curling double in the frying pan. On one recent trip I took along as a bonus, against my better judgment, a featherweight aluminum can of freeze-dried crab meat, with sauce (1½ ounces; $1.25; Apollo Products of Hawthorne, California). Preparation was about as simple as you can get: add cold water. And the taste, to my surprise, was vivid.

On my Grand Canyon walk I included in each cache and airdrop one can of delectables—oysters, lobster, cocktail meatballs, fish appetizers, or frog's legs—and a small bottle of claret. The goodies were great. But the claret, oddly enough, did not really fit in. You simply don't need alcohol in the wilderness. Not when you're on your own, anyway.

But if you feel the need for alcohol (and a little scotch or bourbon in a group can be very welcome at the end of a day) a good container is an aluminum bottle similar to the one I use for white gas (page 110). Get the kind that's anodized and noncorrosive, and so protect both the inside of the bottle and the taste of the booze. In addition, the bottle's bright outside color will obviate (or almost obviate) possible dire confusions. (Anodized bottle, 1⅓ pint, three ounces, $2.50.) Back home after a trip, wash the bottle carefully and leave open until next time.

Food packaging. Most modern materials are pretty effective (see page 67), but some raise a garbage problem. Polyethylene plastic is particularly good because it can be burned. It is moistureproof for reasonable periods, though there is some degree of porosity. In damp climates the packages should if possible be stored or cached in airtight cans, perhaps with some desiccant such as calcium oxide.

For years I was content to consider backpacking gastrology on a *trial and error* basis. Then, quite recently, it occurred to me that the logical approach was the strictly rational, quantitative,

SCIENTIFIC NUTRITIONAL METHOD.

It seemed to me that by tailoring a diet to my exact nutritional requirements under specified conditions and by paring vigorously away as usual at the half ounces I could hardly fail to come up with the most economical menu—economical, that is, in terms of weight and energy. I might have to allow for a few personal fads and fancies, but that was all.

First I disposed of the often-raised mineral and vitamin questions. I knew that the public mind has been obfuscated on both counts by dense, dollar-delivering Madison Avenue smokescreens. I confirmed, as I expected, that unless you are going to walk for a year or more in country known to be deficient in some vital mineral such as iodine or cobalt and are going to live on nothing but locally grown produce (a pretty unlikely combination of events), you can forget the minerals. If you are in normal health you can forget the vitamins for at least a month, and probably forever. My energy bars alone (page 72) just about take care of all the vitamins, and there's a load of vitamin C in Wyler's lemonade mix. I never bother with a supplement, but if you are going on a trip longer than a month you can, if you like, take along multivitamin pills. They weigh very little and may protect your peace of mind.

Next I looked at fat and protein requirements. It seems, though it cannot yet be fully explained, that certain minimum amounts of each are essential. Accepted guideline minima are: fats—20 per cent of total caloric intake; protein—45 grams per day per one hundred pounds bodyweight (though your body cannot assimilate the protein properly if you eat the full requirement at a single sitting). Fats contain 9 calories per unit of weight compared with 4 calories in the same weight of protein or carbohydrate, and they therefore form by far the most efficient food in terms of calories per unit of weight. Although no meaningful figures exist (the technical literature hedges, even cites "fast and slow stomachs"), it seems to be accepted that the energy from fats and protein is released over longer periods than that from carbohydrates, and that they are therefore less efficient for booster snacks but excellent for what might be called all-day or all-night background. As far as is known at present, there seems no purely nutritional reason why calorie-efficient fats should not make up at least 35 per cent of a diet, and perhaps much more.*

But fats can raise a palatability problem. At high elevations in particular, many people cannot face the thought of fatty foods (page 73, footnote)—possibly because the body needs far more oxygen to break down fats than it does for carbohydrates, and in a thin atmosphere simply rebels against the extra demand. This is a pity, because it is usually cold at high elevations, and fat is the most efficient heat-producing food. Perhaps this ability of fat to produce heat is the reason we tend to dislike the idea of eating much of it in hot weather. I know that I tend to want less when walking in deserts.

---

* I am being deliberately vague. At present, the full facts about fats (or "lipids" as nutritionists usually call them) are simply not understood. Neither are the facts about human idiosyncrasies. Just recently I was in the nutritional sciences department of a university checking some figures for this chapter when I saw, on the blackboard in a room of delightfully unstuffy researchers, the plaint: "Lipids are inscrutable." But someone had struck out "Lipids" and substituted "Guinea pigs."

With these minor matters out of the way I turned to the basic problem: total energy supply.

First I set about learning how to calculate the nutritional content of various foods. Almost at once I discovered *Agricultural Handbook No. 8: Composition of Foods,* published by the U. S. Department of Agriculture. I recommend this book to anyone at all interested in a scientific approach to outdoor eating (or, for that matter, indoor eating). Most of its 190 pages consist of two vastly comprehensive tables headed "Composition of foods, 100 grams, edible portion" and (better still for our purposes) "Nutrients in the edible portion of 1 pound of food as purchased." These tables analyze in detail the nutritional make-up of everything from abalone (raw and canned), through muffins, to zwieback. It is worth remembering, though, that the figures for many foods can be only approximations. As a nutrition expert warned me: "No two wheat germs are quite alike." (See, I suspect, the rather surprising figures the table gives for different kinds of trout.)

The book also contains several supplementary tables and some mildly useful notes. It does not contain, as it should, the information that 1 gram = 0.357 ounces, and that therefore 100 grams = 3.57 ounces; or that 1 ounce = 28.35 grams. Even if you are not about to use the full and rather forbidding figures, you need a rough conversion rate.

Public libraries—except, perhaps, very small ones—are likely to have reference copies of *Handbook No. 8.* There is sure to be one in the Nutritional Sciences Library of any university, and with luck you'll be able to buy a copy from the student union book store or its equivalent. Failing that, you can, in the due course of bureaucratic time, get one for $1.50 from The Superintendent of Documents, U. S. Government Printing Office, Washington, D. C. 20402.

By studying *Handbook No. 8,* consulting various manufacturers, and reading much small print on many labels, I managed to calculate the caloric, protein, and fat content of each item on my standard food list (page 68). (In one or two cases, where figures were unobtainable, I substituted guesswork. There's a certain amount of it involved in any such game. It is often difficult, for example, to assess from available figures exactly what percentage of the caloric content of a food is in fat form. Two sources of information may supply widely divergent figures. But a nutrition expert has checked the following table and detects no flagrant errors.)

lbs.	oz.		Energy Value (Calories)	Fat Energy Value (Calories)	Protein (Grams)
2	0	Cereal mixture (Bircher Muesli)	3200	700	90
0	12	Dehydrated fruit (average)	1200	30	14
0	9	Energy bars	1200	480	48
0	4	Beef jerky	410	40	98
1	4	Soup powders (average)*	2400	680	85
0	1	Gravy powder	100	10	5
1	5	Meat food product bars	3590	2420	283
1	4	Dehydrated beans	1930	90	127
0	8	Dehydrated potatoes	800	10	19
0	4	Dehydrated mixed vegetables	400	10	9
0	1	Herbs and spices	0	0	0
1	6	Powdered nonfat milk	2230	40	223
1	8	Granulated sugar	2620	0	0
0	8	Semisweet chocolate	1150	640	10
1	5	Kendal Mint Cake	2290	0	0
1	0	Dry raisins	1310	0	11
0	3	Tea bags	0	0	0
0	6	Fruit drink mix	600	0	0
0	4	Margarine	820	810	1
0	3	Salt	0	0	0
0	1	Salt tablets (30% dextrose)	30	0	0
0	3	Emergency ration (1 meat bar)	510	350	40
		Total for one week	26,790	6310	1063
		Average daily total	3830	900 (23.5%)	152

* The wide variation in food values of different soup flavors was quite a surprise. Here are the figures for Maggi Soups, kindly supplied by the Nestlé Company:

At first glance, the 3830 daily caloric total struck me as a little low, but I postponed judgment. Naturally, I was relieved to find that my diet provided more than the guideline minima for both fats and protein: fats, 23.5 per cent of total caloric intake as against a recommended minimum of 20 per cent; protein, 152 grams as against my personal recommended minimum requirement of 85 grams—based on a bodyweight of 190 pounds.

With these intake figures established, I turned to the second part of the food-to-output tailoring process: calculating what my body needed for maintenance and exercise under various conditions. If I had been starting from scratch, without a food list to evaluate, I should probably have begun on this tack. I'm glad I didn't.

I soon learned that for maintenance alone (basal metabolism) the average person needs about 1100 calories per day per 100 pounds of bodyweight. In city-slob shape—which is the way I seem to start just about every backpacking trip—I now weigh around 190 pounds. So mere maintenance drained off 2090 calories from my daily total of 3830.

During the process of digestion, the body consumes a certain amount of energy as heat. This factor is called, for some reason, "Specific Dynamic Action." It fluctuates between 6 per cent and rather more than 10 per cent of the total caloric intake. For simplicity, it is usually averaged at 10 per cent. So in my case Specific

Soup Flavor	Net Pkg. Wt. (oz.)	Protein (%)	Fat (%)	Carbo-hydrates (%)	Food Energy Value per bag (Calories)
Peas with smoked ham	2¾	17.4	14.2	48.5	334
Onion	2⅝	10.2	12.5	56.2	309
Egg macaroni shell	2⅝	14.2	11.9	54.5	309
Oxtail	2⅝	18.5	13.8	43.2	305
Asparagus	2⅜	14.6	11.4	53.4	276
Mushroom	2⅜	12.2	10.9	56.0	263
Vegetable	2	11.4	13.6	39.0	197
Chicken noodle	2¼	4.2	11.4	53.4	176

Dynamic Action accounted for another 380 calories. 2470 of the total gone; 1360 left. I began to wonder.

Next I got down to assessing energy output over and above these constants. I quickly ran to earth a table of fascinating figures. The moment I began to read the table I thought, Ah, *this* is the answer. Now, nothing can stop me.

THE ENERGY COST OF ACTIVITIES*
(Exclusive of basal metabolism and influence of food)

	Calories per 100 lbs. per hour
Walking: on hard, smooth, level surface, at 2 mph	45
at 3 mph	90
at 4 mph	160
(For walking on rough trails, multiply each figure by a rather arbitrary figure of 2.)	
Standing, relaxed	30
Sitting, quietly	20
Eating	20
Dressing and undressing	30
Lying still, awake	5
Sleeping (basal metabolism only)	0
Shivering, very severe	up to 220
Sawing wood	260
Swimming, at 2 mph	360
Writing	20
Dishwashing	45
Laundry (light)	60
Singing in a loud voice	35

This table lists several other activities that make interesting reading, and all of them might, at a pinch and on a well diversified walking trip, become ancillary pursuits:

* Most of these figures are derived from Carpenter, T. M.: *Factors and Formulas for Computing Respiratory Exchange and Biological Transformations of Energy.* Carnegie Institute, 1948 edition, page 136.

	Calories per 100 lbs. per hour
Typewriting, rapidly	45
Driving an automobile	40
Bicycling (moderate speed)	110
Horseback riding, walk	65
trot	200
gallop	300
Running	320
Boxing	520
Rowing	730

Come to think of it, campfire concerts often feature harmonica and recorder accompaniment, and I suppose there is no reason why it should stop there. So:

	Calories per 100 lbs. per hour
Violin playing	25
Cello playing	60
Piano playing, Mendelssohn's songs	35
Beethoven's *Appassionata*	65
Liszt's *Tarantella*	90

Almost all walking includes some uphill work. And it seems that, assuming a body efficiency of 30 per cent, you use about 110 calories in raising every 100 pounds of bodyweight each 1000 feet of elevation. For practical purposes, you can add the weight of your pack direct to bodyweight.

Armed with all these figures (but already suffering misgivings) I began to work out energy sums for an average fairly hard day's wilderness walking. I pictured myself, at 190 pounds, carrying a fifty-pound pack, walking on a rough trail for seven hours (with halts), gaining a total of 3,000 feet in elevation, and otherwise doing all the things you do on an average day. Juggling with the figures I had gathered, and trying to pin down the hours of a wilderness day along the lines of the table on page 24, I came up with:

Calories

Basal metabolism (190 lbs. @ 1100 cals. per 100 lbs.)	2090
Climbing 3000 feet (240 lbs. @ 110 cals. per 1000 ft.)	760
6 hours actual walking, at 2 mph (240 lbs. @ 45 cals. per hour per 100 lbs., x a factor of 2 for roughness of trail)	1250
3 hours dishwashing, laundering (light), making and striking camp, photography, compulsive dallying, and unmentionable activities (average: 50 cals. per 100 lb.-hours)	290
3 hours dressing and undressing, standing (relaxed), singing in a loud voice, cooking, and such items as evaporated time (quite unaccountable for) (average: 30 cals. per 100 lb.-hours)	160
3 hours eating, writing notes, and sitting quietly (halts, rapt contemplation, worrying, elevated thinking, general sloth) (average: 20 cals. per 100 lb.-hours)	110
1 minute lying still, awake (to nearest cal.)	0
8 hours, 59 minutes sleeping (including catnaps)	0
Total	4660
Plus specific dynamic action, 10%	470
Total day's energy output	5130

Even before I arrived at this figure and stopped to contemplate with dismay the gulf between it and my theoretical daily food consumption of 3830 calories, I knew something was going wrong with my neat little sums. Some of the figures in the energy output table were obviously very rough approximations indeed. The efficiency with which you walk, saw wood, do laundry (light), or sing in a loud voice may vary drastically from day to day, even from hour to hour. And you perform most wilderness activities much more efficiently after you have been out for a week. Altitude tells, too.

But the biggest variable is the individual. All the figures are for average people, and although rough theoretical allowances can apparently be made for discernible differences due to age, build, sex, and even race, the critical question remains, "How do I, personally, function?" The spread, even between apparently similar individuals, can be very wide. About 70 per cent of people fall within a fairly narrow central efficiency range; but if you belong to the 30 per cent in any one function—and the chances are that you do—then any computation may give highly misleading results.

At this point in my investigations I began to suspect that the right approach to the food question was, after all, *trial and error* and not the strict, rational, quantitative, *scientific method*. With considerable misgivings, I voiced this thought to several experienced research workers in the field of human nutrition. To my surprise, they tended to agree. Present knowledge, they said, left too many variables for any very meaningful quantitative balancing of energy input and output. The best way was to "get out in the field and establish bases for your own personal nutrition requirements." To do, in other words, just about what I had done in the first place.

Now the last thing I want to suggest is that the scientific method turns out to be useless. If I thought so I should hardly have inflicted a dozen pages of it on you. I'm convinced, in fact, that even a little knowledge of the principles of human nutrition can be an invaluable aid to anyone striving to evolve a backpack diet that suits his needs. Had I known what I know now, my early trials would have been less tribulatory, my errors less gross. I could have ensured much sooner, for example, that my diet contained enough fats and protein. Early menus, as on the six-month California walk, were almost certainly low in both. The caloric content was considerably lower than in my present diet, too, and I remember feeling a little faint at the end of one or two really long days.

So please do not write off my energy input and output tables as mere stillborn theorizing. Quite apart from anything else, what I've learned about nutrition in the course of preparing them has helped me build some solid-looking bridges across the gap they have revealed between my actual intake and apparent needs.

On long trips, I usually take one day of almost total rest in every week of walking. Often I take two. On these days I normally eat less than on the others. So for the days that really demand energy I have rather more than the standard quota available—more than 4000 calories, almost certainly.

In addition, I tend to nibble away at small quantities of food throughout the day, and this little-and-often kind of intake turns out to be the most efficient, especially for quick-burning carbohydrates.

But the really big factor, in more ways than one, may be my spare tire. I know from happy experience that my midriff begins to deflate after just a few days of walking with a load. On the California and Grand Canyon trips the tire vanished. The Grand Canyon trip was the only time I have ever done a before-and-after weighing, and in those two strenuous months I dropped from 194 to 174 pounds. I am fairly sure that almost all the loss came in the very strenuous first half—a conclusion borne out by nutrition experts who say "Weight loss is usually most marked at the start of any stepped-up exercise." I lost, then, something approaching twenty pounds in thirty days. Up to two thirds of this loss, or about fourteen pounds, is likely to have been fat. (Water would account for most of the balance.) Now it seems that the body uses this fat just as efficiently as it does fat ingested by mouth. That is, it extracts 9 calories per gram, or about 4000 calories per pound. In other words, my fourteen pounds of fat gave me an additional 56,000 calories in thirty days, or close to 2000 calories per day! Too many imponderables are involved in reaching this rather astonishing figure for us to accept it as at all accurate. But, to say the least, it makes the theoretical daily gap of 1300 calories between my apparent needs and actual intake yawn a great deal less capaciously.

In conclusion, then, it seems to me that the way to work out a good backpacking diet is to go on a shakedown cruise and find out by trial and error what suits you. If this sounds too unscientific for your temperament, call it "going out in the field and establishing personal nutritional bases." A good starting point is the U. S. Army allowance of 4500 calories per man for heavy work. (They allocate 3000 for garrison duty.) To translate calories into ounces of food, consult *Agricultural Handbook No. 8* or some simplified list. From there, play it by ear. But keep the ear carefully cocked in the direction of calories and proteins and fats and the like. Think like a rough-and-ready slide rule. And don't forget to sing in a loud voice.

WATER

You can if necessary do without food for days or even weeks and still live, but if you go very long without water you assuredly die. In really hot deserts the limit of survival without water may be barely twenty-four hours. Well before that your brain is likely to become so addled that there is a serious risk of committing some quite irrational act that will kill you.

Dangers of dehydration

Too few people recognize the insidious nature of thirst-induced irrationality. It can swamp you, suddenly and irretrievably, without your being in the least aware of it.

I described one such case in *The Man Who Walked Through Time*. In July 1959, a thirty-two-year-old priest and two teen-age boys tried to follow an old trail down one side of Grand Canyon to the Colorado. They carried little or no water. More than halfway down, hot and tired and already very thirsty, the priest made the barely rational decision to climb back to the rim. Next morning, desperately dehydrated, the trio tried to follow a wash back to the river. Soon they came to a sheer eighty-foot drop-off. The priest, apparently irrational by now, had all three take off their shoes and throw them to the bottom. Then he tried to climb down. A few feet, and he fell to his death. The boys soon found a passable route, but one of them died on the way down to the river. The other was rescued by helicopter a week later, eight miles downstream.

I know only the bare outline of this story. But a few years ago I interviewed many times, and eventually wrote a magazine article about, two boys who were trapped in the Mojave Desert. This is not a walking story, but it is the only case in which I know full details of the kind of irrationality that any dehydrated hiker could all too easily develop. The boys were Gary Beeman, 18, and Jim Twomey, 16. Their car bogged down near midnight in soft sand, two hundred feet off a remote gravel side road. It was June. Daytime temperatures probably approached 120°F. Humidity was virtually zero. The only liquid foods in the car were two cans of soup and one of pineapple juice, plus two pints of water. By the end of the first day—during most of which the boys rested in the shade of some nearby rocks— they had finished all the liquid. That night, working feebly, they moved the car barely fifteen feet back toward the firm gravel.

The second day, back among the rocks, both boys suffered delirium. At sunset, Jim Twomey staggered toward the car. Suddenly he sank to his knees, pitched forward, and lay still. The older boy, Gary, saw him fall. In mid-afternoon he had staggered irrationally out from the shade of the rocks into blazing sunlight in order to "try to find some water," and had finally dug himself into the cool sand. Now, he felt less lightheaded. He went over to his friend and bent over him. Jim's face was deathly pale. His mouth hung open. Dried mucus flecked his scaly white lips. Gary hurried to the car, searched feverishly through the inferno inside it, and at last found a bottle of after-shave lotion. He wrenched off the top and put the bottle to his lips. The shock of what tasted like hot rubbing alcohol brought him up short. He had a brief, horrible comprehension of his unhinged state of mind. Afterward, all he could think was, "We need a drink. We both need a drink."

Desperately, he ran his eyes over the car. For a moment he considered letting air out of the tires and somehow capturing its coolness. Then he was thinking, "My God, the radiator!" He had always known that in the desert your radiator water could save you; yet for two days he had ignored it! Again he had that terrible momentary comprehension of his state of mind. Then he grabbed a saucepan, squirmed under the front bumper, and unscrewed the drainage tap. A stream of rust-brown water poured down over the greasy, dust-encrusted sway bar and splashed into the saucepan. "That water," he told me later, "was the most wonderful sight I had ever seen."

After he had drunk a little, Gary found himself thinking more clearly. He went back and poured some water into Jim's open mouth. Quite quickly, Jim revived. All at once Gary saw what should have been obvious all along: a way to run the car clear, using some old railroad ties they had found much earlier. He spent almost the whole night aligning the ties—five or six hours for a job that would normally have taken him twenty minutes. At sunrise he helped his half-conscious friend into the car and made what he knew—because they had now finished the radiator water—would have to be their last attempt, however it ended. Moments later, with wheels spinning madly and the bucking car threatening to stall at any second, they shot back onto the gravel road. Four hours later, after many sweltering halts for the now dry motor to cool, they hit a highway.

Since that day, Gary has never driven into the desert without stocking up his car with at least fifteen gallons of what he now calls "the most precious liquid in the world."*

How much water to carry

When you're backpacking you can't play it as safe as Gary Beeman now does, and carry fifteen gallons of water (1 U.S. gallon weighs 8⅓ pounds); but in any kind of dry country you'll have to carry more than you would like to.

In the mountains you may not need to pack along any at all— though even in the mountains there are often long, hot stretches without a creek or lake or snowbank, and unless I am quite sure of a regular supply I tend to carry at least a cupful in a canteen. In deserts, water becomes the most precious item in your pack—and often the heaviest. In the drier parts of Grand Canyon I left each widely spaced water source carrying two gallons. Together with the four canteens, that meant a 19¾-pound water load. Several times, at the start of a long dry stretch, I carried a third gallon in a disposable plastic liquid-bleach bottle from food cache or airdrop. On such occasions I

---

* When I asked Jim Twomey how he had felt when his friend came with the radiator water, he said, "Oh, I just wanted him to leave me alone. I was so tired. You know, I'm fairly sure I'd never have regained consciousness if Gary hadn't brought that water, and I guess it sounds a pretty horrible way to die. But it isn't. I wasn't suffering at all—just terribly tired. All I wanted to do was to lie down and go to sleep, quite peacefully, and never have to wake up again."

would walk for a couple of hours in the cool of evening, drink copiously at dinner and breakfast, then leave in the morning, fresh and fully hydrated, on a long and waterless stretch that was now two critical hours shorter than it had been.

The amount of water you need under specific conditions is something you must work out for yourself. As with food, requirements vary a great deal from man to man.*

For me, half a gallon is under normal conditions a comfortable ration for a dry night stop, provided I am sure of finding more by mid-morning. In temperatures around 90°, and in near-zero desert humidity, a gallon once lasted me thirty-six hours, during which I walked a flat but rather soft-surfaced thirty miles or so with no appreciable discomfort, but with no washing or tooth cleaning either.

I always lean toward safety. I can recall only three occasions on which I have been at all uncomfortably thirsty, even in the desert; and lack of water has never even threatened to become a real danger. It pays to remember, though, that only a hair's breadth divides safety from potential tragedy. If you are alone, one moment of carelessness or ill luck could send you stumbling across the threshold: a twisted ankle miles from water would probably be enough; certainly a broken leg or a rattlesnake bite. I try to make some kind of allowance for such possibilities, but in the end you have to rely mostly on caution and luck. Perhaps the two are not altogether unconnected. An ancient Persian proverb has it that "Fortune is infatuated with the efficient."

How often to drink

The old Spartan routine of drinking water at infrequent inter-

---

* Small, wiry men are generally regarded as better adapted to living in deserts than are big, muscular ones. In a sense this is true. As any solid increases in size, its volume is cubed every time its surface area is squared. So the bigger a man's body, the less surface area it has for each unit of volume; and the surface, or skin, is where we lose excess heat, mainly through perspiration. Small men are therefore able to keep their body temperature down more efficiently than are big men. But this extra sweat efficiency also means that small men tend to drink more water for their size than big men do. And because a rough relationship exists in most cases between bodyweight and acceptable load (see page 17), big men can normally carry heavier weights—and therefore more water.

vals, and rarely if ever between meals, is perhaps necessary for military formations: only that way can you satisfactorily impose group discipline. But for individuals the method is inefficient. For one thing, you tend to drink unnecessarily large quantities when at last you get the canteen to your lips. And although thirst may not become an actual physical discomfort, you often walk for hours with your mind blinkered by a kind of dehydrated scum that seals off any vivid appreciation of the world around you.

In well-watered country I take a drink at almost every convenient creek or lake, and I often suck snow or ice as I walk along. In deserts I drink a few sips of water at each hourly halt, swilling it around my mouth before swallowing. I am almost sure I use less water this way. I certainly know that the little-and-often system keeps washing the first traces of that blinkering scum away from the surface of my mind, and so re-hones the edges of my appreciation. And appreciation, after all, is the reason I am walking.

Water sources

In assessing the purity of any water supply, the only safe rule is: "If in doubt, doubt." All still water should be suspect—except perhaps recent rainpockets in rock, and really remote mountain lakes. So should rivers and creeks, no matter how clear, if there seems any chance at all of a permanent settlement upstream, or even an often-used campsite. Most springs are safe. But it is possible for mineral springs, especially in deserts, to be poisonous. One culprit is arsenic. What you do if you suspect an unposted bitter-tasting spring, I really don't know—though a marked lack of insect life would be good reason for doubting its safety. I would guess that if you're in danger of dying from thirst you drink deep; and that if you're not in danger you stand and ruminate for a few minutes, then walk on. Perhaps I should add that in out-of-the-way places I've come across some remarkably evil-looking springs, bubbling and steaming and reeking, and have discovered that the water was drunk regularly by some hardy local. But the only safe rule remains: "If in doubt, doubt."

Do not rely on maps, by the way, for information about springs.

Even the excellent USGS topographical series often show springs that dry out each summer or have vanished altogether due to some subterranean change. Other springs may fail in extra-dry years. Rely only on recent reports from people you feel sure you can trust (see page 247). If any doubts linger, carry enough water to take you not only as far as the hoped-for spring, but also back to the last water source.

Sometimes, of course, snow will be your surest, or only, source of water (see page 133).

Water purification

Consult the purity rule: "If in doubt, doubt," and either boil all doubtful water or treat it with purification tablets.

Ten minutes of boiling should make any water safe, though longer will be needed at high altitudes. But boiling consumes time and energy and fuel, and leaves you with a hot, unquenching drink. So I almost always use chlorine-liberating Halazone tablets. I carry them in a 35 mm. film can, with some cotton wadding to stop them from being pounded to powder. The tablets are stable, light, and cheap (100 tablets weigh less than ½ ounce, cost 54 cents). One tablet disinfects one pint of ordinary water. Heavy pollution may require a double dose. (It's not a bad idea to jot the dosage down on a scrap of paper and keep it in the container you use for the tablets.) To purify water, simply fill a canteen, drop in the tablets, screw down the stopper, and wait thirty minutes.

Some people seem to find the chlorinated water objectionable. Most if not all the taste can be removed by shaking the canteen vigorously and then opening it and allowing it to stand awhile. Or you can mask the taste with fruit drink mix.

Water in an emergency

Cunning ideas are always being propounded about what to do if you run out of water. Typical examples are "Catch the rain in a tarp" and "Shake condensed fog off conifer trees" and "Dig in a damp, low-lying place." Then there are various crafty systems for distilling fresh water from the ocean. Just the other day, in an Armed Forces Research and Development publication, I ran across a description of what at first seemed a practical rig for sea-skirting backpackers: a series of foil sheets between which you heat salt water, either in the sun's rays or "by sitting on them." But right at the end came the killer: "With additional sheets, a survivor can obtain about one pint of water in 16 hours."

Unfortunately, the occasion on which you're really in desperate straits for water is pretty darned sure to come just when there is no rain, no fog, no damp place, and no ocean (not to mention no sheets of special foil). In other words, in the desert, in summer.

The only advice I've heard that sounds even vaguely practical is "Cut open a barrel cactus." One experienced friend of mine says he rather imagines you'd "extract just about enough moisture to make up for the sweat expended in slashing the damned thing open." Mind you, he has never tried it. Neither have I, though I'm always meaning to. I am perhaps a shade less skeptical—but by no means sanguine.

Water caches

On both California and Grand Canyon walks I had to establish several water caches. Bottles, I discovered, kept the water clear and fresh. Whenever possible I buried them—as protection against the hoofs of inquisitive wild burros and the fingers of other thirsty, thieving, or merely thoughtless mammals.*

Unburied bottles are liable to crack from extreme heat (if you leave them in the sun) or from extreme cold (wherever you put them, if temperatures fall low enough for the water to freeze solid). I worried a good deal about the freezing danger in Grand Canyon,

---

* On the California walk, at the southern end of Death Valley, an amateur rockhound operating from a pickup truck kindly gave me a gallon bottle of good drinking water that he had "found under a pile of stones, back up in the hills." The water tasted far sweeter than the alkaline spring water I had camped beside. But it brought on a bad case of the worries. I became highly conscious that for three days ahead I would be relying on water I had cached out as I drove south through the valley two months earlier. I hoped no thoughtless, light-fingered

but found the bottles at both caches intact, in spite of night temperatures several degrees below freezing. The bigger the bottles you use, the less danger that they will freeze solid. One-gallon wine bottles, thoroughly washed, are good; five-gallon bottles, though cumbersome, are better. Plastic bottles such as those used for liquid bleach are lighter and perhaps stronger, but they leave me worrying about rodents.

Water left for even a few weeks in five-gallon metal cans seems to take on a greenish tinge, apparently from algae, though I have no idea why. On the other hand, these five-gallon cans are light and strong, and easily lashed to a packframe when caches have to be made on foot. Twice in Grand Canyon I used five-gallon cans in which my food had been stored (see page 287) to pack water a half day ahead and so break a long waterless trek into two much safer segments.

Canteens

In buying canteens, take no chances. If you find one leaking badly, miles from the nearest desert spring, it may well be about the last thing you ever find.

At one time I used only Swiss-made, all-aluminum, screwtop canteens with felt covers. My half-gallon size weighed thirteen ounces, empty ($5.25), but the ounces seemed a small price to pay for safety. Then, for a summer's walk up England, when drinking water hardly threatened to be a problem but overload did, I bought two polyethylene bottles, each with just under half-gallon capacity.

---

rockhound had stumbled on any of my caches. Fortunately all the caches were buried and camouflaged. I found each one safe.

I also found them without difficulty. People often ask me how you can be sure of finding a cache again. The safest way is to draw in your notebook a sketch map showing important features such as gullies and bushes and rocks, and to pace out and record a few measurements from obvious landmarks. And then to mark the exact spot with a big stone. I did all these things. But I never actually used the maps. Each time, memory took me directly to the right place. City people sometimes express amazement at such a "feat." But once you have lived for a while in any wilderness, its landmarks stand out quite clearly. Even a moderately practiced eye will detect at least as much difference between two neighboring desert gullies as between two neighboring downtown streets.

They weighed only seven ounces each. They had thick walls, a serviceable flattened-and-curved flasklike shape, and strong plastic screwtops. By the end of that English summer I had developed considerable confidence in their strength, and when I made the Grand Canyon journey two years later I took along—as a concession to the pressing weight problem, and in spite of the safety worry—these same two plastic canteens as well as two of the aluminum type. As it turned

out, the polyethylene did better than aluminum. The old and worn felt covers of both metal canteens developed gaping holes, and when the canteens came on side trips—slung from my belt by their convenient little clips—the bared aluminum banged against rocks and developed seep holes. To my surprise, rubber air mattress patches stopped all leakage—but my confidence had been punctured too. The plastic canteens gave no trouble at all, and by the time I came out of Grand Canyon I trusted them more than the aluminum ones. On a recent desert trip I replaced the aluminum canteens with three quart-size, screw-cap, polyethylene bottles (3½ ounces each; 75 cents).

Each kind of canteen has its advantages and drawbacks. The felt covers of the aluminum canteens not only protect the metal but act as insulation and help keep water cool. If the canteens are wetted and put out in the sun, evaporation from the felt soon cools tepid water. Also, the clips are an advantage on packless side trips. But in deserts the cork inserts in the stoppers tend to dry out and crumble. Rubber works much better; inserts cut from an automobile inner tube have lasted me for years. A more serious drawback to these canteens is that the aluminum thread of the neck and stoppers tends to wear away. Cross-threading becomes horribly easy. In the end the stoppers even threaten to flip off.

My trust in the polyethylene bottles, although considerable, is not yet absolute: in extreme cold, many plastics stiffen and even crack, and although my polyethylene canteens have never shown signs of doing so, they have not yet been below 9°F.

When new, and to a lesser degree after being stored for long periods, the polyethylene tends to smell. It may even taint water. As with most things in life, time cures.

Not long ago, after four years of use, the screwtops of these plastic canteens began to leak a little. Padding the inset rim-fitting with string—much as you pad a sleeve-fitting with asbestos—seemed to do the trick. But recently I found that the always damp string apparently harbored bacteria: it had begun to reek.

These flattened plastic canteens make tolerably comfortable pillows, especially if padded with clothing. In weather no worse than cool, the pillow routine also keeps the stopper from freezing (and for an infuriating minor frustration few things equal waking up thirsty in the middle of the night and finding yourself iced off from your drinking water). Simply putting the canteens on air mattress or Ensolite pad (see page 174) may be enough to keep the stopper ice-free, but in really cold weather take one canteen to bed with you. If you think there is any danger at all of the others freezing solid, make sure they are no more than half full. That way, they can hardly burst.

In Grand Canyon I carried, to boost the capacity of the four big canteens to a full two gallons, a wide-mouthed 250 cc. polyethylene Evenflo baby feeder bottle (1 ounce). It turned out to be highly important. Without it I should have been hard put to find an efficient way of collecting water from the shallow rainpockets I often had to depend on. These little bottles are tough too. Once, when this one held my last precious half pint of water, I dropped it on a boulder. It bounced quite beautifully.

An identical bottle came in very useful on a recent two-week trip along the banks of the Colorado River. At each halt I filled it from the river, added one Halazone tablet and a little fruit drink mix, and slipped it into the pack. At the next halt I had, immediately available, just enough safe, palatable water to see me through another hot, dry hour.

These baby bottles are also convenient for taking on short side trips. One will even slip into your pants pocket—though it can also slip out. The two-piece lid (for fitting baby's rubber nipple) is a mild nuisance. To hold it in one piece and so prevent the inner disk from dropping off every time you remove the lid, just slap a piece of Rip-stop tape on top (page 260). The tape will allow the disk to turn a fraction when you replace the lid, and so jam into a watertight joint—provided you keep the rubber nipple in place.

KITCHEN UTENSILS

Keep your utensils as few and as simple as you can, consistent with your own personal requirements of weight, comfort, convenience, and obscure inner satisfaction. Naturally, no two backpackers are likely to make identical choices. I know one man-and-wife hiking team who never carry more than one cup and one spoon between them. At least, so they say. Other people like to pack everything along, including the kitchen sink. My own list reads:

	lbs.	*oz.*
2 Nesting cooking pots	I	4
Stainless steel cup		3
Spoon		2
Sheath knife		6
Salt and pepper shaker		½
Sugar container		2
Margarine container		2
Detergent container		I
Milk squirter		I
Book matches—7 per week		I
Waterproof matchsafe		I
Miniature can opener		⅛
Total	2	7⅝

In trout country I often add:

Steel frying pan with detachable handle (9¾ inches diameter; 15 ounces; $2.50). Aluminum pans are lighter, but are much less efficient heat spreaders.

My nesting cooking pots (3½ and 2½ pint capacities) are polished aluminum, with lids that double as plates or pans. The bail handles lock firmly into an upright position.

These are simple, highly practical units. The corners are rounded and easily cleaned. The low profiles and broad bases promote rapid heating. And these pots are tough. The larger one once bounced 150 feet down a steep talus slope and pulled up with only a couple of minor dents. But after ten years' brutal use the outer pot, which I use much more often, is at last beginning to wilt, and one of these years I guess I'll have to buy a new one. It will be like losing an old friend.

These Swiss-made pots, by Sigg, also come in 5¼, 7, and 8¾ pint sizes (15, 17, and 20 ounces). The catalogues sometimes call them "kettles." (My sizes, 1 pound, 4 ounces the pair; $7.25.)

The *Sierra Club stainless steel cup* (3 ounces, $1) is one of those simple but gloriously successful devices that man occasionally invents. It is tough. It cleans easily. Its rim rarely burns your lips, even with the hottest food or drink—a feature that anyone who has suffered an aluminum cup will appreciate. The open-end steel wire handle stays cool too, hooks over belt or bough or cord, and snaps easily and securely onto a belt clip (see page 267).

For reserve cup in case of loss or company, see cover of Svea stove (page 110).

Unfortunately the Sierra Club cup has in certain wilderness circles become a badge of conformity: you are not considered "in" if you do not sport one dangling from your belt. A dismal fate for a first-class article. But it is entirely possible, I assure you, to be a member of the very worthwhile Sierra Club and to carry one of their excellent cups and yet not qualify as what has been aptly called a cup-carrying member.

Spoon. Any tough, light spoon will do. One from a clip-together knife-fork-and-spoon set will have two little protuberances that are not only ideal for hooking on pot rims when you leave the spoon standing in one, but also unbeatable for collecting dirt.

Fork. Redundant.

Knife. I am sometimes a little surprised to find myself still carrying a six-ounce sheath knife. On the rare occasions I use it for eating, a much lighter tool would do. Even for other jobs, I find I use it rather infrequently. But I can recall several occasions when, lacking such a solid blade and handle, I should have been hard put to it to gouge out dry kindling, or even to clean especially large fish. And there is no denying that, especially in game country such as East Africa, it is comforting to have some sort of a defensive weapon along.

Most outdoor equipment catalogues feature ultra-functional knives festooned with gadgets. One Swiss army model embodies large blade, nail file, scissors, saw, fire-starting glass, can opener, screwdriver, cap lifter, tweezers, toothpick, Phillips screwdriver, awl, and lanyard shackle—all for 4¾ ounces and $13.95. But color TV is extra.

Small carborundum stone (3-inch, 1-ounce, 50 cents). For knife-sharpening. An alternative is a small tungsten-carbide steel shaft, four-sided, hollow-ground, with handle. It is said to be highly efficient as well as very light.

Salt and pepper shaker. For years I've used a two-compartment, noncorrosive, anodized aluminum shaker, made by Sigg of Switzerland (½ ounce; 95 cents). But I hear they are no longer available. A good-looking alternative is this strong plastic shaker, the "Tokyo-Top," made in Japan. Although heavier, it has the advantage of letting you see how much salt and pepper is left (1 ounce; 75 cents).

Containers for sugar, margarine, and detergent. The strongest and lightest, not to mention the cheapest, are polyethylene. The best, such as Tupperware, wear surprisingly well. My sugar container is ten years old.

Make sure all your containers are easily distinguishable, by sight and touch: I can heartily unrecommend predawn cereal sleepily sweetened with detergent powder. My sugar now travels in a square container that holds 1¼ pounds; the margarine in a round one that just takes a squeezed-down ¼-pound bar; and the detergent in a bottle of flat, distinctive shape.

Milk squirter. One of those pliable, squeezable polyethylene containers in which honey and mustard are sometimes sold. For re-filling with milk powder, unscrew main top. For making milk, re-move only the little dunce-cap top and squirt powder down onto water or tea. Even in a raging gale you suffer virtually no loss. A simple but valuable device.

Bookmatches, though useless in a high wind, are otherwise more convenient than wooden ones. I find a book a day more than enough.

A waterproof matchsafe holds about twenty large wooden strike-anywhere matches for use in wind or wet. I'm always rather surprised at how rarely I use mine. The matchsafe is also a safe place to keep needles and a little thread (see page 261).

My matchsafe is the metal kind, made by Marble's of Gladstone, Michigan (1 ounce, $1.75). I've carried it for years, but have for some time been unhappy with both the difficulty of opening it and also the way the metal attachment loop can pull loose. If it weren't for the usefulness of this loop, which permits you to tie the match-safe to your belt, or to an inflatable vest on river crossings (see page 279), I would probably switch to a simpler plastic model (¾ ounce; 45 cents), though I mistrust the screw-on lid. 120-size film cans are said to be useful makeshift matchsafes.

A prospector's magnifying glass, most often useful for examining rock samples and such sights as the horrifying head of a dragonfly, forms an emergency reserve for fire-lighting (page 119). Mine is 10-power, weighs 2 ounces.

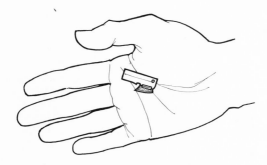

A can opener—U.S. Army type—is worth carrying, even though ordinary canned foods make hopelessly inefficient backpacking fare. You may need the opener for canned goodies that you include in cache or airdrop, or buy as a welcome change at a wayside store, or are given by some kind, heavy-toting, back-country horseman. These tiny can openers (⅛ ounce; two for 25 cents) are astonishingly efficient. The Trailwise catalogue calls them "one of the noblest products of the U.S. Army."

Warning: these can openers are easily lost, especially in sand, so thread a small piece of red rag through the key-chain hole. My opener goes into my wallet when I carry one, otherwise into the office (page 256).

One end of the opener doubles as a not particularly effective screwdriver.

Flint stick. This catalogue item caught my eye recently (and has me halfway convinced, especially as I'm told it's a very effective little device). It gives off a fat, high-temperature spark that will ignite flammable gases or tinder. It comes in a kit with flint, striker, tinder, and key-ring (¾ ounce, ninety-eight cents. Flint stick alone;

¼ ounce. Made by the Flint Stick Company, Box 82, Lakewood, California 90714.) "The size of a house key," says the catalogue, "but it could save your life." Maybe it could too.

HEAT SOURCES

Stove or open fire?

The obvious and traditional way to cook outdoor food is on an open fire. But ten years ago I bought a small gas-burning stove for use in a fuelless mountain area above timberline, and the stove turned out to be so efficient that I have virtually given up open-fire cooking.

A stove wins on every count except weight and esthetics. In selecting a campsite, you no longer have to worry about fuel supply or to hunt for wood as soon as you stop—an important advantage when you want to push ahead until dark, and a comfort in rattlesnake country. Instead, you light up the stove (an operation that takes about a minute), then leave the meal to cook by itself while you set up camp—another advantage, especially when you're flop-down tired. And heat control is as easy and instant and exact as on the gas stove back home. On a stove, too, the outside of your pot stays bright and clean. You won't write this off as a minor gain if you've ever discovered that the plastic bag sheathing your fire-blackened pots in the pack has sprung a leak, next door to the sleeping bag; or if you have woken up one morning to find that you unsuspectingly went to sleep the night before with one hand soot-black from handling a cooking pot in the dark. Finally—and at certain times and in certain places this may be vital—a properly handled stove constitutes no fire hazard.

For groups, a fire yields one important practical advantage: you can heat more than one pot at a time—especially if you carry a grill or grate, as many experienced backpackers do.

On purely esthetic grounds—and don't forget that you are, fundamentally, walking for esthetic reasons—most people find a fire preferable (for a dissenting view, see pages 115–16). A fire is at once a relaxing and yet stimulating change from modern home life—including its own emasculated shadow, the suburban barbecue. At night, its pulsing mysteries never pall. Then there are the smells. And food cooked on it often picks up a genuinely delightful tang. To some people, half the fun of camping seems to be cooking on an open fire. A fire can also warm you, cheer you up, promote community spirit within a heterogeneous party, wrap you in choking clouds of smoke, and spit red-hot sparks onto your sleeping bag. But there is no need to forgo all these delights if you happen to prefer a stove for cooking. Simply build a fire whenever you feel the need for warmth or cheer. I do so fairly often. But for cooking I rely, almost always, on my

Stove.

The complete rig, primed for a week, consists of:

	lbs.	oz.
Svea 123 stove, with cover	1	2
⅓ pint white gas in stove		4
Stove cover handle (for use when cover acts as cup or pot)		¼
Stove nozzle cleaner		¼
Aluminum white gas bottle (holds 1⅓ pints) (see page 110)		3
1⅓ pints white gas	1	
Small aluminum or plastic funnel (for filling stove) (see page 110)		⅛
Total	2	9⅝

(If I expect to have to melt much snow or ice for water, I carry a second bottleful of white gas.)

Other lightweight gas-burning stoves you may like to consider include a simple Borde, the Primus 71L, and the Optimus 80 and 8RF. The Swiss Borde (9 ounces, $7.50) is essentially for use with its own special set of pots and windshields and has no pot stand above the flame. A few backpackers seem to swear by it. Others find it a temperamental starter, fear the lack of a safety valve, and complain that the steel—as opposed to brass—nozzle needle sometimes rusts. The other three stoves are roughly comparable to my Svea. All three are Swedish-made, have safety valves, and require no pumping (once started, they generate their own pressure). The Optimus 8RF has a self-cleaning orifice. Comparative statistics:*

				Burning	*Boils*	
		Weight	*Capacity*	*Time*	*Qt. Water*	
Stove	*lbs.*	*oz.*	*(pints)*	*(hours)*	*(minutes)*	*Price*
Optimus 8RF	1	9	⅓	1¼	6 to 7	$12.00
Primus 71L	1	6	½	1¼	7 to 8	9.95
Optimus 80	1	4	½	1½	7 to 8	9.95
Svea 123	1	2	⅓	¾	6 to 7	8.95

The not quite comparable figures for another stove (page 111) are:

| | | | | | | |
| Bluet 200 | 1 | 9 | cart-ridge | 3(?) | 8 to 9 | 8.85 |

As with most equipment, a lot of chance is involved in what kind of stove you start with. And most of us tend, humanly, to develop a blind, or at least blinkered, loyalty toward the kind we use. (It's the same with automobiles: who really likes to admit he's made a bad choice?)

I bought a Svea originally because a friend recommended it. I found it sturdy and reliable and surprisingly stable (though it pays

---

* These figures by kind permission of Recreational Equipment Inc., Seattle, and The Ski Hut, Berkeley. In my own trials with the Svea I found that it boiled 1½ pints of cold (50°) water at sea level in five to six minutes.

to level off a firm base pad). And I stuck with it. One filling sees me conveniently through a full day's cooking; but if your menu is more elaborate than mine the three-quarter-hour burning time may be frustratingly short, and you may choose instead to pack along the extra two ounces of the slower heating Optimus 80 or the extra four ounces of the Primus or even the extra seven ounces of the Optimus 8RF.

When I bought my Svea I was told, "In the end, any of these stoves will begin to show its age. Once it begins to give trouble, the thing is to ditch it and buy a new one." After five years' pretty concentrated use, including three months of the California walk and four months solid in England, my Svea began to give trouble. A little belatedly, I remembered the ditching advice—which I pass on, fortissimo. My second Svea is now five years old and going strong.

You light the Svea, and the Primus and Optimus as well, by opening the valve and warming the bowl a little and so forcing out liquid gasoline which collects in a depression at the foot of the generator and when ignited (after you have closed the valve again) heats the generator sufficiently to vaporize some fuel. All you have to do then is to reopen the valve and apply a match. The stove lights. And the heat of burning maintains pressure as long as the fuel lasts. In general, the system works well—especially if you remember, as I almost never do, to open the valve when the stove has cooled after use, and so nullify the internal vacuum.

But beware of two things. First, the business of "warming the bowl." The instructions say that cradling the bowl in the palms of your hands is enough. But, except when temperatures are cool but not cold, you run into difficulties. At one extreme, the cold metal murders your hands. At the other, the gasoline is already so warm that the increase in temperature, if any, is too small to force out fuel, and you sit there for minutes on end, as solemn and expectant as Aladdin, and nothing happens. Nowadays I rarely bother with the warm-hands routine. Sometimes I just put the stove in the sun on a hot rock for a few moments and just sometimes it works. More often I light a fragment of paper under the bowl. Toilet paper does fine, but—in one of those old-womanish habits that seem so impor-

tant in the wilderness, and are—I hoard in a pants pocket every
discarded paper wrapper from tea bags and meat bars and mintcake,
and I reach for one automatically when I want to light the stove.
Occasionally, no heating is necessary: when temperature or altitude
is much higher than on the last occasion you used the stove, especially if you refilled it then or remembered the de-vacuum business,
the fuel often wells out as soon as you open the valve.

But the big difficulty in lighting a stove is wind. A guttering
warm-up flame does precious little warming up, and the stove will
burn feebly, if at all. So make sure you shield it adequately. The wind
may remain a problem even when the stove is well alight. It drastically reduces the effective heat. And, because this is something you
cannot see, the only way you know about it is that after a while you
find the wretched water still hasn't come to a boil. Most of us, I
fancy, tend to become careless about protecting our stoves from wind.
Every now and then I get a reminder. Not long ago I spent a night
on a mountain in winds that I later learned had gusted to fifty miles
an hour, and was forced to sleep in a sheltered rock crevice. At the
back of the crevice I found a beautiful little grotto of a kitchen that
might have been made for my Svea. In that perfectly protected place
the stove burned with the healthiest and boomingest roar I have ever
heard it make, as if it was overjoyed at being given this chance to
defy the rage outside. And my dinner stew that night seemed to start
bubbling and steaming much more quickly than usual.

Sometimes a gust of wind will blow a stove clean out, particularly before the burner ring becomes red hot, or when you lower the
flame for simmering. At such times, and especially when you are
relighting it, a match left across the burner helps keep the flame alive.

For use of cloth windscreen, see page 113.

Snow (or very cold rock or earth) may cool the stove so severely
that even after it has been burning well it will weaken and finally
go out. If I foresee any such danger I carry a small square of Ensolite
cut from a foam bed pad (see page 174). At night, if you're sleeping
on a pad, simply put the stove on one corner of it.

The Svea is protected by a perforated windshield and a removable top cover. This aluminum cover is designed to double as a small

pot or cup (hellishly hot to the lips, but a useful reserve in case of company or the loss of your regular cup). I sometimes carry the pot on sidetrips away from my pack and brew tea in it over a small wood fire. But my stove cover's main use is as a stand for the Sierra Club cup. By rotating the open end a couple of times on any rough surface except rock I can dig it in enough to form a raised and stable platform. Anyone who has watched precious tea or coffee spill from his tilted cup will understand its value. In snow, where a hot cup quickly melts its own hole, I invert the cover and rest the cup in its hollow. The heat dissipates much more gradually, the food stays hot longer, and the cover, kept cool, sinks into the snow only very slowly. To correct even that minor fault, I put the Ensolite pad underneath once it is no longer needed for the stove.

The fine-jet nozzle of my Svea has given remarkably little trouble. But the wrong fuel (see below) may block it. So may blown sand. Always keep your stove-cleaner handy.

The stove-cleaner—a little wire pricker in its own metal casing —travels in my office, wrapped in a small plastic bag and taped to the cardboard stiffener (see page 256).

White gas for refilling stove. My spare gas travels in a non-anodized aluminum bottle or bottles (see page 106) that hold $1\frac{1}{3}$ pints (3 ounces; $1.75). The gasketed screwtops never leak, and that is the vital thing. My first-line bottle is now ten years old and battered like a pug, but still sound.

In cities, white gas is becoming less and less easy to find. Special fuels, such as Coleman Appliance Fuel, are often sold in sports stores. They're expensive, but said to be very efficient. Ordinary automobile gas is leaded and in time will block the stove jet. Use only in an emergency. And get the cheapest grade; it contains the least additives.

I carry a tiny funnel for filling the stove direct from the bottle. It doesn't matter much whether the funnel is plastic or aluminum, but clean it carefully before use. No matter how carefully I pour, I find that when the bottle is full I always spill a little gas; but once the level drops the difficulty vanishes (see page 128).

Much the same details of usage apply, I imagine, to the Primus and both Optimus stoves, which all operate inside their own steel carrying boxes.

For large groups, bigger stoves are more efficient. Stoves with pumps are recommended for high altitude (above 12,000 feet), though I've used my Svea without difficulty at over 14,000 feet.

Kerosene fuel, used in some larger stoves, produces more heat per pound; but it has a lingering odor and must be primed with alcohol.

The French-made Bluet stove illustrated below is only now becoming well known in America. This stove operates on disposable pressurized butane cartridges, and therefore requires no filling or preheating. It is said to burn for 2½ to three hours. (Complete with windshield and full cartridge: 1 pound, 11 ounces; $8.85. Replacement cartridge: 11 ounces; 69 cents each, or $3.98 for box of six.)

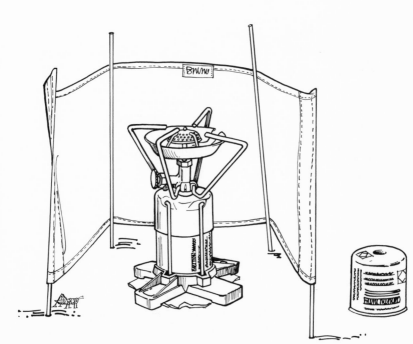

When I began to experiment with a Bluet, I figured that two cartridges would take me through a week with something to spare. The first tests were inexact and inconclusive, but they raised doubts in my mind. A two-week desert trip confirmed the doubts. An allowance of two cartridges per week (renewed halfway by airdrop) proved inadequate. Temperatures rose to over a hundred degrees almost every day, and I now understand that this may have reduced efficiency. A letter from the makers recommends that "to reduce the influence of high temperatures, simply adjust the tap for a smaller flame." I assume that by "tap" they mean the main control valve. But further experiments suggest that, under most conditions, two cartridges will not last me for a full week. The relative merits of Svea and Bluet revolve very much around this question. Comparative figures are:

	At start, full		At end, empty	
	lbs.	*oz.*	*lbs.*	*oz.*
Svea rig, complete, with gas	2	9⅝	1	5⅝
Bluet, with windshield and two cartridges	2	6	1	7
Bluet, with windshield and three cartridges	3	1	1	10

"Empty" figures for the Bluet assume that you cannot find a place to ditch empty cartridges without desecrating the countryside. If you expect to call in at a ranger station or some other place with garbage disposal, deduct three ounces for each empty cartridge.

Of course, weight is not the only criterion. The Bluet is simpler to light, cleaner, less noisy, and needs no daily refilling. In cold weather you can use it with no trouble at all for a minute or two of reheating half-chilled food—an operation that's quite a chore if you have to reprime a gasoline stove.

On the other hand, there is some danger of leakage with a Bluet. On that desert trip, the second cartridge definitely leaked. I could smell it. But since then, each time I've changed a cartridge I have carefully cleaned both the penetration point of the new cartridge and the pressure seating on the stove, and I have had no further trouble.

A minor annoyance with the Bluet is that it is dangerous to remove a part-full cartridge, and if the stove is in that state when you want to start a trip you either have to light it and let the cartridge burn empty or, alternatively, pack along an uncertain amount of fuel in an inefficient form, weightwise. Empty cartridges, by the way, reek so strongly of butane that you may get whiffs of it from your pack as you walk along. Remedy: seal exit hole with a piece of Rip-stop tape (see page 260).

Early Bluets had no windshield, but a burner-enclosing fitting is now standard—and very necessary (2 ounces; 85 cents). My first trials were without a windshield, so I carried a fireproof

Cloth windscreen.

(See illustration, page 111.) It worked well, provided the ground was soft enough to accept the metal legs. The simplest way to keep the sides reasonably taut is to remove the two middle legs from the fabric, plant the two outer legs firmly, leaving the screen slack, and then force the screen outward as you plant the middle legs. In really high-wind country this screen might just be worth carrying for any stove (3 ounces; $2.25).

The Svea's big advantages over the Bluet are that it definitely produces more heat, and that in most country areas of the U.S. white gas is easier to find than a Bluet cartridge. (For alternatives to white gas, see page 110.) The Svea is also cheaper to operate.

I haven't finally made up my mind about the comparative merits of the Bluet and Svea. In general, I'm coming down on the side of the Svea, though the Bluet, with one cartridge, would seem better for short trips up to one weekend—and perhaps, with three cartridges, for snow trips. But these are only *my* feelings—and tentative ones at that. What matters in the end, as usual, is how the respective rigs function in *your* hands for *your* kind of cooking.

Keeping cooked food warm when you're using a stove can pose a problem. You can't normally leave the stove on low: fuel is too valuable. And relighting a Svea, or any stove that needs priming, is next door to unthinkable, though relighting a Bluet is simple. In cold or windy weather you can wrap the cooking pot in the sleeping bag or some other spare insulator. But the one really satisfactory solution is to have a large campfire (not for cooking, see below) and put the pot of cooked food beside it—close enough to keep warm, far enough away to keep clean. You have to keep reversing the pot, so that half the food doesn't get cold, but you can do this very simply each time you pour or ladle out another cupful of food.

FIRES

Cooking fire

Except when stove fuel runs low or I brew tea on sidetrips away from my pack, the only time I cook on an open fire nowadays is for frying—and that generally means frying fish. A stove is not really satisfactory for this job: its concentrated heat makes fish stick to the pan. So I resign myself to having a blackened frying pan, and before putting it in the pack I wrap it carefully in two large plastic bags.

For frying, I find that the best hearth is a two- or three-stone affair with a shallow trough for the fire. The stones must be flat enough to form a stable rest for the pan, and deep enough to leave space for a sizable fire. Wind direction and strength dictate the angle of the trough. A light breeze blowing down its length keeps flame and glow healthy; a high wind is best blocked off by the side stones, perhaps with an assist from others.

On the rare occasions I use an open fire with my cooking pots, I usually make a two- or three-stone hearth. A useful alternative that makes it easier to build and replenish a sizable fire and to control its heat is a double-Y-stick-with-crossbar rig:

The two forked (or, more often, branched) sticks must be planted firmly, and far enough apart to be safe from burning. As a precaution, I may splash them from time to time with water. The crossbar must be tolerably straight and either green or wet enough not to burn too readily.

If there is any hint of fire hazard, I carefully seal off my fire, no matter which kind, with a circle of stones (page 120).

The hottest fire comes from small sticks; the best are those that burn fairly slowly and/or remain glowing for a long time.

Another satisfactory cooking method that I occasionally use, especially for frying, is to build a small extension to the stone ring around a big campfire. It's simple, then, to transfer a few glowing embers from the main fire, and to keep replenishing them.

Campfires: to have or not to have

A campfire is one of the long-standing traditions of outdoor life. Understandably so. For cheer and warmth—not to mention drying out wet clothes—there is nothing quite like it. The warmth is not very efficient—you tend to be toasted on one side, iceberged on the other—but there's no doubt about the cheer. Beside your fire, you live in a private, glowing little world. All around you, fire-shapes dance across rocks and bushes and tree trunks. A grasshopper that you have been watching as it basks on one verge, motionless, leaps without warning clear over the flames and out into the darkness. But most of the time you just sit and gaze into the caverns that form and crumble and then form again between the incandescent logs. You build fantastic worlds among those pulsating walls and arches and colonnades. No, not quite "build," for that is too active and definite a word. Rather, you let your mind slip away, free and un- restricted, roaming wide yet completely at rest, unconnected with your conscious self yet reporting back quite clearly at some low, quiet, strangely decisive level. You sit, in other words, and dream. The East African has an almost limitless capacity for this masterly and delightful form of inactivity, and when his friends see him squatting there, lost, they understand and say in Swahili, poetically, that he is "dreaming the fire."

Yet as often as not I do without a campfire. Perhaps laziness has a lot to do with it. But I am very aware that a fire cuts you off from the night. Within the fire's domain you exist in a special, private, personal, isolated world. It is only when you walk away and stand for a while as a part of the silence and immensity beyond that you understand the restriction. And then you find that the silent, infinite, mysterious world that exists beyond the campfire is truer than the restricted world that exists around it—and that in the end it is more rewarding. I walk out into wilderness primarily, I think, to re-establish a sense of unity with the rest of the world—with the rock and the trees and the animals and the sky and its stars. Or perhaps I mean only that when I return to the city a renewed sense of this affinity is, above all, what I bring back with me. A campfire, by its very charms, disrupts my sense of inclusion.

But if I do not build a fire I build no lasting barriers. After I have cooked the evening meal and switched off the hissing stove and registered the unfailing astonishment I experience at the noisiness of that hissing, I am alone in and with the night. I can hear, now, the magnified sounds of its silence: a field mouse thinly complaining; a dry leaf rustling; a wedge of wind sliding down the far slope of the valley. And I can look deep into the shadowy blackness or the starlit dimness or the moonlit clarity. Or, best of all, I can watch the moon lever itself up and flood the starlit dimness into landscape.

Always, over each of these separate mysteries, spreads the sky, total. And I, at the center—my center of it—am small and insignificant; but at the same time a part of it and therefore significant.

Lighting a fire

An outdoorsman's ability to start a fire—anywhere, anytime—is the traditional criterion for judging his competence, and I suppose I have always accepted the criterion in an unthinking, uncritical sort of way. But now that I try to assess my own competence I find it surprisingly difficult to award a grade. Perhaps it is just because I am not a prolific lighter of fires. But I suspect that the traditional criterion has outlived its validity.

Every modern outdoorsman should be able to light a fire, but the act is not, it seems to me, a particularly important or testing part of his life. There are exceptions, of course. In cold, wet country where you are always needing a fire for warmth or for drying out clothes, getting one alight quickly is both a testing and an important business. And doubly so in an emergency, without matches. But the generalization stands.

I certainly seem to have survived without undue discomfort on a meager and rather incoherent grab bag of fire-lighting rules that I've made up as I went along: Carry plenty of matches, and *keep them dry.* The kindling is what matters; once you've got a small but healthy fire going, almost anything will burn on it. Unless your kindling is very dry indeed and very small, use paper as a starter. If the whole place is dripping wet, look for big stuff that will be dry in the center and from which you can cut out slivers that are easily split and shaved into serviceable kindling (the dry side of a dead cedar is a good bet, and so are the dead and sheltered twigs at the foot of many conifers), but don't overlook sheltered rock crevices and hollow trees (mice or other small animals will often store small sticks there, and you can rob them with remarkably little guilt). If you anticipate real trouble in starting a fire (if, for example, you had just one hell of a time doing so last night), carry along some kindling from wood that you dried out on last night's hard-won fire; and don't just stuff it into your pack; wrap it in a plastic bag and keep out the damp air. If necessary, do the same with some fire-dried paper too; in really wet weather, even paper can be hard to light. Some people, when they expect bad conditions, take along some kind of starter: candles (which are dual purpose tools), heat tablets, or tubes of barbecue igniter paste.

The rules for lighting a fire are simple and fairly obvious: Have plenty of wood ready in small, graduated sizes. Arrange the sticks of kindling more or less upright, wigwamwise, so that the flame will creep up them, preheating as it climbs. Keep the wigwam small. Apply your match at the bottom. In the first critical moments, carefully shield the flame from wind.

With these simple rules I seem to have got by without serious trouble. Oddly enough, the only real difficulties I can recall have been 'in the desert. Lighting a fire there is normally simple: you just break off a few twigs of almost any growth, dead or alive, and it lights. But desert plant life must, to survive, be adapted to absorb every drop of moisture. And it does so alive or dead. One sharp shower of rain, and every plant or fragment of plant you break off will feel like damp blotting paper. I vividly remember one cold and windy evening in Grand Canyon when a day of intermittent rain had ended with a snowstorm. At dusk I found a shallow rock overhang that offered shelter from both wind and snow but fell distinctly short of total coziness. Tired and damp and cold after a long day, I wanted a fire more than anything else. But every piece of wood I could find under the thin blanket of snow was soggy, clean through. I made a few abortive attempts at starting a fire with the driest wood, but even the scraps of paper from my pocket did little more than smolder. I was running desperately short of white gas too, and could not afford to use the stove as wood drier. Eventually I found the fairly thick stem of a cactus-like century plant or agave and managed to whittle some shreds of dry kindling from its center. It lit first time, and I spent a cheerful and almost luxuriously warm evening.

It is only common sense to site a fire so that the smoke from it will blow away from your campsite—but it is also common sense to expect that the moment you light the fire the wind will reverse itself. Impartial research would probably confirm the existence of something more statistically verifiable behind this expectation than the orneriness of inanimate objects: campfires tend to be lit around dusk, and winds tend to change direction at that time, particularly in mountain country.

Some men speak learnedly about the virtues of different firewoods. Frankly, I know almost none by name. But it does not seem to matter too much. It is no doubt more efficient to know at a glance the burning properties of each kind of wood you find; but you have only to heft a piece of dead wood to get a good idea of how it will burn. Generally speaking, light wood tends to catch easily and burn fast. Heavy wood will last well, though the heaviest may be the devil to get started, even in a roaring blaze.

I have never, thank God, had to produce a flame without matches. I have not even given the matter the thought it deserved. The magnifying glass that I carry primarily for other purposes (page 103) is always there as an emergency concentrator of sunlight onto paper or tinder, but I have never, in spite of intermittent good resolves, actually tried it out. In any case, the day on which you need a fire most desperately is likely to be wet and cold, and a magnifying glass would be about as useful as a station wagon in outer space. A flint-stick (page 104) might be just the answer.

In an emergency, it is theoretically possible to do the trick with a piece of string or bootlace that you wrap around a rotator of a stick whose end is held in a depression in a slab of wood. The idea is to twirl the stick fast enough and long enough to create by friction enough heat to ignite some scraps of tinder dropped into the depression. Simple, primitive men certainly started fires this way; but I have an idea that we clever bastards might find it quite difficult.

To be honest, I'm singularly unimpressed by the woodsy fanatic who's rich in this kind of caveman lore, especially if he'll pass it all on at the drop of a snowflake. I always suspect that he'll turn out to be the sort of man who under actual field conditions can stop almost anywhere, any time, and have a pot of water on the very brink of boiling within two hours and thirty-five minutes—provided it isn't actually raining, and he has plenty of matches. But maybe you'd be right to chalk my cynicism up to plain jealousy.

FIRE HAZARDS

These days, the way a man guards and leaves his fire may well be a more valid criterion for judging his outdoor competence than the way he starts one. A deliberately apprehensive common sense is your best guide; but the Forest Service lays down some useful rules:

Never build a fire on deep litter, such as pine needles. It can smolder
for days, then erupt into a catastrophic forest blaze.
Clear all inflammable organic material from an area appreciably
bigger than your fire, scraping right down to bare earth.

Generally speaking, and where possible, build a ring of stones around your fire. It will contain the ash and considerably reduce the chances of spread.

Never leave a fire unattended.

Where a fire hazard exists, do not built a fire on a windy day.

Avoid wood that generates a lot of sparks. The sparks can start fires in surrounding vegetation—and your sleeping bag.

Above all, *don't just put your fire out—kill it, dead.* Stir the ashes, deep and thoroughly, even though the fire seems to have been out for hours. Then douse it with dirt and water. You can safely stop when it's so doused you could take a swim in it.

Oddly enough, you can forgo such precautions in most kinds of desert. The place is curiously immune to arson. I have only once seen an extensive "burn" in treeless desert. Individual bushes may catch fire rather easily, but vegetation is so widely spaced (a necessary adaptation to acute moisture shortage) that the fire rarely spreads. The heat and dryness of deserts would seem sure to cause fires in mass-inflammable vegetation, so susceptible species have no doubt been selected out by the natural process of destruction by fire.

General fire precautions

Cultivate the habit of breaking all matches in two before you throw them away. The idea is not that half a match is much less dangerous than a whole one, but that the breaking makes you aware of the match and conscious of any lingering flame or heat. Book matches are rather difficult to break, but as I use mine only for fires or the stove, I always put used matches into the former or under the latter.

The big match danger comes from smokers (with a seven-year nonsmoking halo now tilted rakishly over my bald patch I feel comfortably smug). In some critical fire areas you are forbidden to carry cigarettes at certain times of year. In many forests you are not allowed to smoke while on the move, and can do so only on a site with at least three-foot clearance all around—such as a bare rock or a broad trail. Make absolutely sure you put your cigarette stub OUT. Soak it in water; or pull it to shreds. If you doubt the necessity of following such irritating rules to the letter, make yourself go and see the corpse of a recently burned forest.

THE KITCHEN IN ACTION

Packaging and packing

My kitchen travels, almost exclusively, in plastic freezer bags. The most useful sizes are small (pint and quart), medium (half gallon and one gallon) and capacious (the thick, pillow-size kind you can get for twenty-five cents from machines in some laundromats). Before knotting small and medium-size bags with food in them (or securing with a rubber band if they are too full) expel most of the air. And secure as high as possible, so that bag and contents can adjust to external pressures and occupy the minimum and most convenient space. To avoid frustration, knot bags loosely.

Into small bags go herbs and spices, spare salt, book matches, and the stove nozzle cleaner (page 110). Just about everything else goes into medium-size bags: dry cereal mixture (emptied from its heavy cardboard box); soup and gravy packages (they tend to split open); powdered milk packages (they split too, and you can picture, I'm sure, a faintly milk-coated kitchen on a rainy day); the week's supply of meat bars (for convenience rather than protection); the complete collection of little bags containing herbs and spices; spare sugar; chocolate; energy bars; beef jerky; dry raisins in bulk; dry raisins and mintcake together, for the current day's consumption; mintcake for the rest of the week; tea bags; fruit drink mixes; margarine container (always mildly greasy); and the stove. The more rebellious items (cereal, soups, sugar, milk, chocolate) get double-bag protection. The blackened frying pan, when it comes along, slips inside two medium-large bags.

All the food is now divided between two pillow-size bags. Into one bag goes everything needed for the current day. Into the other goes the balance of the week's rations. (If you put the whole lot into one bag you'll never be able to find what you want.) Once a day I choose the morrow's menu and transfer the rations (page 127).

Into one of the pack's upper outside pockets (my "nibble" pocket—page 272) go the between-meal snacks: the day's allowance of mintcakes and raisins, one energy bar, some beef jerky, chocolate (in cool weather), a package of fruit drink mix (under certain conditions, see page 99), and the canister of salt tablets. Also one meat bar, so that if there's no time to stop for a regular lunch, I need not unpack the main food.

The can of Halazone tablets goes, if it is likely to be used a lot, into the flap pocket, otherwise into one of the lower side pockets.

The nesting cooking pots travel in a pillow-size bag, folded around so that no residual water can escape. Well, not much anyway. Spoon and cup fit inside the inner pot, though in well-watered country I often carry the cup ready for use on a belt clip (see page 267).

Garbage

No matter how carefully you select food that comes in burnable packages, you'll always find small items that can't be burned. And burying is no solution to litter: animals will soon smell the adhering food and dig it up. I stow all unburnable garbage into a medium-size plastic bag that travels, easily get-at-able, in the back pocket of the pack. Into it go empty foil bags from soups, meat food product, energy bars, milk, and the like. Also, on the rare occasions I use them, cans. I don't like packing the extra weight but the self-righteous glow is well worth it.

I used to feel nothing but contempt for those who desecrate the countryside with litter. But nowadays I'm uncomfortably aware that once, in a mild alcoholic haze and pleasantly provocative company, I heaved an empty bottle out into the virgin desert sand—and did it maliciously, with delight, and with satisfaction. Like a good, rabid, antilitter man, I retrieved the bottle later. But the memory is still there, and, although I continue to look on litter louts with contempt and loathing, I can in my more charitable moments feel twinges of understanding. But only in the more charitable moments.

A SAMPLE DAY IN THE KITCHEN *

(Not to mention the bedroom, and most other departments too.) (Meticulously applicable only to those who operate on the Fletcher in-sleeping-bag culinary system.)

Something stirs inside you, and you half-open one eye. Stars and blackness, nothing more. You close the eye. But the something keeps on stirring, and after a moment you slide another inch toward consciousness and turn your head to the east and reopen the eye. It is there all right, a pale blue backing to the distant peaks. You sigh, pull up one arm inside the mummy bag, and check that the luminous hands of your watch say five o'clock.

After a decent interval you loosen the drawstrings of the mummy bag so that there is just enough room for you to slip on the shirt (which has been keeping the draft off your shoulders all night) and the down jacket (which you have been lying on). Then, still half-cocooned in the mummy bag, you sit up, reach back into the pack (which is propped up against the staff, just behind your head), and take out your shorts (which are waiting on top of everything else) and the pillow-size bag containing the day's rations (which is just underneath the shorts). From the ticket pocket of the shorts you fumble out book matches and an empty Lipton tea-bag wrapper. You stuff the shorts down into the mummy bag to warm. Next you take the flashlight out of one of your boots (which are standing just off to the left of the air mattress). Then you put the tea-bag wrapper down in the little patch you cleared for the stove last night (on the right side of the bed, because the wind was blowing from the left last night; and very close to the groundsheet so that you don't have to stretch). You set the tea-bag wrapper alight and hold the stove (which is waiting close by) by its handle, just above the burning paper. Soon, you see in the beam of the flashlight that gasoline is welling up from the nozzle. You put the stove down on the tea bag, snuffing out the flame. Gasoline seeps down the generator of the stove and into the little

* There are several similarities, here, to an account in *The Man Who Walked Through Time* (pages 19–24) of how I prepared an evening meal.

depression in the bowl, encircling the generator. When the depression is full, you close the stove valve and ignite the gasoline. When it has almost burned away, you reopen the valve. If you time it dead right, the last guttering flame ignites the jet. Otherwise, you light it with another match. The stove roars healthily, almost waking you up.

You check that the roaring stove is standing quite firm, reach out for the larger of the cooking pots (which you half-filled with water after dinner last night—because you know what you are like in the morning—and which spent the night back near the pack, off to one side, where no restless movement of your body could possibly knock it over). You put the pot on the stove. Next you put on your hat (which was hanging by its chin band from the top of the pack-frame) because you are now conscious enough to feel chilly on the back of your head where there used to be plenty of hair when you were younger. Then you reach out for the smaller cooking pot (which is also back in safety beside the pack, and in which you last night put two ounces of dehydrated fruit cocktail and a shade more water than was necessary to reconstitute it). You remove the cup from inside this pot (it stayed clean there overnight) and put it ready on the stove-cover platform (which is still beside the stove, where you used it for dinner last night). You leave the spoon in the pot (it too stayed clean and safe there overnight). You pour a little more water into the pot from a canteen, squirt in some milk powder (the squirter stood all night beside the pot), stir, and add about two ounces of cereal mix. Then you lean back against the pack, still warm and comfortable in the mummy bag, and begin to eat the fruit and cereal mixture. The pale blue band along the eastern horizon broadens.

Soon—without needing to use the flashlight now—you see steam jetting out from the pot on the stove. You remove the pot, lift its cover and drop in one tea bag (which you put ready on top of the pot at the same time as you took the cereal out of the day's-ration bag). You leave the label hanging outside so that later, when the tea is strong enough, you can lift the bag out. Then you turn off the stove. And suddenly the world is very quiet and very beautiful, and for the first time that morning you really look at the silhouetted peaks and at the shadows that are the valleys. You swirl the teapot a couple of times to suffuse the tea, take a few more mouthfuls of fruit-and-cereal, then pour a cupful of tea, squirt-add milk, spoon in copious sugar (the sugar container also spent the night beside the pots), and take the first luxurious sip. Warmth flows down your throat, spreads outward. Your brain responds. Still sluggishly, it takes another step toward full focus.

And so, sitting there at ease, leaning back against the pack, you eat breakfast. You eat it fairly fast today, because you have twenty miles to go, and by eleven o'clock it will be hot. You keep pouring fresh cups of hot tea, and each one tells. Spoonful by spoonful, you eat the fruit-and-cereal. It is very sweet, and it tastes good. When it is finished you chew a stick of beef jerky. And all the time the world and the day are unfolding above and below and around you. The light eases from gray toward blue. The valleys begin to emerge from their shadow, the peaks to gain a third dimension. The night, you realize, has already slipped away.

Do not let the menu deceive you: there is no better kind of breakfast.

When the meal is over you wash up rather sketchily (there is plenty of water, but time presses). You re-bag the food and utensils and stove and stow them away in the pack. The light moves on from blue toward pink. Still inside the mummy bag, you put on your shorts. And (because this is a day in a book) you time it just right. The sun moves majestically up from behind those distant peaks, exploding the blue and the pink into gold, at the very moment you need its warmth—at the very moment that the time arrives for you to pluck up your courage and forsake the mummy bag and put on socks and boots. Ten minutes later you are walking. Another half hour and you are wide awake.

(This is only a sample morning, of course—a not-too-cold morning on which you know there is a hot and fairly long day ahead. If the night had been really cold, or the dew so heavy that it soaked the mummy bag and everything else, you would probably have waited for the sun to make the world bearable or to dry out all that extra and unnecessary load of water. If, on the other hand, the day promised to be horribly long, or its noonday heat burningly hot, you would have set the something to stir inside you even earlier —probably suffering a restless night thereby, unless you are a more efficient alarm clock than I am—and would have finished breakfast in time to start walking as soon as it was light enough to do so safely. By contrast, this might have been a rest day. Then, you would simply have dozed until you got tired of dozing, and afterward made breakfast—or have woken yourself up first by diving into lake or river. But whatever the variations—unless you decided to catch fish for breakfast and succeeded—the basic food theme would have remained very much the same.)

You walk all morning, following a trail that twists along beside a pure, rushing mountain creek. Every hour, you halt for ten minutes. At every halt you take the cup from the belt clip at your waist and dip it into the creek and drink as much of the sensuously cool water as you want. And at every halt—except perhaps the first, when breakfast is still adequately with you—you take the bag of raisins-and-mintcake out of the nibble pocket and munch a few raisins and fragments of mintcake. At each succeeding halt you tend to eat rather more; but, without giving the matter much direct thought, you ration against the hours ahead. In mid-morning, a stick of beef jerky helps replenish the protein supply. Later, you boost the quickly available energy, and the fats too, with a piece of chocolate.

Just after noon, you stop for lunch. You choose the place carefully—almost more carefully than the site for a night camp, because you will spend more waking hours there. You most often organize the day with a long midday halt, not only because it means that you avoid walking through the worst of the heat but also because you have found noon a more comfortable and rewarding time than late evening to swim and wash and launder and doze and read and write notes and dream and mosey around looking at rocks and stones and fish and lizards and sandflies and trees and panoramas and cloud shadows and all the other important things. A long lunch halt also means that you split the day's effort into two slabs, with a good long rest in between. Come to think of it, perhaps this after all is the really critical factor.

Anyway, you choose your lunch site carefully. You find a perfect place, in a shady hollow beside the creek, to prop up the pack and roll out the groundsheet and then the air mattress and mummy bag (yes, mummy bag, for cushioning effect), and within three minutes of halting you have a set-up virtually identical to the one you woke up in that morning.

The soup of the day is mushroom. The directions could hardly be simpler: "Empty the contents into 1 liter (4 measuring cups) of hot water and bring to the boil. Cover and simmer for 5–10 minutes." So you light the stove and boil as much water as you know from experience you need for soup (what *you* need, not necessarily four measuring cups). You stir in the soup powder, add a smidgen of thyme (after rubbing it lightly in the palm of your hand), replace the cover at a very slight tilt so that the simmering soup will not boil over, reduce the heat as far as it will go (a mildly delicate business), and meditate for five minutes, stretched out tiredly but luxuriously on the mummy bag. After five minutes you add a dollop of margarine to the soup, stir, and pour out the first cupful. You leave the rest simmering. When you pour the second cup you turn off the stove and put the pot in the warmest place around—a patch of dry, sandy soil that happens to lie in a shaft of sunlight. Within half an hour of halting you have finished the soup and dropped off into a catnap.

When you wake up you wash all pots and utensils—thoroughly now, because there is time as well as water. You use sand as a scourer, grass as a cleaning cloth, detergent powder as detergent powder, and the creek for rinsing. (If the pots had looked very dirty and you had been "out" for a long time, or if an upset stomach had made you suspicious about cleanliness, you might—if there was fuel to spare—have put spoon and cup into the small pot and the small pot and some water into the big pot and boil-sterilized the whole caboosh.)

Next you do a couple of chores that you have made more or less automatic action after lunch, so that you will not overlook them. You decide on the menu for the next twenty-four hours and make the necessary transfers from bulk-ration bag to current-day's bag—including the refilling from the bagged reserve of the containers of milk (an everyday chore) and sugar and salt (once a week). You also replenish the nibble pocket: raisins, mintcake, energy bar. If necessary, you put a new book of matches in the ticket pocket of your shorts or long pants or both. (You carry a book in each.)

Then you refill the stove. You use the funnel and take great care not to spill precious fuel, but the aluminum bottle is brimful and some gasoline dribbles down its side. Still, you expected this slight wastage; and you know that it won't happen in a day or two, once the level in the bottle drops.

(Naturally, it does not matter much what time of day you choose to do these chores. In winter, for example, when the days are short, you'll probably just snatch a quick lunch and will do the reapportionment and refilling during the early hours of the long, long darkness. But on each trip you try to get into the habit of doing the chores at about the same time each day, because you know that otherwise you may find yourself fumbling down into the pack for the bulk-food bag in the middle of a meal, and at the same moment hear the dying bleat of an almost empty stove.)

For the next two or three or four or even five hours you either do some of the many make-and-mend chores that always keep piling up (washing, laundering, writing notes, and so on), or you mosey around and do the important matters that you came for (rocks, lizards, cloud shadows), or you simply sit and contemplate. Or you devote the time to a combination of all these things. But at the end of that time, when you know you ought to be walking again within half an hour, you brew up a sizable pot of tea (this particular day, you too are walking on a British passport). And because there are still four hours to darkness and night camp and dinner, you eat half an energy bar. Then you pack everything away, hoist up the pack, and start walking—leaving behind as the only signs of occupation a rectangle of crushed grass that will recover within hours, and, where the stove stood, a tiny circle that you manage to conceal anyway by pulling the grass stems together.

You find yourself walking in desert now (a shade miraculously, it's true, but it suits our book purposes better to have it happen that way) and it is very hot. Because you expect to find no more water until you come to a spring about noon the following day, you have filled all three half-gallon canteens you brought with you. Now, you go easy on the water. You still drink as well as munch at every hourly halt. And you drink enough. But only just enough. Enough, that is, to take the edge off any emerging hint of thirst. At the first couple of halts this blunting process calls for only a very small sip or two. Later you need a little more. But always, before you swallow the precious liquid, you swirl it around your mouth to wash away the dryness and the scum.

One canteen has to be non-fumble available at halts, but direct sunlight would quickly turn its water tepid. So you put it inside the pack—on top, but insulated by a down jacket.

With an hour to go to darkness, and a promise already there of the coolness that will come when the sun drops behind the parched, encircling hills, you begin to feel tired—not so much muscle-weary as plain running out of energy. So at the hourly halt you pour some water into the lid of one cooking pot, squirt-add milk, and pour in some cereal mixture. (Looked at objectively, this cereal snack always seems a highly inefficient business. It ought to be enough to take from the nibble pocket a booster bonus of raisins or chocolate or the remaining half energy bar. But the cereal snack seems to work better, so you go on doing it.)

At this final pre-camp halt you empty into the inner cooking pot the dehydrated beans and mixed vegetables that are on the day's dinner menu, and add salt and just enough water to reconstitute them. (Presoaked like this, they cook in ten minutes rather than half an hour.) You know from experience how much water to add. It is surprisingly little: barely enough to cover them. You add as little as possible, to reduce the danger of spillage, and from now on, when you take the pack off, you are careful to keep it upright.

You walk until it is too dark to go on (keeping a canny rattlesnake-watch during the last hour, because this is their time of day —see page 300). You camp in any convenient place that is level enough, though it is a kitchen advantage, stovewise, to have adequate shelter from desert winds (usually *down* canyons at night).

Dinner is the main meal of the day, but it is very simple to prepare. It has to be. You are tired now. And because the rising sun will be coercing you on your way again in less than eight hours, you don't want to waste time. So as soon as you halt you roll out the groundsheet and air mattress and sleeping bag and sit thankfully down and set up the kitchen just as you did last night and at lunchtime, except that because of a hump in the ground and a gentle but growing crosswind you find it expedient to put everything on the other side of the bed. Even before you take off your boots, you empty the already soft vegetables out of the small pot into the big one, scraping the stickily reluctant scraps out with the spoon and swirling the small pot clean with the water you're going to need to cook the meal anyway. You add a little or a lot of water according to whether you fancy tonight's stew in the form of a near-soup or an off-putty goo. (Only experience will teach you how much water achieves what consistency. For painless experience, start with near-soups that won't burn, and then work down toward goo. Your methods are rough and ready, so you will from time to time add the pleasures of surprise to those of variety.) You light the stove (using the flashlight to check when the gasoline wells up) and put the big pot on it, uncovered. Then you crumble one meat bar onto the vegetables and sprinkle in about one fifth of a package of oxtail soup and a couple of shakes of pepper and a healthy dose of hand-rubbed oregano. You stir and cover. Next you take off your boots and put them within easy reach, on the opposite side of the bed from the kitchen, and put your socks in the boots. Then you anoint your feet with rubbing alcohol, taking care to keep it well away from the stove, and blow up the air mattress (whatever you do, don't leave this breath-demanding chore until after dinner).

At this point, steam issues from the stew pot. You reduce the heat to dead-low or thereabouts (taking care not to turn the stove off in the process), stir the compound a couple of times, inhale appreciatively and replace the cover. While dinner simmers toward fruition you empty two ounces of dehydrated peaches and a little water into the small cooking pot and put it ready for breakfast, up alongside the pack. Then you jot down a few thoughts in your notebook, stir the stew and sample it, find the beans are not quite soft yet. So you study the map and worry a bit about the morning's route,

put map and pen and pencil and eyeglasses and thermometer into
the bedside boots, take off your shorts and slide halfway down into
the mummy bag out of the wind, and stir the stew again and find all
ready. You pour-and-spoon out a cupful, leaving the balance on the
stove because the wind is blowing distinctly cool now. And then,
leaning comfortably back against the pack and watching the sky and
the black peaks meld, you eat, cupful by cupful, your dinner. You
finish it—just. Then you spoon-scrape out every last possible fragment and polish-clean the pot and cup and spoon with a piece of
toilet paper. You put the paper under the stove so that you can burn
it in the morning. Then you put cup and spoon into the breakfast-
readied small pot, pour the morning tea water into the big pot, set
the big pot alongside the small one and the sugar and milk containers
alongside them both, put the current day's ration bag into the pack
(where it is moderately safe from mice and their night allies) and

your shorts on top of it, lean one canteen against the boots so that you can reach out and grasp it during the night without doing more than loosen the mummy-bag drawstrings, zipper and drawstring yourself into the bag, wind your watch, belch once, remind yourself what time you want the something to stir in the morning, and go to sleep.*

THE KITCHEN IN ACTION
UNDER SPECIAL CONDITIONS

High altitude

At sea level, water boils at 100°C. But the boiling point falls 1°C. for every rise of 1000 feet. At 5000 feet: 95°. At 10,000: 90°. At 15,000: 85°. (These figures are for pure water under average barometric pressures. When the water contains salt or other impurities, the boiling point rises slightly. Marked weather changes may raise or lower it.)

As most outdoor cooking depends on the boiling point of water, food therefore takes longer to cook at high altitudes than at sea level. With my simple menus, and at the maximum elevations I normally reach (little over 14,000 feet), I pay almost no attention to the differences. I just sample and go by the taste. But with more complicated dishes you should probably work out some kind of graduated compensation. The only time I ever noted any figures was at 14,246 feet. There, an egg boiled for ten minutes turned out to be still slightly underdone. It would be difficult, I imagine, to find a more superbly useless item of information.

For the vagaries of appetite at high altitude, see page 73, footnote.

---

* The elapsed time between halting and going to sleep will obviously vary with many factors, including how eager you are to get to sleep. It is difficult to give meaningful average times. You just don't measure such things very often. The only time I remember doing so was under conditions markedly similar to those of our sample evening. I was in no particular hurry, but I did not dally. And I happened to notice as I wound my watch that it was exactly forty minutes since I had halted.

In snow

For keeping canteens de-iced, see page 98; for insulation of stove bowl with Ensolite pad, page 109; and for use of inverted stove cover as cup platform, page 110. But the big problem in snow —or, rather, the big labor—is water.

Even in mid-winter you can, in clear weather and while the sun is high, often find little runnels of water on rock surfaces or at sharp drop-offs in the snow. And a few places that drip slowly but steadily will enable you, given time, to collect all the water you need by putting pots and pot lids and cup and canteens under the drips. Or you may be able to spread out a groundsheet or poncho or both, anywhere but on the snow and scatter snow on it for the sun to melt. Sometimes you'll find a creek appearing intermittently at small openings, far down in deep drifts, and a cooking pot lowered on a nylon cord will land you all the water you need. Where such creeks are common, some backpackers carry tin cans with baling-wire handles.

Traveling up high in summer or fall, you may sometimes have to melt snow for water (though you naturally stand a good chance of finding the liquid form). The winter's snow will by then have compacted, and a potful of it may produce as much as a half potful of water. Under these amiable conditions you need adopt no tight melting techniques. Just pack snow into a pot, heat, and pour the water into your canteens.

But in winter, in powdery snow, you need to apply a little more thought. The object is to produce a reasonable volume of water with the least possible expenditure of time, gasoline, energy, and fret. From limited experience I have evolved this procedure for tent camping:

Before you crawl inside the tent, pile up a heap of snow just outside the entrance and within easy reach of your lying position inside (and on the opposite side from that on which the zipper opening has just jammed halfway). Stamp the pile of snow down to a reasonably compact consistency. When you are safely inside and have the stove set up, reach out and, using your cup as a scoop, fill both cooking pots with the compacted snow and also build tall piles on both inverted pot lids. Tamp the snow in the big pot firmly down. Light the stove and heat the big pot. Wait until water appears at the surface of the snow—which will by that time have shrunk almost to the bottom of the pot—and then begin to add spoonfuls of snow from the small pot. (You wait for the water to appear because once it has a chance to permeate the new snow it conducts heat far more efficiently than the dry crystals do.)

Continue spooning in more snow. Keep matches ready for immediate use, because water tends to condense on the outside of the pot and drip down, and it may occasionally douse the flame. Replenish the lids from the snowpile outside the tent. When the pot is almost half full of water, stop adding snow. Just before the last snowbergs disappear, pour all the water except about an inch depth into the small and now empty pot. Quickly replace the big pot on the stove and refill with snow from the waiting lids. Replenish lids, rather feverishly, from the outside dump. At a convenient pause in the rush, pour the water with tremendous care from the small pot into a canteen. Leave small dirt particles in bottom of pot. Restopper canteen and place on Ensolite pad or air mattress. (By transferring the water from big pot to small you reduce wastage of gasoline, keep the big pot hot, introduce a double-sedimentation process for removal of inevitable dirt particles, obviate the pouring hazard of floating snowbergs [if one or two flop down into the small pot, wait until they dissolve before filling the canteen], and also give yourself a more sharply curved and therefore better-pouring vessel with which to transfer water into the canteen.) Continue adding snow to big pot. When half full, transfer again. Continue ad nauseam.

Do not expect to do much all this time except melt snow. For one thing, you will find yourself quite fully occupied. For another, you can bet your bottom layer of clothing that if you take your mind off the stove and pot for more than ten seconds straight you are, in those cramped quarters, going to swing a careless arm and send the whole caboodle flying.

This kind of snow-melting is a long and tedious business. The time needed to produce a given volume of water varies with, among other things, the consistency of the snow and the efficiency of your stove and technique. As a guide on the first attempt, allow twice as long as seems reasonable. Then double this allowance. And don't be so naïve as to imagine you'll really do that well.

In a tent (especially, but not necessarily, in snow)

Two kitchen dangers must not be forgotten.

One is fire. In the cramped confines of a tent you are hardly likely to be absent-minded enough to drop a still-glowing match. But a stove—and especially a kerosene stove—being lit in low temperatures is liable to send an oversize flame shooting upward. So it is wise to be ready at any moment to hurl the complete fiery article outside. As you often have to batten down tight while lighting the stove in order to cut wind disturbance to the minimum, you can hardly leave a zipper or drawstring undone. But at least you can be mentally ready, somewhere in the far recesses of your mind, to pull them open at the first sign of trouble.

A more serious danger, and one more likely to occur, is carbon monoxide poisoning.

Unless you ensure adequate ventilation, a burning stove can very quickly consume almost all the free oxygen in your battened-down little world. And a stove burning in a confined space that lacks a free oxygen supply will give off carbon monoxide.

It is important to understand the distinction between asphyxiation (lack of oxygen; presence of too much carbon dioxide) and carbon monoxide poisoning. If you are starved of oxygen, your breathing will in time fill the space around you with carbon dioxide, and you will usually be warned of the danger of asphyxiation—even awakened from sleep—by being made to gasp for breath (see page 152—but also page 164). But carbon monoxide is a colorless, odorless, highly poisonous gas—the gas that occasionally kills people in enclosed garages. It does not warn you of danger by making you gasp for breath. And it does not extinguish or even dim a flame.

Carbon monoxide poisoning is no mere theoretical hazard for campers—especially in snow, which can very effectively cut off all ventilation. Down the years there have been many tragedies and near tragedies. Vilhjalmur Stefansson, in his book *Unsolved Mysteries of the Arctic* (1938), gives some graphic examples. The gas almost killed Willem Barents and his entire polar party when they holed up in a snow-encased cabin on Novaya Zemlya in the winter of 1596 and tried to keep themselves warm with "sea-coles which we had brought out of the ship." Stefansson himself was lucky to escape in 1911 when his four-man party found an old Eskimo snowhouse, sealed the doorway too tight, and began cooking on a kerosene-burning stove. A kerosene-burning heater almost killed a man on the first Byrd Antarctic Expedition of 1938, when a blizzard partially blocked the flue pipe. Stefansson maintains that the two men of the ill-fated Andrée arctic balloon party of 1897, whose bodies were not found until 1930, probably died from carbon monoxide poisoning: a kerosene-burning Primus stove stood between their bodies, and there seems every reason to believe that their tent may have been partly covered by drifting snow.

Only a year or two ago, two young men apparently died from carbon monoxide poisoning while camping in the Inyo National Forest of California. It seems almost certain that, in unexpectedly cold weather, they battened down their impermeable plastic tube tent (page 159) and for warmth left their Sterno stove (canned heat) burning when they went to sleep. They never woke up.

Now I do not want to make you afraid of cooking in a confined space. But I do want to make you keenly aware of the dangers. It is vital to remember that, as becomes clear from the accounts of survivors from near-tragedies, you get no warning of carbon monoxide poisoning beyond, perhaps, "a slight feeling of pressure on the temples, a little bit as if from an elastic band or cap." Unconsciousness may follow within seconds. Unless someone else recognizes the danger in time and lets in fresh air before he succumbs himself, you die.

The necessary precautions are simple. When you are cooking in a tent or other enclosed space, especially in snow, always make sure that you have adequate airflow. In a high wind, that is hardly likely to be a problem. But if snow is falling, keep checking that the air vents do not become blocked, and keep clearing away drifted snow, so that the entrance is never in danger of being completely buried (see also page 151).

Bedroom

THE ROOF

Under most conditions, the best roof for your bedroom is the sky. This common-sensible arrangement saves weight, time, energy, and money. It also keeps you in intimate contact with the world you are presumably walking through in order to come into intimate contact with.

That world often mounts to its most sublime moments of beauty at the fringes of darkness; and the important thing, I find, is not just to see such beauty but to see it happen—to watch the slow and almost imperceptible transitions of shine and shadow, form and shapelessness. You cannot see such events by peering out occasionally from under a roof. Certainly you cannot lie under a roof and let yourself become a part of them, so that their meanings, or whatever it is that is important about them, move deep inside you. You must be out under the sky.

For me, the supreme place to watch beauty happen is a mountaintop.

I shall never forget a calm and cloudless autumn night when I camped roofless and free, yet warm and comfortable, on the very summit of Mount Shasta. Shasta is an isolated volcanic pyramid that rises 10,000 feet from a broken plain. Its apex stands 14,162 feet above sea level. From this apex, as the sun eased downward, I watched the huge shadow of the pyramid begin to move out across the humps and bubukles of the darkening plain. At first the shadow was squat and blunt. And its color was the color of the blue-gray plain, only darker. As the sun sank lower, the shadow reached slowly out toward the horizon until it seemed to cover half the eastward plain. Its color deepened. The pyramid grew longer, taller, narrower. At last the slender apex touched the gray and hazy horizon. There, for a long and perfect moment the huge shape halted; lay passive on the plain. Its color deepened to a luminous, sumptuous, majestic, royal blue. Then the light went out. The shadow faded. Night took over the gray but still humped and bubukled plain. And slowly, as the western sky darkened, the shapeless shadows moved deeper into everything and smoothed the plain into a blackboard. Soon, a few small lights bloomed out of the dusk. But the real happenings were over, and after a while I went to sleep, high above the stage and yet a part of it.

But you do not have to climb a 14,000-foot peak in order to sleep above and yet in the night. Sometimes, quite late at night, when I feel the need for a new perspective on my tight little urban life, I go to the place in which I wrote the opening chapter of this book. I heave my pack into the station wagon, drive for an hour, and park the wagon on a dirt road that winds steeply through a stretch of still-untrampled ranch country, recently set aside as a public park. An hour later, aided by a flashlight and the pleasurable excitements of change and darkness, I climb up onto the flat, grassy summit of an isolated and "unimproved" hill. This little tableland stands almost 1,700 feet above sea level, and from it I can see the sprawling blaze of lights that now rings San Francisco Bay. I can watch tiny headlights creeping in and out of this web, like unsuspecting fireflies, along the freeways that link it, eastward, with the black and mysterious continent. And when I have rolled out my mummy bag and cocooned myself inside it against the cold wind sweeping in from the Pacific, I can sometimes see as well, quite effortlessly, in the moments before I fall asleep, both a time when the shores of the Bay were as black as the rest of the continent, and a time when the eastward view from this hill will blaze almost as brightly and beautifully and senselessly as the present thin ring around the blackness that is the Bay. I should find it quite pointless to camp on that hill in a tent.

But there is more to rooflessness than panoramas. Some worlds only come alive after dark, and my memory often cheers me with warm little cameos it would not hold if I always cut myself off from the night in a tent. Deep in Grand Canyon, inches from my eyes, floodlit by flashlight, a pair of quick, clean little deer mice scamper with thistledown delicacy along slender willow shoots. On a Cornish hillside, with the Atlantic pounding away at the cliffs below, the shadowy shape of a fox ambles unconcernedly out of and then back into the darkness. On the flank of a California mountain, in sharp moonlight, a raccoon emerges from behind a bush, stops short and peers through its mask at my cocooned figure, then performs a long and comically exaggerated mime of indecision before turning away and, still not altogether sure it is doing the right thing, sea-rolls back behind the bush.

Without a roof, you wake directly into the new day. Sometimes I open my eyes in the morning to see a rabbit bobbing and nibbling its way through breakfast. Once I woke at dawn to find, ten feet from my head, a doe browsing among dew-covered ferns. Near the start of my California walk, camped beside a levee that protected some rich farmland that had been created from desert by irrigation with Colorado River water, I woke in a pale early light to find myself looking into the rather surprised eye of a desert road runner that stood on top of the levee, as still and striking as a national emblem. There was a light frost in my little hollow, and I lay warm and snug in my bag, only eyes and nose exposed, and watched the bird. It watched me back. After a while I heard a noise off to the left. The road runner came to life and retreated over the levee. The noise increased. Suddenly, sunshine streamed over the dike. Soon a tractor pulled up, twenty feet from my bedroom, beyond some low bushes. A large and cheerful and voluminously wrapped Negro got down and swung his arms for warmth and made an adjustment to the motor. Then, seeing me for the first time, he grinned hugely and enviously and said, "Well, *you* look warm enough. That's one of us, anyways."

Yet in spite of the obvious advantages of rooflessness a majority of indoorsmen—and quite a few outdoorsmen—seem to assume that camping means sleeping in a tent.*

TENTS

There are, of course, certain conditions under which a tent becomes desirable or even essential.

Very cold weather is one of them—the kind of weather in which you need to retain every possible calorie that your body generates. But, unless a wicked wind is blowing, such conditions occur only when the temperature falls really low. That night I camped on the peak of Mount Shasta, the thermometer read 9°F. at sunrise. Yet with nothing for a bedroom except an Ensolite pad and a good sleeping bag, I slept warm and snug. But that night was dead calm. In any kind of strong wind, even when the temperature is up close to freezing, you need walled shelter: all but the warmest sleeping bags, unprotected, lose too much heat. You also find it virtually impossible to cook food or do any other part-way-out-of-the-bag chores. A cave may be the best hideout, but in most places good caves are rare. When you're on the move, a tent is unfortunately the only dependable solution.

You also need a tent in any appreciable snowfall—if you want to be sure of reasonable comfort. And under really bad conditions of cold and snow a tent may be necessary for survival.†

---

* In this connection I always recall the instinctive remark of a young lady whose forte was indoor rather than outdoor sports but who was for a time the very close friend of an experienced outdoorsman. One close and friendly evening she lifted the sheets above them both with the tips of her pink toes so that it formed a neat little pup tent, and exclaimed, "Look! Camping out!"

No, come to think of it, it was a friendly afternoon.

† I suspect, though, that a safely constructed snow cave may be as good if not better. Not long ago, in a Sierra Nevada storm that brought four feet of snow but left temperatures up around 25°, I found a U.S. Air Force survival training group dug in, apparently without sleeping bags, on a steep ridge. As far as I could make out (when I stumbled on them, visibility was down to about ten yards), they seemed reasonably comfortable. They certainly sounded cheerful.

But you do not really need a tent in rain, except perhaps when the rain is heavy and prolonged and wind-driven. There are, as we shall see, better bedrooms. One of the difficulties of a tent in wet weather is that you need a fly sheet. Without one you simply can't keep dry. And a tent and fly sheet together tend to be prohibitively heavy, even when dry.

There is one other occasion on which a tent may be worth packing along. If you are going to set up a semipermanent camp and move out from it each day—for fishing, hunting, climbing, or whatever—it is convenient to be able to leave your gear unpacked and ready for use but still protected. Protected, that is, from any weather that may blow up, and also from animals. Naturally, no tent will keep out every kind of animal. Ants can usually find a way in. So, less certainly, can mice. But a properly battened-down tent, especially one with a sewn-in floor, will keep out most middle-size creatures that can be a daytime nuisance: birds (especially jays, which are sometimes called "camp robbers") and such inquisitive mammals as chipmunks and squirrels and, worst of all, pack rats. Fortunately, most of the big mammals—deer, coyote, bobcat, cougar—seem to steer well clear of anything that smells of man. The dire exception is bear—and a tent, unfortunately, won't stop a bear.*

Outside North America, the animal situation may be rather different. For some considerations in East Africa, see page 145.

Car campers often carry tents to give them privacy in crowded campsites; but if you go backpacking and camp in crowded places, don't worry about a tent. Consult a psychiatrist.

Kinds of tents

My experience with tents is limited, but I suppose I must attempt to lay down guidelines for those even less experienced.

I own one tent, a model now sold by Trailwise in an improved

---

* Just the other day, I glimpsed a way out of the bear hazard. We carry insect repellent; why not bear repellent?—something neutral or pleasing to a human nose but obnoxious to a bear's. (Tincture of bear mother-in-law?) Just spread or spray the mixture lightly on your tent or packbag and then go fishing all day without a bear-worry in the world.

version as their "One Man Mountain Tent." Occasionally I pack this tent on high mountain trips. Very occasionally.

Made of bright yellow nylon fabric, with a lightweight coated nylon floor, it is forty inches high and forty inches wide at the head At the foot it tapers to sixteen by sixteen inches. When the zipper is closed, a front alcove extends out about twenty-two inches from the head. In theory, you stow pack and gear into this alcove. In practice, you are hard put to it to fit the stove and pots in there. The tent does a fairly good job of conserving warmth in high winds, though I don't think I'd trust its stability in a full-scale storm. The whole structure lacks the necessary reserve of strength. Several times I have slept in sheltered rock niches rather than trust it—though part of the choice can be attributed to the difficulty of erecting a tent in high winds. In rain, without a fly sheet, this tent is several grades worse than useless: water seeps in, collects on the waterproof floor, and leaves you wallowing in a puddle.

But the tent is very light. The whole rig—tent, guys, alloy poles and pegs, and carrying bag—weighs just two pounds, fourteen ounces ($62.50). A fly sheet of waterproof Nylport-coated nylon weighs twenty ounces, costs $18.75.

Of its kind, this tent is excellent. But, ounce-parer though I am, I'm inclined to regard it as too light for the sort of conditions under which you normally need a tent. To face a long siege from a winter storm you must have plenty of reserve strength in fabric and attachments. And strength means weight. What's more, it's not just a matter of catalogue weight. The bundle that goes into or onto your pack is often a snow-and-ice-caked mess, half again as heavy as the original.

Then there's the size question. A geographer friend of mine who does a great deal of winter mountain work maintains that for real efficiency, let alone comfort, a man on his own needs what the catalogues call a "two-man tent." I agree. Two years ago, a snowstorm kept me mostly in my tent for four straight days. But it was a two-man tent, and I was both warm and tolerably comfortable. I would not have liked to spend those four days cooped up in my little one-man tent.

Last winter, on a week's solo cross-country ski trip, I packed along a two-man tent. (Yes, you're quite right, skiing is not walking. But as far as the tent was concerned I could just as easily have been using snowshoes. And snowshoeing, we decided, *is* walking.)

The tent I used (see illustration) was a prototype by Sierra Designs of Point Richmond, California, which they now put out in improved form under the name "Wilderness Tent."

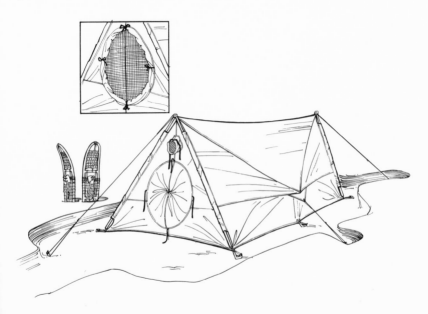

This tent proved highly satisfactory. I found the floor space (4½ by 7½ feet) plenty big enough for myself, my outspread gear, my pack, and my actions. The headroom (45 inches) and footroom (36 inches) were entirely adequate. Side pullouts kept the walls from sagging too markedly under one overnight snowfall of about a foot. The fabric of thin Rip-stop nylon stood up without sign of strain to the quite gentle weather I experienced (no howling winds, no heavy snowfalls, temperature never below 16°). There was a certain amount of condensation on the walls, especially during two hours of unexpected rain, but it never became a problem. A projecting vent at each apex provided good ventilation. Each vent was fly-screened with fine nylon mesh, and could be tape-tied shut from inside or out. Later versions of the tent have a clothesline attachment in the ridge (see page 219). The floor, and the sidewalls and endwalls up to a height of 12 inches, were made of tough, waterproof Nylport. All stitching was with nylon thread.

The two sets of aluminum A-frame poles were of a "self-erecting" type: a thick shock-cord ran through the three sections of each pole, preventing single sections being lost and also tending at all times to spring them into the joined, or erect, position. At first I scoffed at this fancy device. But the week's use made me a tentative convert. The poles proved very convenient compared with the usual unattached sections, which acquire wills of their own as soon as you start trying to put up a tent in a wind or a hurry.

For me, the outstanding features of this tent—beyond the lightweight and apparently effective fabric—were the entrance and the cookhole.

The entrance was drawstring type, a foolproof, easily adjustable system that I had not used before but which I found a vast improvement over zipped doorways, which in foul weather can freeze, jam, break, and utterly infuriate. (An alternative model of this tent has a zipper doorway. It is six ounces and $9 extra and is not for me. But see page 151 for dangers of sleeve—or drawstring—entrances in very heavy snowfall.) The entrance had a zipper nylon mesh screen door that sealed off the tent completely, for use in insect country. I did not have to use it.

The cookhole was simply a thirty-inch semicircular, nylon-zippered flap on the floor of the tent. I found it admirable, not only for cooking (to keep food scraps and condensed water off the floor) and for garbage disposal (just sweep snow and debris into it—see pages 150 and 151) but also for indoor sanitation (though to perform you need to be half brother to a contortionist). The cookhole is normally put on the left side of the tent: if you are right-handed, you probably find it easiest to cook lying on your left side, using your right arm for most of the work.

From my limited experience, I would say that a tent of this type comes pretty close to the ideal for one man operating in snow country or in cold, strong winds. If there are two of you . . . well, this *is* a two-man tent.

"Wilderness" tent: 2 pounds, 12 ounces; $64. Poles: 1 pound, 6 ounces; $16. Ten snow pegs: 1 pound, 1 ounce; cost included in tent. Total: 5 pounds, 3 ounces; $80. A waterproof Rip-stop nylon fly sheet for this tent, recommended for prolonged and heavy rain: 1 pound, 4 ounces; $24.50.

The Wilderness is Sierra Designs' middle-price model. Since drafting this book I have given a prolonged trial, under very different conditions, to their topline "Glacier" tent—similar to the Wilderness but forty-five inches high at both ends and with a drawstring entrance at one end, zipper door at the other.

I used this tent fairly often during a recent six-month return visit to East Africa, when I spent much of the time watching wild game in Kenya, Uganda, and Tanzania. Because it is dangerous—not to mention illegal—to walk in most game reserves and all parks, I car-camped. Generally, I slept in the tent—not because you need protection from weather on most East African nights, but because it is unwise, on account of lions and hyenas, to sleep in the open on your own. You do not need much protection: almost anything that completely surrounds you seems to keep the predators off (a mosquito net is probably, though not quite certainly, enough). But it is important that you are *completely* surrounded. Lions, in particular, have been known to wander in through the open doors of tents. The point of all this is that I had to have a tent that would, even when closed, be well enough ventilated on nights that, although usually cool, occasionally remained quite warm (most game areas of East Africa lie at elevations between 3000 and 7000 feet above sea level). The Glacier filled the bill. By closing the lower halves of both zipper and tunnel doors and fully closing their mosquito-net coverings, and by leaving the mosquito-netted air vent above the tunnel door open, I maintained adequate ventilation. And the lions and hyenas that were often around camp at night never bothered me.

When there was a danger of rain I used the very simply erected fly sheet. With it, the tent withstood several tropical downpours. Once, when an all-night storm left the ground half an inch deep in water, there was some seepage through the cookhole, but a shallow drainage ditch around the tent's perimeter would have prevented this contretemps.

This was the first tent I've used that dispenses with line tighteners. You just tie a loop in the nylon cord at a convenient place, pass the free end of line (coming up from its peg) through the loop, pull to tighten, and jam with a slip knot. Simple. Brilliant.

All in all, my trial convinced me that the makers are not exaggerating when they describe this tent as "suitable for use in Alpine or Tropical conditions in all weather." I also became a full-blooded convert to the shock-cord-joined, self-erecting aluminum poles.

(Glacier tent: 3 pounds, 4 ounces; $88.50. Poles: 1 pound, 8 ounces; $16.75. Ten snow pegs: 1 pound, 1 ounce—ten aluminum wire pegs weigh 4 ounces; cost included in tent. Total 5 pounds, 13 ounces; $105.25. Fly sheet: 1 pound, 5 ounces; $24.50.)

High prices like this are normal for first-rate tents—and remember that cheap tents are usually bad tents. So if there's a store close to you that rents equipment it pays to rent the model you're considering buying and give it a thorough trial. But renting such expensive and fragile items is not cheap (see page 19).

Care of tents

A nylon tent needs far less looking after than the old canvas type with rope guy lines. For one thing, you do not have to keep loosening and tightening the lines to meet humidity changes. And once the weather swings around on your side the tent dries out very quickly.

Damp does not harm nylon the way it does canvas and rope, but if you arrive home with a wet nylon tent it's best to dry it out. The simplest way is to erect it on the lawn, wash it if necessary with the garden hose, and just leave it to dry. If you have to do the job indoors, hang the tent by its normal suspension points. (Since writing this paragraph, I've been told by Sierra Designs that they wash their Rip-stop nylon tents after use in an ordinary washing machine, with mild detergent, then dry them in a spin drier. To avoid grisly tangles, they remove all guy lines.)

TENTS IN ACTION

Tent poles

Most modern poles are hollow aluminum tubes that break down into convenient sections of less than three feet. Carry them tied to one side of your packframe. I find this method best: bundle the poles together as a unit with three rubber bands (at top, middle, and bottom) so that they will not slip and slide. Then lash the bundle tightly to one side of the packframe with a three- or four-foot length of nylon cord (page 264). Knot one end of the cord to the lowest aluminum eyebolt on the packframe (illustration, page 53). (For knot, see page 265). Lay the bundled poles snugly along the packframe, upright, close to the packbag. Then, maintaining all possible tension, wind the cord upward around the packframe outer bar and the poles. Wind in open turns about six inches apart. Five or six turns bring you to the packframe crossbar. Make several securing turns around the bar and finish off with a knot through the nearest eyebolt. I find that, secured this way, the poles often stay firmly lashed without re-tightening for several days and nights on which I do not use them.

For instant-erect tent poles joined by shock cord, see page 144. Most good backpacking tents come in convenient stuff bags.

Tent pegs

Ultralightweight pegs made from solid round duralumin rods (usually known as "wire pegs") are satisfactory for most purposes. They average ½ ounce each, cost 15 cents. If a campsite is too soft to hold them firm (sand) or too hard for you to drive them in (yes, rock), and if the wind is not too strong (if it is, try to go someplace else), tie the guy lines to the middle of the pegs, lay them flat, and block them from sliding toward the tent with heavy rocks. If strong sticks are available, use them instead of the pegs: their greater friction reduces the chances of slippage. Either method works better than trying to tie guy lines directly onto all but ideally shaped stones.

Pitching a tent in a high wind

Every tent has its own stratagems for driving you to the brink of lunacy when you try to erect it in a high wind. But there are standard defensive measures with which you can counter. Before you unroll the tent itself and allow the wind to breathe berserk life into its billowing folds, have all the support weapons ready and waiting— poles, pegs, and an assortment of articles from pack or nature that are heavy enough to help hold down the wind-filled tent and yet smooth enough not to tear it. Then drive in the first peg, part way. For obvious reasons, wind- and door-wise, this peg should be the one for the center guy line of the foot end of the tent. If possible, hook this line over the peg before you unfold the tent. Drive the peg fully home, so that the line cannot by any devilish means flap free. Then take a deep breath and unfold the tent. Unfold it slowly, close to the ground, and onto each foot or so of unfolding fabric put one or more of the heavy, smooth articles. Their size and nature will depend on wind strength and campsite: sometimes all you can use is the full pack; big stones, when available, are godsends, but they must be smooth. Failing adequate heavy support weapons, sprawl yourself over the whistling, flapping bedlam. Slowly, painfully, drive in the pegs that hold down the edges of the stretched-out floor. If no stones are handy, drive in the pegs with your heels. Unless you've attempted this maneuver from the prone position in a thirty-mile-an-hour wind—brother, you haven't lived.

The sequence in which you tackle pole-erection and the securing of the other guy lines will depend on the structure of your tent and the vagaries of your temperament, but in general you fix the windward end first and you try to keep everything flat on the ground until you are ready to lift the fabric quickly into a taut, unflappable position. You can't possibly accomplish such an act, but you might as well aim for it. Once you've come anywhere close, your troubles are almost over. But if you get the tent up within double the time you figured on, count yourself a candidate for the Tent of Fame.

Once the tent is up you should check several times that no pegs are threatening to pull out. And, because even the tautest tent will flap in a high wind, you may have to tighten the lines occasionally. End-to-end stability is the most vital factor, and it pays to place the head-end peg so that the line tightener comes close to the apex of the tent and you can adjust it by simply reaching out from inside. If necessary, shorten the line by tying in a sheepshank.

Pitching a tent in snow

In hard snow, the only vital difference from pitching a tent elsewhere (unless you have to level a site) lies in the pegs. Ordinary round tent pegs are useless in snow. Use the special angle pegs (1¾ ounces each; 45 cents). They're astonishingly efficient. Once you've driven them in, in fact, the only difficulty tends to be getting them out when you strike camp. The best extractor is the point of an ice ax. It is also a highly efficient tool for making holes in tent fabric.

In case of lost pegs, snowshoes or skis or ice axes make good emergency replacements. Some people even use them regularly, and so cut down on tent pegs.

I have heard of, but not yet seen, a new type of "dish" peg—six or eight inches in diameter, made of light alloy or of fiberglass, with a central hole for tying in the guy line. You slide it sideways into soft snow that has been stamped down. You remove it by . . . well, your guess is as good as mine.

In soft snow it is essential that before you attempt to pitch a tent you stamp out the site. Do the job before you take anything out of your pack, and make sure you know beforehand how many paces or boot lengths you need for length and for width, allowing room for you to move around outside the tent during the pitching operation. Stamp out narrow extensions for all guy lines, and a broad one around the entrance. In bad weather, this stamped-down entrance area will reduce the risk of drifting snow blocking all ventilation (see pages 135–6, and 151). In good weather you'll find it invaluable as a place you can probably stand up in without snowshoes or skis. A little alleyway extension as a john is a worthwhile refinement.

The tent in action in snow

In snow camping, your tent is your castle. Outside, the world howls, white and hostile. Inside, you create a little domain of your own—cramped, imperfectly dry, and frigid by town-indoor standards; but livable and surprisingly snug. Of course, you have to work to keep it that way. Above all, you have to work at keeping things reasonably dry. Primarily, that means keeping the snow out. Before you crawl inside, brush all the snow you can off clothing and person. Stamp as much as you can off your boots too. And do not wear them all the way inside: swivel around before they come more than an inch or two over the threshold, take them off (less easily done than written), and immediately slip your feet down into the sleeping bag. Legs and body probably go into the bag too. Then bang the boots together and get most of the remaining snow off them. In good weather, hold the boots outside for this operation. In vile weather, bang the snow onto something waterproof, laid out just inside the entrance, and empty it outside when you get a chance. A cookhole (page 145) makes it very simple to dispose of such snow as collects on the waterproof floor, and you can relax some of these precautions. But you still have to be careful not to get sleeping bag or clothing wet.

Boot de-snowing is not the only reason for having a waterproof mat of some kind just inside the entrance. (I use the large, tough plastic bag that wraps my cooking pots—see page 122.) This door-mat collects most of the snow that inevitably comes with you when you crawl in, and also the smaller but by no means negligible amounts that dribble in whenever you have a small opening for ventilation. It also serves as an interim garbage can for all the for-eign matter you'd just as soon didn't lie around inside: gas spilled when you're refilling the stove; water spilled when you're filling can-teens after melting snow; food fragments; even, if you're feeling house-proud, the inevitable stray feathers from sleeping bag and down clothing. At convenient intervals, you empty all this debris outside—or into the cookhole, if you have one.

Your waterproof mat also acts as a doormat when the weather is good enough for you to put on your boots outside: you tread on it in stockinged feet while you put on the boots. You can also stand on it in stockinged feet, just outside, when you have to answer the liquid calls of nature. The right kind of gloves make even better slippers (see page 211). The ideal is a pair of down booties (page 206).

For techniques and precautions when cooking in a tent, see pages 132 and 135.

The most vital precaution of all when camping in snow is to keep the tent from getting buried. You can even buy lightweight aluminum shovels (1½ pounds; $3.95) to carry along for the job —and, of course, for clearing tent sites, digging snow caves, or even clearing a route. But a snowshoe is a very efficient tool for keeping your tent unburied. In extremely heavy snow it may even be neces-sary, if the snow keeps falling for a day or two, to take down your tent, raise the platform by shoveling in snow and stamping it flat, and then re-pitch the tent.

In mid-July 1958, a party of four climbers camped in stormy weather on an exposed Alaskan ridge at about 11,500 feet. They had two two-man tents: a Gerry model made of permeable material and with two entrances, and an impermeable army mountain tent with only a sleeve entrance. On the second stormbound night a very heavy fall of snow formed a ten-inch-thick windslab over the tents so quickly that none of the climbers appreciated the danger before morning. Around six a.m., one of the men in the army tent woke, breathing rapidly, and realized that the air was foul. Unable to find knife, boots or gloves in the semi-collapsed tent, he just managed to dig his way out through the clinging folds of the sleeve-entrance, barehanded, then had to slide back inside to rest and warm up. (The outside temperature was around $-10°$.) Suddenly, he and his companion found themselves gasping for breath. The first man immediately started out the entrance again, but was unable to free himself from the door, stopped digging to rest—and lost consciousness. Around eight thirty a.m., one of the men in the Gerry tent dug free and saw him lying halfway out of the entrance, with evidence of frostbite. Carried into the Gerry tent, he soon recovered consciousness. His companion was found, still inside the army tent, motionless and not breathing. Four to five hours' artificial respiration failed to revive him. He had died, of course, from asphyxiation (lack of oxygen, presence of carbon dioxide) due to the tent's being buried.

Extremely bad snow conditions caused this accident, but contributory factors included the impermeable tent fabric, the clinging nature of the only exit, and a guying system that failed to preserve adequate internal air space. (For full report and analysis see "Accidents in American Mountaineering"; Twelfth Annual Report of the Safety Committee of the American Alpine Club, 1959, pages 22–24.) The story is a vivid object lesson in how alert you must remain —under conditions horribly conducive to weariness and boredom— when there is any danger of your tent's being buried by snow.

For more on blocked ventilation see pages 135–6.

NON-TENTS

Your roof need not be a tent, of course. The several alternatives are all lighter than tents and easier to erect. All perform more efficiently as cool retreats in hot weather. And all are much cheaper. On the other hand, none can approach the efficiency of a tent in blocking out a really high wind or in conserving warmth (though it is often overlooked that all of them, except in a very high wind, reduce the rate at which warm air from your body can escape, and so increase your warmth at night to a surprising degree). Although some of them repel the average rainstorm as well as most tents do, or even better, there is nothing to compare with a good tent *with* fly sheet for comfort in prolonged rain, whether it is a heavy downpour or a swirling, penetrating mountain drizzle.

You choose your roof, then, to suit expected conditions.

A fly sheet alone

(Tarps and pup tents amount to much the same thing—though they sometimes have end-walls.)

A few years ago I used nothing but a fly sheet for night protection during a four-month walk up England—through the very maw of what the British sportingly call summer.

I had a serviceable unit made up from two pieces of cream-colored, 3½-ounce, untreated nylon fabric, joined down their length:

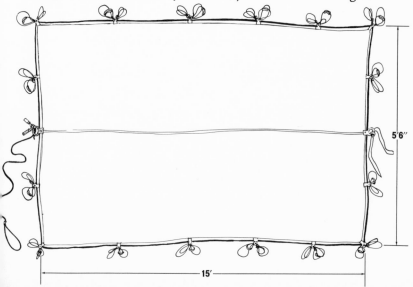

The center join and all edges were strengthened with ¾-inch herringbone twill tape. The center join was waterproofed. I had small aluminum rings attached by loops of tape, stoutly stitched. To all rings on the long edges I tied on three-foot guy lines of ³⁄₃₂-inch braided nylon. To keep these thin lines from snarling, they had to be gathered up in rough slip knots every time the fly sheet was packed away. Each line had a small, ultralightweight aluminum tightener. They were of the old kind, straight but bent. (The newer triangular tighteners [twelve to an ounce] are more efficient. But see page 146 for a way of dispensing with tighteners.) To one of the rings at the ridge I tied on the two metal pole sockets from my one-man tent (see illustration, page 142). To the other I tied on two one-foot lengths of strong tape. The whole rig weighed one pound, ten ounces. I can't find a record of the cost, but it was very low.

Along with my fly sheet I carried the two aluminum tent poles from my one-man tent (each four feet long, but breaking into two sections), and sixteen of the small pegs from that tent (two as spares).

This bedroom was very simple to erect. My walking staff, tied to one end of the ridge by the lengths of tape (and held upright by three lengths of nylon cord attached to three pegs or other convenient points such as trees or bushes) held the ridge high at the head-end. The tent poles, inserted in their metal sockets, held the sheet high enough over my feet. The side lines kept the sheet spread wide and taut. The small aluminum rings on the short edges enabled me to pull one or both ends of the structure in with lengths of nylon cord, and so form rough end-walls that could be further buttressed, once I was inside, by a poncho.

The fly sheet made a surprisingly effective house, even in a soggy English summer. The side lines unfortunately tended to pull the ridge down into a depression midway between its ends, and in very wet weather moisture occasionally collected there and dropped off. But for the most part the roof was rainproof. When rain drove in from one side I could lower the ridge, drop the eaves on the windward flank, plug the small ground-level gap with anything handy (from brush to poncho), and stay remarkably snug. In extremely heavy rain the force of big drops sometimes drove a fine spray through the nylon. But on such occasions my outspread poncho kept the sleeping bag dry, and the spray was too fine to harm anything else. I remember in particular a nighttime thunderstorm just outside Nottingham when the rain lashed down for several hours with tropical intensity. I remember it vividly because it is the only time I have *heard* lightning hitting the ground all around me. The rain matched the ferocity of the flashes and crackling explosions, but under my little fly sheet I slept as dry as a dehydrated bean.

The fly sheet was strong enough to stand up to prolonged use and to strong winds (though not, of course, to full-scale mountain storms). And it was a reasonably flexible unit. I could make a high-roofed, airy bedroom or a low, snug retreat simply by raising and lowering the point at which I tied the tapes to my staff and by splaying the aluminum poles more or less widely. Once, when I stayed several days on a Cornish headland and a wind blew steadily in from the Atlantic, I used my poncho as a roof and the fly sheet as side-walls.

All in all, the fly sheet set-up made a good bedroom, especially where there were no trees or other hitching posts. Today, I would have the fly sheet made from coated nylon. I suppose I ought to have the old one treated, but nowadays I tend to use instead a

Plastic sheet with Visklamp attachment.

This cunning and convenient, though unlikely-looking, rig is strong, light, and very cheap. The plastic sheet is smooth, white, translucent .004-inch polyethylene, known as Visqueen, that is absolutely watertight and a very great deal tougher than it looks. (Make sure, though, that you buy good quality sheeting. One sample I tried recently soon began to tear. And check that the material is translucent, not semitransparent, or it will make a scurvy sun awning.)

The sheeting comes in several sizes including 6 by 8 feet (1 pound; $1), 8 by 9 feet (1½ pounds—according to the catalogue though my present one is 3 ounces lighter; $1.49) and 9 by 12 feet (2 pounds; $2.10). You can also buy it even more cheaply in 100-foot rolls, either 12 or 24 feet wide. With the 8-by-9 size, I live luxuriously.

The sheets are quite plain, without grommets or attachments

of any kind. You secure them with improbable little two-part devices called Visklamps (¾ ounce and 10 cents each):

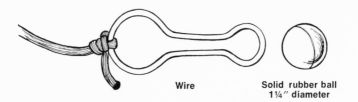

Wire   **Solid rubber ball
                        1¼″ diameter**

A Visklamp is extremely easy to use. At whatever point you want to attach a guy line, you simply wrap the rubber ball in the sheet and twist a couple of times so that the ball and the plastic envelope around it form an isolated isthmus. Then you pass the enveloped ball through the larger metal loop and slide the twisted neck of the isthmus down the narrow connecting channel until the ball is held in the smaller loop. Attach a nylon cord to the larger loop, and you have a guy line that will take remarkable strain.

The great advantage of this system is its flexibility. You can build an orthodox, tent-like bedroom:

or a sort of eccentric rotunda (though you have to be careful about the angles, or you end up with almost no roof—only folds):

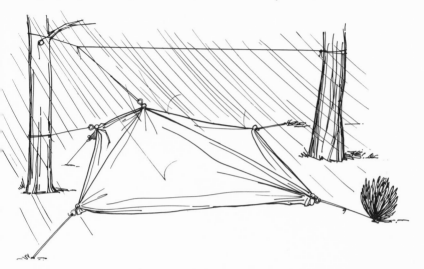

or a useful lunchtime shelter in wind-driven drizzle:

For other ideas, see variations on the poncho theme, pages 160–62.

An advantage of this rig is that you can, by moving one or two Visklamps, very simply make a major readjustment to meet new conditions of wind or rain. And in most set-ups you can, while still in bed, slip one Visklamp loose and lift aside the roof for cooking or working or for looking around, and can immediately replace it if rain threatens or you want more warmth.

If rain catches you unawares, you can as an emergency measure simply spread the sheet over yourself. Or you can wrap it loosely around everything—taking care to leave an opening at your head for ventilation. (For details, diagram, and dangers, see pages 163 and 164.) This wrap-around system, by the way, will help keep you warm, rain or no rain.

I usually carry five Visklamps and four aluminum tent pegs for this set-up, but in really cramped and awkward corners a couple extra of each can make all the difference. If you lose a metal attachment, just tie the nylon directly around the twisted isthmus below the rubber ball. The polyethylene sheeting is so tough that it seems to stand up quite satisfactorily to this makeshift arrangement. Once or twice, when I needed more attachment points than I had Visklamps, I have just twisted up a tumor of plastic and tied the nylon directly to its neck. And I have never yet torn or even worn a hole in the sheeting.

Still, the thin polyethylene does not yet inspire me with total confidence. I would not trust it in a full-scale mountain gale. But I always take it now on summer trips of a week or so when there seems a chance of heavy rain. I am not sure I would rely on the sheeting for a really long trip when I could not replace it, but on short trips the wear factor can hardly become serious.

Because the sheeting is white, it does not make your den dark and dismal, even in oppressive weather. And because it is translucent it makes an excellent sun awning.

The sheeting is versatile stuff. It's exactly what you need for waterproofing your pack contents on major river crossings (pages 273–82). And if you have to swim across a river on a packless side-

trip you can wrap all your clothes and gear in the sheet, tie it with
cord, and have yourself a buoyant, watertight bundle that you can
push or pull along (page 275). In any kind of terrain not covered by
snow, the sheeting also makes a first-class marker for airdrops (page
290).

Visklamps and polyethylene sheets are made by the Visqueen
Division of the Ethyl Corporation of Baton Rouge, Louisiana, and
are becoming increasingly available in equipment stores.

I see that several makers (Sierra Designs, Holubar of Boulder,
Colorado, and Himalayan Industries of Monterey, California) now
catalogue large coated-nylon tarps with a grommet at each end and
doubled tapes attached at various points. They look as though they
would be almost as flexible as the Visklamp set-up and somewhat
stronger. But they are heavier and much more expensive. (Range:
from 1¾ to 3½ pounds; from $22 to $37.50.)

A popular device I have often seen but never tried is the

Tube or instant tent.

The tube of inexpensive polyethylene is usually .0035-inch
gauge or lighter, about nine feet long, and eight to ten feet in circum-

ference. It can be quickly strung up on any ridge line. The weight of your gear and body—perhaps with an assist from smooth stones— anchor the floor. Some models have three grommets at each end for drawing the gap more or less closed. Weight varies from one to two pounds, price from $2.50 to $3.50. Tube tents are obviously useful for thunderstorm weather, but if the ridge line sags beware of the suffocation hazard, and of carbon monoxide poisoning (see page 136).

Unless the rain threat is serious, I generally rely for an emergency roof on my

Poncho or groundsheet.

Most heavy ponchos have grommets along their edges, and it is a simple matter to string them up with nylon cord. Lightweight ponchos often lack grommets, but I have up to six or eight specially inserted. To build your roof you can string a ridge rope between trees and make an orthodox tent-like bedroom (see illustration, page 156), or you can attach the poncho by its corners to surrounding bushes and branches, or to sticks held in position by stones. In heavy or driving rain you can stay surprisingly dry if you keep the roof so low that

there is only just room for you underneath. Recently I have taken to carrying one Visklamp as a roof-lifter for the poncho. With the low-level, battened-down roof, it makes life much more comfortable.

Under milder conditions you can use your staff either as an external upright or as an inside prop to force the roof pleasantly high above your head and also to keep it taut, so that rain does not collect in sagging hollows. When you use the staff this way, pad it at the top with something soft so that it will not cut the poncho.

The poncho rig is especially useful in open desert, when you may find yourself in desperate need of an awning at midday halts. The difference between the sun-scorched ground and the little coffin-shaped patch of shade under your poncho will seem like the difference between hell and . . . well, something a comfortable half-hitch short of hell. (See figures for desert ground temperatures: page 45, foot-note.) The awning will certainly make a critical difference to your sense of well-being, and therefore to what you are capable of doing in the cool of evening, and under certain conditions it could be the difference between life and death.

On desert afternoons a strong wind often blows for hour after hour. When it does, the continuous flapping of the poncho makes a hideous din, always threatens to tear grommets loose, and sometimes does. One way of reducing both noise and strain is to secure only three corners of the poncho to fixed points and to tie a large rock on the downwind corner with a cord of such a length that the stone will just rest on the ground under normal conditions but will lift, and so ease the strain, when the poncho billows under an especially strong gust.

A grommeted *groundsheet* (see page 169) can make as effective a rain roof as a poncho. As it is usually bigger, it will when new make an even better one—but groundsheets rarely stay unpunctured for very long.

Economy-size groundsheets (which in our peculiar modern tongue are distinctly large ones) can be folded so that they act both in their normal role and at the same time as an angled wall that will protect you from driven rain (and from a cold wind, dry or rainbearing).

As awnings, clear plastic groundsheets are, of course, comprehensively useless.

Whether you choose to use groundsheet or poncho as your emergency rain roof depends on conditions. If you can race an approaching storm you will probably be wise to rig up your capacious groundsheet over a dry piece of ground and do without anything under your mattress. Then you'll be able to wear the poncho when necessary. Try to resist the temptation to use it as a groundsheet; it will certainly develop holes. If the ground is already wet you will need the groundsheet as a floor, and the poncho goes up as roof.

Finally there is the problem of what to do about a roof when you go to sleep in the open, confident that no rain will fall, and wake up an hour later to the pitter-patter of tiny raindrops or the clammy drift of drizzle. One solution is to unwrap your groundsheet (which is doubled under you) and cover yourself over, with the open side to leeward. If the weather gets worse, you can quickly improve this makeshift cocoon by lacing the open side with nylon cord threaded through the grommets (you get only mildly wet in the process). Another solution is to use the poncho in the same way, laced or unlaced. (If I harbor any doubts at all about the weather I go to sleep with the poncho ready, close at hand.) Better still is a combination of groundsheet and poncho: the groundsheet as main cocoon, the poncho wrapped like an elephant's foot around the bottom of your sleeping bag, which otherwise persists, steadfastly, in pushing out into the open. Provided the rain is not too heavy, such a makeshift shelter can keep your sleeping bag surprisingly dry, and yourself totally so. (One good friend of mine, an experienced backpacker, holds with ferocity to the childiotic notion that if he erects any rain shelter more complicated than a poncho-groundsheet cocoon he is pandering to his weaker instincts.)

The extent of the action you take when surprised by rain during the night depends on your sleepy estimate of the probable heaviness of the rain. If you think it is going to come down but good, it pays to make the hard decision early and get up and rig poncho or groundsheet into an adequate roof. Of course, any man with an ounce of sense will rig a roof whenever there's any real doubt about the weather. I suppose I'll learn one day.

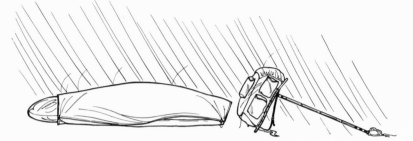

The cocoon bedroom in all its variants is also a useful makeshift measure in unexpected light snow. Even in dry weather, it gives you a surprising degree of extra warmth, particularly in high winds.

But a cocoon—or a tarp or groundsheet just spread over your sleeping bag—can be dangerous. In early April 1961, a co-ed from the University of New Hampshire camped beside the parking lot of a New England ski resort. She had considerable winter camping experience. The weather had been warm, and there was melt water on the packed snow. It rained during the night. Then the weather cleared, and the temperature fell. Presumably to keep the rain off, the girl had covered her sleeping bag with an impermeable plastic tarp. In the morning she was found dead. It was presumed that she had suffocated, for the edges of the tarp were frozen to the ground ice, and she had been sealed in. The carbon dioxide that would normally have awakened her by making her struggle for breath may have been absorbed by the moisture collected under the tarp. Lesson: always leave plenty of ventilation at your head, especially if there is any danger of the tarp's being frozen to the ground.

In the advertising material for old-type, open-mouth sleeping bags you still find, occasionally, neat little pictures of

Head roofs.

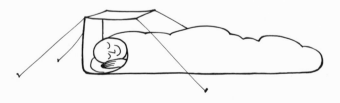

I suspect that the whole tradition is nurtured by advertiser-indoorsmen. I certainly can't remember seeing such a device actually being used. Yet heavy sleeping bags often have special flaps for just this purpose. I suppose they would help shield you from a head-to-toes wind, but anyone who uses an open-mouth bag rather than a mummy type is presumably not too worried about keeping warm.

SELECTING CAMPSITES

Level beds

There are few simpler ways of ensuring a bad night's sleep than choosing a bedroom that slopes. If the slope is sideways, you spend the night in a thinly conscious hassle with gravity; and you wake, tired and aching, to find yourself still pressing fiercely on the downslope with arms and knees and a battery of assistant muscles. If the slope is from feet to head you don't go to sleep at all. No matter how gentle the incline (and it is sure to be gentle, or you would never have over-looked it) you discover the horrible truth the moment you lie down. The feeling that all the blood is going to rush to your head is so disturbing that after a few feeble attempts at telling yourself that it's all imagination you gruntle up and switch head and feet.

If you can't possibly avoid a sloping bed, sleep with your feet downhill. That way, if the slope is not too severe, you spend a passably comfortable night: several times you find yourself a yard and a half downhill from pillow and groundsheet, and have to do an undignified wriggle back uphill; but you wake with nothing worse than mildly aching leg muscles.

Do everything you can, then, to organize a level bed. If you have to camp on sloping ground, try to do so on a trail or just above a tree or in some other place where there is a ready-made level platform. Or go to considerable pains to make a platform. Often, you can find a place with soil loose enough to kick away with your heels. You can always do so on talus.

Shelter from wind

This level bed business is so important that when I camp at nightfall and expect to move on again first thing in the morning, it is often the only campsite feature I worry about. In fair weather, that is. But when the wind rises to gale force or feels like a disembodied iceberg—a combination all too common on mountains—then shelter from wind supplants level ground as the one thing you absolutely must have.

Unless you have both a tent and confidence that you can erect it in the teeth of the gale, go to great pains to find natural shelter. I tend to do so anyway. It's much simpler, and often warmer. A clump of trees or bushes will deflect the full fury of any wind. And, even in exposed places, quite minor irregularities, if themselves total windbreaks, make remarkably good refuges. I have spent comfortable nights, well sheltered from icy gales, in the troughs of shallow gullies, behind low walls, even tucked in close to a cattle trough. But the best hideout of all is an overhanging rockledge. (A full-fledged cave protects you better, of course; but caves tend to be both rare and unappetizing.) Even a quite shallow ledge, provided it's on the lee side of a hill or rockpile, can be a snug place. The rock retains much of its daytime warmth, and after one comfortable night in such a place you understand why cold-blooded rattlesnakes like to live among rocks. The floor of the ledge is rarely as level as you would like it to be, but there are often small rocks lying around for a rough construction job. In any case, if the wind outside is icebergial enough, you will not be worrying all that much about a level bed.

Shelter from rain

Rockledges make good shelters from rain too—and caves are even better. But beware of shallow caves in thunderstorms (see page 309). Hollow tree trunks are traditional wilderness shelters, but to be honest I have never tried one. In rain I just tend to put up whatever roof I've brought along. Naturally I choose the most sheltered site I can find.

Shelter from snow

In heavy and prolonged snowstorms, an obvious campsite in the lee of a cliff or steep rise may just possibly be dangerous: drifting snow could bury your tent while you slept. At least, so they say.

"They" also say that properly constructed snow caves are very warm and tolerably comfortable (see page 140, second footnote). I'm afraid my experience is zero.

Cold bedrooms

Meadows, especially when cradled in hollows, collect not only cold but damp air. They're delightful places to camp, though, and should not necessarily be avoided. A hillock or rockslab a few feet above the grass is often enough to ward off discomfort—and to improve the view.

Riverbanks also tend to be damp and therefore cold places— and to provide richly rewarding campsites.

Siting your bedroom to catch
—or avoid—the morning sun

It can occasionally be important that your bed should catch the first rays of morning sunshine. Sometimes only the sun's warmth will make a bitter world habitable. Sometimes you go to sleep without a roof—because you are tired or lazy or just because you like it that way—expecting heavy dew during the night but knowing that morning sunshine will quickly dry it off and save you packing along pounds of water. Or it may be that a tent needs drying. And on days on which you are planning not to move camp, or to move late, it is always more pleasant to start the day in sunshine. At least, almost always. In deserts, in summer, you will want to avoid the sun.

Anyway, whatever your reason for wanting to know where the sun will rise, the solution is simple: on the first day of the trip— or before you start, if you can remember it—measure with your compass the exact bearing on which the sun rises over a flat horizon.

Pencil the bearing on the back of the compass. Then, at any night camp, all you have to do is take out the compass, sight along the correct bearing, make due allowance for close or distant heightening of the horizon, and site your camp in the right place. With a little experience you can prophesy accurately enough to make use of even narrow gaps in trees.

Minor factors in choosing a campsite

Your criteria for a good campsite will vary a lot with the kind of country, your probable length of stay, and your personal preferences. I've described some of them in *The Thousand-Mile Summer*. For the first day or two of a trip, especially in strange country, you may find yourself circling around a promising area like a dog stirred by ancestral memories. But before long you are once more recognizing a good site at a glance: not only a flat bedroom and reasonable protection from wind but also a soft bed or material for making a mattress (if you're not carrying one) and plenty of firewood (if you want a fire). Also, where there's water, a bathroom.

Don't underrate the importance of a good bathroom. There is a yawning gap between a camp with running bedside water (where you can without effort scoop out drinking water, wash, wash up, and wash your feet) and a place in which you have to crash through tangled undergrowth and yards of sucking swamp to reach a tepid out-puddle of a river. By comparison, the difference between hotel rooms with and without a private bath is so much fiddle-faddle.

You earn, by the way, an oddly satisfying bonus if you succeed in choosing a memorable camp from the map—as you can sometimes do once you grow used to a certain kind of country. If you play the percentages and the hunches and manage to get everything right—level bed, shelter from wind, firewood, water, morning sunshine, pleasing surroundings, even (and this is what makes a camp truly memorable) the stimulation or mystery or magic than can come from an isthmus of woodland or an oddly shaped hillock or a quietly gurgling backwater—if you get all these right, you experience the same slightly surprised pleasure as from finding that your checkbook total tallies with the bank statement.

GROUNDSHEETS

It is quite possible to operate without a groundsheet. But you need one in many places to keep out the damp, in even more places to reduce wear and tear on such fragile items as air mattress and sleeping bag, and just about everywhere, in my opinion, as a general keep-clean-and-keep-from-losing-things area for the gear you take out of the pack. A slippery groundsheet also forms a natural defense zone against ants and ticks and scorpions and their brethren. And on top of all this there is the groundsheet-as-roof-and-walls (see pages 162–3).

When your weight problem is acute and the chances of rain slight (a combination that applied on my Grand Canyon trip) you can carry a light poncho that doubles as groundsheet. A groundsheet does highly abrasive duty, so do not expect the dual-purpose article to last very long as a waterproof poncho. In Grand Canyon, mine, sure enough, didn't. But all the rain and snow fell near the start, just as I had expected, and the arrangement worked out fine.

For a long trip on which you cannot get equipment replaced you need a strong, though still lightweight, groundsheet. Nylport tarps (urethene-coated, fine-weave nylon) are at present the best bet. But they are expensive. A 5-by-7-foot sheet weighs 13 ounces, costs $11.50; the 7-by-9-foot size weighs 1 pound, 8 ounces, costs $16.50. For short trips I use lighter and cheaper polyethylene sheets (.003 inch)—semi-transparent, watertight when unpunctured, and expendable. (5-by-8 feet: 12 ounces; $1.75. 8 by 10: 1 pound 4 ounces; $2.95.) These sheets come with four self-adhesive grommet tabs, and are invaluable in wind or rain as an emergency cocoon or sidewall (see pages 162 and 164).

MATTRESSES

When you are young and eager and tough, and the weather is not too perishingly cold, you do without a mattress. I did so all through the six months of my California walk (except for the first few days when, to cushion the shock of changing from soft city life, I carried a cheap plastic air mattress that I didn't expect to last long, and which didn't). I soon got used to sleeping with my mummy bag directly on all kinds of hard ground, but I often padded the bag inside with a sweater or other clothes. On that trip, temperatures rarely fell more than a degree or two below freezing, though on one occasion I slept on stones at 25°F. (That night I had a floored tent and a few sheets of newspaper, which make a very useful emergency insulator.)

But if you have grown used to an ordinary bed the change to mummy-bag-on-the-ground is likely to ruin your sleep for at least a few nights. This will reduce your efficiency, and also your enjoyment, and the saving in weight just isn't worth it—unless you can be sure of finding some soft, dry sand for a bed. Then, all you need is a couple of wriggles to dig shallow depressions for shoulders and rump, and you've got yourself a comfortable sleep. But even on sand the lack of a mattress seriously reduces the warmth-conserving efficiency of your sleeping bag.

The traditional woodsman and boy scout routine was to build a mattress from natural materials: soft and pliable bough tips, or moss, or thick grass. On the California walk I did for a while use branches from desert creosote bushes. But in many of today's heavily traveled camping areas the cutting of plant life is not merely illegal but downright immoral—an atrocity committed only by the sort of feeble-minded citizen who scatters empty beer cans and carves his name on trees. Besides, the method is inefficient. Even when you can find suitable materials, you waste time in preparing a bed. And the bed is rarely as warm or as comfortable as a modern, lightweight pad or air mattress.

For something like two decades now the standard equipment under almost all conditions has been an

Air mattress.

An air mattress can amplify the efficiency of your sleeping bag, neutralize the sharpest stones, support your body luxuriously at all the right places, convert into an easy chair, float you and your pack across a river, and get punctures.

As far as the punctures go, all you have to do is keep a wary eye open for thorns, pray, and carry a repair outfit (4 ounces; $1). Traditionally, such outfits seem to include a wild selection of patches but nothing like enough adhesive. Consider carrying an extra tube of rubber solution—or two complementary tubes of Epoxy, which will repair not only your air mattress but everything from sunglasses through boot soles to packbag and even aluminum packframe. But beware of crushed tubes!

Inflating an air mattress is easy—but not quite as easy as it sounds. For sleeping, the mattress should be fairly soft. Inexperienced campers tend to blow their mattresses up far too tight, spend a night or two bobbing around like corks on a rough sea, then give up the great outdoors for good. The trick is to inflate the mattress just hard enough to keep every segment of you off the ground—and no harder. The easiest way to achieve this end is to blow the mattress up considerably harder than it will finally need to be, wait for the hot air from your lungs to cool and therefore contract, lie on your side on the mattress and press down unnaturally hard with your hip, and slowly let air out of the valve until your hip just touches the ground. Then close the valve. The mattress will now be firm enough to hold your hip clear of the ground when you're lying naturally, but soft enough to accept your body into its bosom rather than to send you bobbing around or rolling off to one side. And because the protruding portions of your body compress the air, the mattress will support the parts that need support: knees, small of back, and neck. If your mattress has a pillow section as a separate compartment, inflate it rather hard. Again, overinflate, and when you lie down reduce the pressure to what feels right.

Rather to my surprise, I have come to the conclusion that a separately inflatable pillow section is worth having. It certainly makes for a more comfortable bed. And it also means that you carry along, without extra weight, an excellent easy chair.

For the chair, reverse the inflation routine for the bed: blow the main section up hard but leave the pillow soft. Then reverse the mattress too, propping the main section up against your pack as backrest and laying the pillow flat as a seat. You can hardly make the backrest too firm. The best way to get the pillow right is once more to overinflate and then to fine-adjust with your butt in position. You may possibly classify a wilderness easy chair as rampant hedonism—until you have sampled the difference between eating the evening meal with and without a comfortable backrest, or have spent an afternoon leaning against a tree and writing notes.

For techniques of river crossing with an air mattress raft, see page 275.

Air mattress materials: Unless you want an air mattress only for a night or two, avoid at all costs the cheap, thin, plastic jobs. They puncture at the drop of a twig, tear almost without provocation, and often don't get the chance to do either before a seam pulls open. Most backpackers seem to find coated nylon mattresses satisfactory. They are certainly light and should be strong. But the only one I have owned gave me continual trouble with leaky seams, and I remain prejudiced. Rubberized canvas, though heavier, is very tough. It gets my vote.

Size: The choice lies between three-quarter or hip-length (supporting butt, shoulders, and possibly head; in cold weather you keep your feet off the ground with spare clothing or your pack or whatever else you can lay hands on) and full-length (accommodating the whole body, but weighing about half as much again). Some years ago, after several miserable nights on a hip-length mattress, I vowed a solemn vow that I would never again carry anything but a full-length. Today, the only backpacking air mattress I own is a small hip-length. And it is some time since I even thought about changing. I can offer no explanation for this phenomenon, unless it is that in time a man gets used to just about anything. There is no need, by the way, for a wide mattress. A flat width of twenty-eight inches—rather less when inflated—is entirely adequate. Provided you keep the pressure down, you will not roll off. Not often enough to matter, anyway.

Valves: The simpler and stronger the better. Not too much can go wrong with stout rubber tubes and solid plug stoppers attached with stout nylon. Even if you lose a stopper, a makeshift wooden plug shouldn't be beyond your powers. One-piece metal screw tops fill me with distrust; I am always afraid they may jam, particularly in sand. And they let air out miserably slowly. The process may take three or four minutes. With the stopper type, you just pull the plug while lying on the mattress; within seconds the bulk of the air is out, you are more or less forced to get up, and the mattress is ready for packing.

Models: My present choice is a rubberized canvas mattress with separate pillow section and four longitudinal tubes that are "wave-joined" to help keep all parts of your body clear of the ground:

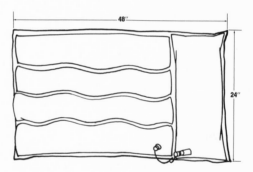

Weight: 1 pound, 14 ounces. Color: Green. Cost: $8.95. Name: "Good Companions"—though the maker (Thomas Black) now markets what seems to be an almost identical model under the name "Scottie."

I carried a Good Companions all through the two-month traverse of Grand Canyon, and treated it brutally. Night after night it supported me in comfort on bedrock or gravel or sand. Sometimes a thin poncho protected it; sometimes, nothing. Day after day it was my easy chair for reading, writing, and sloth. Five times it was my raft for river-detours around unclimbable outcrops; and once it floated me clear across the Colorado. The only puncture came three days from the end when I lived for twenty-four hours in a cliff dwelling;

then, as I sat at ease in my chair on the chip-strewn floor, the pillow protested at last with an explosive three-inch rent. My present Good Companion, already four years old, has yet to suffer its second puncture.

There is a line of nylon mattresses (the Stebco Backpackers), rubber vulcanized on the inside, without pillows, that many experienced backpackers seem to find good, though it was one of these that gave me trouble with leaking seams. All are twenty-two inches wide, inflated. They come in three lengths: 48-inch—1 pound, 12 ounces, $9.50; 60-inch—2 pounds, 5 ounces, $10.50; 72-inch—2 pounds, 10 ounces, $11.50. There is also a coffin-shaped G.I. nylon mattress (73 by 27 inches, 2 pounds, 14 ounces, $13.50) that one friend of mine has used a great deal for over four years without trouble.

There are any number of big, luxurious, and very strong models in every catalogue, with refinements such as large outer and foot tubes to give a cradle effect. But they weigh anything from four pounds on up. They are excellent for car camping, though, and I always take one along when I drive to my starting point. That way, I save wear and tear on the lighter backpacking mattress until I hike away from the car.

Inflators: Concertina-type pumps that "will inflate your mattress in a few minutes" appear in every catalogue. And the propaganda goes on to say that they are "very necessary at high altitudes and a big help at any altitude." A big help, possibly; but also 7½ ounces. I use my lungs, no matter what the altitude. But I always do the job *before* a meal.

Air mattresses have in recent years been challenged as the standard sub-sleeping-bag equipment by

Foam pads.

The best material now available seems to be Ensolite—a lightweight unicellular foam synthetic that insulates very efficiently and will not soak up water. It comes in thicknesses from ³⁄₁₆ inch up, and sheets can be laminated with any good adhesive. The ⅜-inch single sheets I have tried seem a good compromise between insulation and comfort on one hand and weight and bulk on the other.

Ensolite is warmer and lighter than an air mattress, but less comfortable on most surfaces and appreciably bulkier. It cannot puncture, of course, and therefore needs no repair outfit. But neither can it float you across a river.

It makes sense, then, to carry Ensolite in cold weather when the surface you sleep on is soft. It makes so much sense that Ensolite pads have virtually replaced air mattresses for use on snow, where they are definitely warmer and at least as comfortable. The one disadvantage is bulk—and, because of heavy clothing and a tent, your pack always seems to be overflowing in snow country.

I also tend to carry an Ensolite pad instead of the heavier air mattress when I expect to sleep on reasonably soft surfaces such as grassland or sand, or when I can prepare a good bed by smoothing away any minor unevenness. And I would carry it in thorn country. But I stay with my air mattress when I expect to sleep on rock or to raft a river.

Ensolite comes in sheets of various size, and, within reason, you can cut it to suit your fancies. I have two pads:

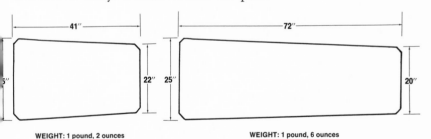

WEIGHT: 1 pound, 2 ounces   WEIGHT: 1 pound, 6 ounces

The hip-length pad is for general use under fairly friendly conditions, when weight and/or bulk is a major problem. It folds down quite easily to fit flat inside my packbag. In cold weather I keep my feet off the ground with whatever is handy—spare clothing, pack, thin boughs.

The full-length pad is for snow country. (Many snow campers prefer to cut down on weight and bulk by carrying only a hip-length pad.) There is just too much of this big pad to fold, so I carry it rolled. It is bulky and a damned nuisance—until the time comes to lie down.

For pillows with Ensolite pads, see page 192.

SLEEPING BAGS

No modern backpacker would seriously consider carrying blankets, as the old-timer had to. Yet some people still carry old-style, rectangular, open-end sleeping bags, which are in my opinion as outdated compared with mummy bags as blankets are with the old-style bags.

It was natural enough that the first sleeping bags should be the rectangular shape of a normal bed: they obviously evolved from the idea of stitching two or more blankets together. But were it not for the innate conservatism of mankind, virtually all outdoorsmen would surely have switched long ago to mummy bags. They are, after all, designed to contain human forms rather than small upright pianos.

I have heard only two mildly valid objections to mummy bags.

A few people feel uncomfortably confined in them. At least, so they say. I am not sure that they have always given mummies a fair trial; if they have, and just cannot get used to any real or imagined constriction, they probably have no alternative but to put up with the inefficiencies of the old rectangular piano-envelope.

Some outdoor lovers complain that mummy bags do not leave enough room for maneuver. Opportunists may certainly face a problem here. But those who plan their amatory operations with care should note that it is possible to order two sidezippered mummy bags with zippers on opposite sides that will join convivially together. There are also double mummy bags—lighter, less bulky, warmer, and cheaper than two individual bags. At a pinch, one can be carried for solo use.

But do not get wrong ideas about how mummy bags earned their name. It is simply that any human lying on his back in one of these roughly contoured bags, with the tapes on the rounded head-flap pulled so tight that only his nose peeks through a small hole, is a dead ringer for an Egyptian mummy:

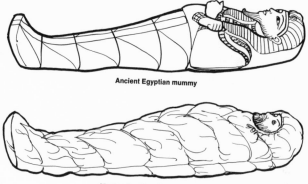

Ancient Egyptian mummy

Modern American in mummy bag

Mummy bags are more efficient than the old-style rectangular envelopes not only because they eliminate a great deal of superfluous material (though that is important enough) but, even more vitally, because they do a far better job of conserving your body heat.

The old-style bag gives your head no protection at all, and your shoulders precious little. (You can wrap the mouth of the bag around them neatly enough at first, and some bags have cloth flaps attached for the purpose; but on a cold night you're likely to wake up half an hour later and find your shoulders exposed to the elements—though the down-filled hood [page 191] looks as if it may help.) This head-and-shoulders business is bad enough, but what matters at least as much is that the bag's wide mouth allows a large and quite unmeasurable amount of precious body heat to escape.

A mummy bag eliminates all these faults. It can cover your head completely in the same all-inclusive envelope that conserves the heat from the rest of your body. You just pull on the draw tapes of the hood and tie them in a bow or other simple quick-release knot. On a cold night you pull until the opening contracts to a small hole around your nose and mouth. If, like me, you prefer to sleep naked because you wake feeling fresher, you may sometimes find cold air seeping down through the hole and moving uncomfortably around your bare shoulders. All you need do is wrap a shirt loosely around your shoulders. But this arrangement often holds the warm air in so well that you soon find you are too hot. To reduce the inside temperature (whether you are using a shoulder wrap or not) simply slacken the hood tapes a little. In warm weather you can leave the tapes undrawn, so that the mouth of the bag remains as open as in old-style envelopes. In hot weather you can go two steps further—if you have the right kind of bag.

Mummy bags designed for use only in cold weather (that is, for polar exploration, high-altitude mountaineering, and winter hunting) do not normally have zipper openings: an uninterrupted shell is not only the lightest possible design but also conserves heat the most efficiently. But such a bag lacks versatility. In anything but chilly weather you are liable to find yourself sweating even with the mouth of the bag open, and to face no alternatives except getting partly or wholly out. A zipper opening solves the problem. The modification is not pure gain, however. To prevent air passage through the closed zipper, it has to be faced inside with a down-filled draft flap. A 72-inch zipper and its flap can add several ounces to the weight of a bag, and no matter how good the flap, there is bound to be some slight loss in heat-conserving efficiency. But it seems to me that if you expect to operate at times in temperatures much above freezing the very great gain in versatility is well worth such minor drawbacks. (For more about adjusting to wide temperature ranges, see pages 194–6.)

Sleeping-bag materials

What matters most is the fill. The fill must hold within itself as many pockets of air as possible, to act as an insulant between the warm inner and cold outer air. For backpacking purposes, the best material is obviously that which does this job most efficiently for the least weight.

Reliable comparative insulation values for different materials are hard to come by, but there seems to be no doubt that by far the best is good quality down. Dacron—probably next on the scale—imposes construction difficulties: to stop it cuddling up in corners, it must be stitched in place. Dacron bags seem satisfactory when weight and bulk do not matter, as in car camping, and it's generally accepted that you double up in Dacron for the recommended fill weight in down. But down remains the only practical filling material for back-packers' bags.

Two kinds of material are now used for the shells of high-quality mummy bags: cotton and nylon. A really good cotton cover-ing, such as Egyptian cotton or element cloth, is surprisingly water-repellent, and I much prefer the feel of it, compared with nylon, on my skin. But nylon is rather lighter, appreciably more wind-resistant, and wears far better. It is also more expensive. Nylon linings tend to pick up a peculiar odor from the human body—an odor that I at first attributed to some terrible private uncleanliness, but later found, to my relief, was experienced by other people. It is a very minor prob-lem. Out in the field I rarely notice the odor. If I do, spreading the bag out in the sunshine soon dispels it. Back home, I just put the bag out to air (page 192) or, at the most, wash the inside with soap and warm water.

I now buy bags with nylon shells. But if you often camp in wet weather you might well be right to choose cotton, especially if you don't expect to use the bag frequently enough for wear and tear to matter much.

A sleeping-bag zipper must obviously be of very high quality and must have a draw tab inside as well as out. The newest and best bags tend to have nylon zippers, which run more smoothly than metal ones and are reputed to give less trouble.

Construction

With use, any kind of fill tends to move away from the points of greatest wear, notably from under your butt and shoulders, and in time you are left with nothing to protect you at vital places except a couple of layers of the thin shell. To minimize this effect, the shell is divided into a series of self-contained tubes that keep the fill from moving very far. Because of a general tendency for fill to migrate from the head toward the foot of the bag, transverse tubes work better than longitudinal ones. And an angled or chevron plan is said by some makers to be even more effective than transverse tubing.

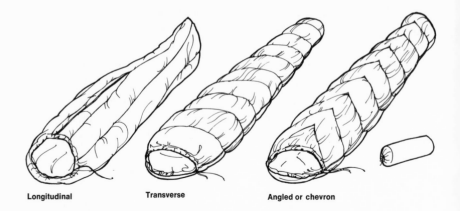

Longitudinal   **Transverse**   **Angled or chevron**

If tubes are made by simply stitching through the inner and outer walls of the shell,

you are obviously left unprotected at the stitch-through points.

If some form of batting is inserted at the stitch-through points (a simple and cheap system),

there is some improvement. But not much.

The difficulty can be overcome in two ways:

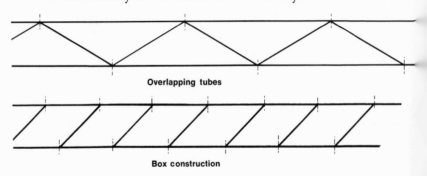

Overlapping tubes

Box construction

All really good modern sleeping bags embody one or the other of these systems, or some variation.

To conserve weight, the best mummy bags are now made widest at the shoulders and narrowest at the ankles, and flare out again to accommodate the feet. Their inner shells are cut smaller than the outer shells. This "differential cut," which allows the down to "loft" properly (see illustration and text, page 182), is particularly important in close-fitting bags.

Costs

Any good sleeping bag is an expensive item. The reasons: construction and materials. Simple, inefficient, single-tube bags can be stitched, with or without batting, by machine; a bag with baffled or overlapping tubes demands many hours of trained hand labor. Then there is the fill. In just about every case, cost varies in direct proportion to efficiency. A fairly good backpacker's bag filled with three pounds of Dacron is likely to cost little more than one third of its equivalent with a down filling—though the down bag is likely to be much better made, because the makers know that a backpacker who wants a good bag is unlikely to settle for Dacron.

It is difficult to give any very meaningful sample costs without specifying the construction and materials of each bag, for the details are what count. But you can pick up a fancy-looking rectangular bag filled with several pounds of some reassuringly named synthetic material for $15 or less—and can shiver through many a long night regretting it. With luck and patience you may be able to buy a not very well constructed mummy bag filled with four pounds of Dacron for about $20—and maybe get away with it. An extra $5 for better shell construction will almost certainly be worth it. Any really well-made mummy bag with, say, 2½ pounds of high-quality down fill, is going to cost around $50. The very best models, in which nothing has been spared in materials or construction, may run over $100. And there are intermediate models on every rung.

As far as cost goes, you must as usual make your own decisions. All I can tell you is that when you take a sleeping bag out of your pack as night falls on the windswept slopes of a 10,000-foot mountain, you understand without even having to think about it that dollars are meaningless frivolities.

Choosing a bag that will suit your purposes

The usual criterion for gauging the efficiency of a sleeping bag is the lowest temperature at which it can be used with comfort. "This bag is excellent for use down to 25°F.," the catalogue may proclaim. And the general rule is sometimes promulgated: "For summer use, with temperatures above freezing—two pounds of high-quality down; for temperatures down to 0°F.—three pounds."

Such generalizations have their uses. Beginners need guidelines. But there is a danger that people will take the figures too literally. For there are so many other factors involved that a wide variation in one or more of them can throw out the whole works.

First and simplest factor is construction. Two and a half pounds of down is not going to keep you warm in freezing temperatures, let alone down to 0°F., if the bag's shell is so constructed that the fill can migrate from the places it is most needed, or if single holding tubes are used, whether stitched with or without batting. You can check the construction of most bags light enough for backpacking by simply holding the shell up to a strong light.

One way sometimes recommended for checking the probable efficiency of both fill and construction is to measure what is called "free loft." Unroll the bag on a flat surface and shake its edges with a gentle fluffing action that allows air to become entrapped in the fill. Then measure the height of the bag at its mid-section.

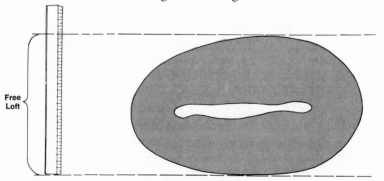

Free
Loft

The amount of loft depends on both the quality of the fill and the efficiency of the shell construction (see, especially, differential cut, page 181). The highest quality bag with a 2½-pound fill may have an 8½-inch loft, while even a very good similar model may manage only 6 inches. It seems reasonable to assume that, as is claimed, a relationship exists between free loft and heat-retaining efficiency. What the exact relationship is I have no idea, and I doubt if anyone has.

An even more vital matter that you cannot allow for if you try to give a tolerance temperature for a sleeping bag is the way you camp. A bag that keeps you comfortably warm at 32°F. on a full-length Ensolite pad will not come near to doing so if you roll it out on bare ground. And the same kind of difference exists between different roofs—tent, sky, or intermediate. The temperature inside a tent may run ten or twenty degrees higher than outside. Again, much depends on what clothes, if any, you choose to sleep in. My solution to all this is always to carry a pad or air mattress and to take a sleeping bag that under normal conditions for the time and place will keep me warm if I sleep without clothes or roof (except in snow), and that will just about do so under the worst recorded conditions if I wear every garment in my pack and protect the bag with every form of shelter I am carrying—whether mere poncho or a Visklamp-and-polyethylene roof or a tent. Nowadays I seem to guess about right. I cannot remember a single night in the past ten years when I have slept in a sleeping bag and been at all seriously cold.

Another difficulty with the straight temperature criterion for sleeping bags is that the relationship between air temperature and what the human body feels is a remarkably tenuous one.

First, weather is much more than just temperature. A bag that keeps you snugly warm in the open on a calm 10°F. night may be frigidly inadequate at 32°F. in a thirty-mile-an-hour wind. Humidity comes into it too. Dry air is a poor conductor of heat, damp air a good one. So in wet weather the air pockets held in the fill of your sleeping bag insulate less efficiently than in dry. This is no idle theorizing. Using equipment that has proved entirely adequate in dry weather at freezing and below, you may find yourself decidedly cool in a temperature of 40° after heavy rain has saturated the atmosphere. It is even possible for a drop in temperature to make you feel warmer. I remember one snow trip when my thermometer readings ranged from 24° to about 34°. At 34°, with the air full of water vapor, the weather was rawly cold. When the temperature fell a few degrees and the moisture that was ruining the insulation froze, I felt appreciably warmer.

But the most variable factor of all is the individual. It is not just that individuals vary; that some "sleep cold," as mountaineers put it. At different times the same person may react to similar conditions quite differently. Often, it is largely a matter of whether or not he is used to the cold or the heat or the elevation or whatever. Our bodies need time to adapt to radically changed conditions. Two or three days' acclimation may be plenty; but if the change is too abrupt those two or three days can be distressing.

The solution is to get used to a new environment gradually. One word for this process is "training." In Europe during World War II we often used to sleep in the open or in slit trenches in subfreezing weather with nothing over our distinctly temperate-country clothing except a thin anti-gas cape. I don't say we liked it. And I don't say we slept very well. But we slept. We were young, we were fit—and we got used to it (mainly, perhaps, because we had to). By the time I made the California walk I was a dozen years less young; but after a month of walking I was probably just as fit. Yet I remember a night in Death Valley that might make you wonder if I were the same person. That warm desert night I put on all the clothing I had— which was certainly as warm, if not warmer, than British battle dress. Then I wrapped my poncho around me and curled up in a little gully. I had just finished a twenty-mile day, and I promptly fell asleep. But before long I came half-awake and tried to pull the poncho more closely around me. There was no wind; nothing that could even be called a breeze. But cool night air was moving slowly and steadily across the desert's surface. Like the tide advancing across mudflats, it penetrated every corner. It passed over me. It passed around me. It passed underneath me. Soon it seemed to be passing through me as well. Minute by minute it sucked my warmth away.

No matter how closely I cuddled to the gully wall, the cold bit deeper and deeper. For shapeless hours I fought the sleep battle. Occasionally I dozed. More often I lay three-quarters awake, telling myself I was half-asleep. By two o'clock the dozes had become unreal memories. And at three thirty I got up, packed my bag, and headed north into the darkness.*

Later, I learned that the temperature that night never fell below 58°. This is admittedly an official reading, taken five feet off the ground; but a thermometer lying beside my bed just before I left would probably have registered about the same. Now 58° is a very mild temperature. But the reason I felt so bitterly cold is simple: I wasn't used to it. I had been walking through deserts for more than a month, in day temperatures that had risen to a peak of 105°. Recently, the nights had been warm too, and the day I entered Death Valley the minimum temperature had been 80°. But what mattered most was that all this time I had been sleeping in a highly efficient 2½ pounds-of-goose-down mummy bag. Then, two days earlier— wanting to cut my load, and feeling I did not need a bag in night temperatures that seemed likely to fall no lower than 80°—I had given it to two Death Valley rangers who checked my arrival at a spring at the south end of the valley. I arranged to collect the bag when I passed through a ranger station a couple of weeks later. But that same night an unexpected storm sent temperatures plunging. The next night I found myself curling up in that miserable little gully with no protection except my clothes and poncho—and, what was even more important, with my body unprepared for the shock of sleeping in what were, in objective fact, quite pleasantly warm conditions.

Acclimation can also work the other way. Last September I spent a week walking along a mountain crest that rarely fell below 12,000 feet and rose at one point to 14,000. In clear autumnal weather the panoramas and the wind were both breathtaking. On the third night my route took me down off the crest for the only time all week, and I camped in a sidecanyon at 10,000 feet. At dusk, my bedside thermometer read a bare degree or two below freezing.

* From *The Thousand-Mile Summer,* page 86.

Because I was trying out a very efficient experimental mummy bag (with three pounds of down and no side zipper) that had been designed for Alaskan mountaineering, I did not bother about shelter, except to camp just below some bushes. The bushes, I felt sure, would blunt the almost inevitable down-canyon wind. To my surprise, no wind blew. Soon, I was far too hot to sleep. I slipped into my wool shirt and a very thick, hooded down parka, then eased up part way out of the sleeping bag and pulled on long johns and pants. With the sleeping bag pulled loosely up around my midriff and a pair of big leather gauntlets to protect my hands, I immediately fell asleep.

I woke at dawn, glowingly warm, to find the thermometer registering 22°. But what really surprised me was that during the night one glove had come off and my bare hand, lying on the grass quite unprotected, felt perfectly warm. The circulation in my hands has always been rather poor in cold weather, and I would not have believed it possible for one of them to feel pleasantly warm at 22°—even though the rest of my body was glowing, and the air was undeniably very dry. The point is, I think, that I had been up in cold, windy country for two days. I very much doubt if the hand would have felt so warm under identical conditions on the night I left the car.

I hope all this discussion has not confused the issue. Temperature tolerance has its uses as a means of expressing the efficiency of a sleeping bag. It's just that temperature figures alone can be dangerously misleading. Bear this fact steadily in mind when you are choosing a sleeping bag. And ponder ponderously. Buying a sleeping bag is a serious business. If you make a mistake, you will have many long, slow, purgatorial hours in which to repent.

Models

I now own a very close-fitting mummy bag that weighs only two pounds, eleven ounces but which I take confidently on all trips on which it seems from weather records that the temperature (here we go already!) is almost certain to go no lower than about 15°F. and is unlikely to fall more than a few degrees below freezing. I have never yet had to test this bag anywhere close to 15°; but I have slept naked in it with total comfort at a windless 30°, when it was simply rolled out in the open on my air mattress; and I feel sure that with warm clothing on and a tent or other good cover for the bag and my poncho wrapped around it I could be comfortable at a windless 15° and would even get by in a fairly considerable wind.*

The bag is a Trailwise Slimline—a beautifully made little bag that has a nylon shell, differentially cut and chevron baffled, and, originally, twenty ounces of the best white goose-down fill. Mine is the larger size Slimline, for people up to six feet three inches and 190 pounds. New models of this bag have twenty-six ounces of fill; the smaller size (for those up to six feet and 175 pounds) twenty-four ounces. The basic models have no side zippers. They weigh, respectively, two pounds, eleven ounces and two pounds, six ounces.

Because I wanted a bag that would be comfortable in hot as well as cold weather (I bought it for the Grand Canyon trip), I had a 72-inch side zipper and draft flap inserted in the old standard model. The extra five ounces proved well worth it. After a couple of light snowstorms near the start, night temperatures in the Canyon rose steadily. At first I merely opened the zipper part way; then all the way; later, on calm nights when the temperature held up in the sixties, I often lay naked on my air mattress with the opened bag loosely over me. For Grand Canyon conditions the bag was perfect. Since then I have taken it on all but really cold trips and it has never let me down. Naturally, the Slimline is not cheap. The basic larger size costs $67.75; the smaller, $62.75. Seventy-two-inch zippers are now optional, for about five ounces and $5 extra.

You can buy a cover and pad that are said to extend the range of the Slimline down to 0°F. I have never used this combination, but it sounds worth a trial. The cover is waterproof nylon below and lightweight nylon above. It is pocketed to take a 2-by-20-by-30-inch foam pad. Cover (10 ounces zipperless, 12 ounces with 72-inch

---

* I have recently had six ounces of extra down fill put in this bag and have slept warmly in it—roofless, but wearing a wool shirt and a down jacket and long whipcord pants and down booties (see page 206)—at 10,000 feet on a windless night when the temperature fell to 11°F. I was carrying a large plastic sheet and a pair of down pants but used neither.

zipper) and pad (17 ounces) together cost $20.05 zipperless, $23.95 zippered.

Ultralight mummy bags rather similar to the Slimline are now sold by many of the leading makers. And almost all makers have a line of larger, heavier mummy bags in a wide range of prices and qualities. These larger bags, usually weighing between five and six pounds, may be a better bet for those who habitually go backpacking in winter, or who "sleep cold," or who find that the very slim Slimline type tends to cause claustrophobia or physical restriction.

Naturally, it is impossible to mention every maker of good sleeping bags. But Alp Sport of Boulder, Colorado, is fast gaining a fine reputation. And a couple of years ago I was impressed by the look of some bags made by the then new firm of Sierra Designs of Point Richmond, California. I have now tried out a bag of theirs, similar to the Slimline, under what turned out to be surprisingly friendly conditions on both Fujiyama and Kilimanjaro. It seemed excellent. A useful innovation on these bags is a pair of leather sliders on the hood drawstrings that allow you to get out of bed without having to untie the hood closure. (Model 100, large size, with 66-inch zip: 2 pounds, 12 ounces; $75.50.) Future models will have more down, lighter shells.

I am aware that many people who use their camping equipment only once or twice a year may not feel justified in view of other responsibilities in spending $60 or so on a sleeping bag. Unfortunately I have no experience of cheaper modern bags suitable for backpacking, and can give no advice about specific models. But I hope I have said enough to indicate what are the important things to look for, irrespective of trade name or price tag.

Double mummy bags

See page 176.

Children's sleeping bags

These bags are usually made of cheaper materials than full-size ones, and are more simply constructed, no doubt on the reasonable assumption that if you are going to invest in a high-quality bag you are not going to buy something your children will grow out of in a year or two.

Yet the lower-quality children's bags apparently sell very well. One possible reason is that children tend to sleep warmer than adults. In theory, they should sleep colder: their smaller bodies, with a wider surface-to-volume ratio, should lose heat faster. But, to balance this factor, their metabolism tends to operate at a higher rate. What happens in practice is a matter of opinion, but a limited poll I conducted among friends tended to support the opinion of one mother of five children ranging from four to thirteen years old, whose family seems to spend half its young life camping or cabining in the mountains. "Yes," said this seasoned troop leader, "I'd say there may well be something to the sleeping-warmer business—certainly when the kids are young and covered in puppy fat. I've found our four-year-old almost out of his bag on quite cold nights, still fast asleep. Once children start beanstalking up into their teens, though, it's rather different. It could easily be that at that stringy stage they tend to sleep somewhat colder than adults."

If you want a really warm bag for a child, there seem to be two alternatives. One is a small adult bag. The other, for children up to about four feet, two inches tall, is a footsack.

SUBSTITUTES AND SUPPLEMENTS FOR SLEEPING BAGS

The footsack or elephant's foot

This is a crafty device I have never used but which offers obvious possibilities. Essentially, a footsack is the bottom half of a Slimline-type mummy bag with a drawstring at the top. Good models are cut higher in the rear than in front, both to protect the sensitive small of your back when you are lying down and also to keep it covered in the sitting position, when everything covering your rear midriff tends to pull apart in a quite infuriating way. A footsack is designed as an emergency bag for use with a good down-filled parka (on occasions when you do not plan to sleep out but just might have to) or as a straight substitute for a bag (when you really have to cut down the weight and think you can trust the weather). Don't forget that you need warm gloves with this rig—unless, like one friend of mine, you can sleep tolerably comfortably all night with hands down in the bag in a kind of fig-leaf position.

A first-rate footsack, with baffled nylon shell and about twelve ounces of goose-down fill, weighs and costs around 1½ pounds and $30.

A high-quality footsack—say fifty inches long in front and sixty inches in back—makes an excellent mummy bag for a child up to about four feet two inches tall. Two factors make this a popular choice for a really warm child's bag. The drawstring pulls the top of the sack into a hood just like that on an ordinary mummy bag. And parents can help justify the expense with the knowledge that they are also buying something that will come in useful for themselves.

Cagoule-and-footsack bivouac

The knee-length parka or cagoule (see page 209) is designed for use as a bivouac—either alone (when you draw your knees up inside it) or with a companion footsack.

The idea is presumably to use the combination when nights are really warm, but there are few climates I would trust. As an emergency bivouac the rig looks ideal. But "emergency bivouac" means sleeping out when you do not expect to—and therefore are unlikely to be carrying equipment for the job. Still, it is possible to imagine certain situations in which the complete rig might be worth packing along. Anyway, the world would be poorer without it. It is one of those intriguing items that make catalogue-browsing the dreamy, time-wasting, utterly delightful pursuit it is.

Down-filled hood

Said to be a useful supplement for any sleeping bag in extreme cold or wind. An intriguing item that looks as if it might almost convert a rectangular sleeping bag into an efficient unit, especially if there is some kind of drawstring at the mouth of the bag (six ounces; $7.95).

Stuff bags

Many people stuff their sleeping bags, every morning, into small cylindrical bags with drawcord closure. Perhaps because I tend to roll out my mummy bag at lunchtime halts, I have in the past rarely used one. But I am coming around. Stuff bags certainly protect down clothing and sleeping bags from wear and tear and from rain. They also reduce the bulk.

The best stuff bags are now made of waterproof-coated nylon. (Typical range: 7 inches diameter by 18 inches long: 1¼ ounces; $1.75; through 11 inches diameter by 21 inches long: 2¼ ounces; $3).

Pillows

Some people do not mind sleeping without a pillow; others even prefer it that way. Unless I am too tired to notice, I find it quite disconcerting not to have one. For me, the little air mattress with pillow (see page 173) is ideal. When I'm using an Ensolite pad, I normally just roll up my long pants or down jacket or both and stuff them under my head. Sometimes I bolster the clothing with a plastic canteen or the day's-ration food bag. If the night is cold enough to make me wear all the clothes I have brought, I may use a canteen alone. This arrangement helps keep the canteen unfrozen; and because I am wearing my Balaclava helmet and possibly a hooded parka as well, it is tolerably comfortable. Or I may pad the canteen with the packbag or ration bag—making sure that soft food such as cereal is directly under my head. On sand or other loose soil the simplest and most comfortable pillow is a roughly banked-up guillotine block. If pillows really mean a lot to you, and you're not too bone-weary, you may want to cut bough tips or collect moss, especially if you enjoy doing such things.

Care of sleeping bags

Any sleeping bag should be aired after use. A nylon one must be (see page 179). Just open the bag and leave it spread out, preferably up off the ground. With nylon bags, two or three days is not too long. Outdoor airing, especially in sunshine, is best.

It is best not to store a bag for long periods compressed in its stuff bag. Lay it out flat, hang in a closet, or roll loosely.

Normally, cleaning should amount to no more than sponging lining and cover with a mild soap and tepid water. Dry thoroughly. If a bag becomes so soiled that it demands more stringent cleaning, one way is washing. Take the bag to reputable launderers, accustomed to down clothing, and have them wash it in soap or mild detergent and then tumble dry.

An alternative is dry cleaning. Ever since one favorite old bag of mine lost a great deal of its virtue after two or three widely spaced visits to the cleaners, I have been inclined to avoid commercial cleaning. But so that I should not pass on pure hunch, I made careful inquiries before writing this section. The manager of one dry-cleaning plant, who owns both down and Dacron sleeping bags (the latter for car camping), advised me that only dry cleaning will do a really satisfactory job on badly soiled shells. And Dacron fill, he said, remains unaffected by cleaning. No harm comes to down if the solvents used are petroleum-based and are not chlorinated hydrocarbons (which, though excellent for most jobs, are just too efficient at removing greases and therefore remove essential oils from the down). It seems that only small cleaning firms use chlorinated hydrocarbon solvents; the process is too expensive for big plants. So have your bag cleaned, if at all, at a big plant. But make local inquiries first; a good outdoor-equipment store should know which firms do a restrained but effective job on sleeping bags.

One reason it sometimes seems advisable to have a bag cleaned is that in time the down begins to mat. Clumps of it coagulate, and large areas in each baffle tube are left empty. Dry cleaning certainly seems to redistribute the down effectively. But the plant manager I quoted (and he can hardly be accused of commercial bias in this opinion) maintained that the redistribution was purely the result of mechanical tumbling in the drier. In other words, the way to redistribute the down in your bag is to put it in the tumble drier at low heat—back home or at a laundromat.

Warning: almost any kind of patch will come off a bag during dry cleaning, and fill will escape. So if your bag has been patched, have the plant wash rather than clean it. Or else wash it at home. I am told that it's possible to do the job in a bath of tepid soapy water. Rinse the bag well, and dry outdoors in fair weather, fluffing the fill as it dries out. Or dry at low heat in a tumble drier.

All these instructions apply equally to down clothing.

THE BEDROOM IN ACTION

We examined almost all details of how the bedroom operates in "The Kitchen in Action" (pages 121–2 and 129–32). For modifications under various kinds of roof, see their separate subheadings in this chapter. But a few minor points remain unmade:

Keeping tabs on the flashlight

After dark, you must always know exactly where the flashlight is. Otherwise, chaos. My flashlight spends the night in an easy-to-feel position in one bedside boot. And I have a rule that when it is in intermittent use, such as before and during dinner, I never let go my grasp on it without putting it in the pocket designated for the night (*which* pocket depends on what I'm wearing). This rule is so strict that I rarely break it more than three or four times a night.

Come to think of it, it might be worth tying the flashlight to a loop of nylon cord large enough to slip over your head.

For more on flashlights, see page 221.

Fluffing up the sleeping bag

Although I am told that quite a lot of people fail to do so, it seems only common sense that before you get into bed at night you should always shake the sleeping bag by the edges and so fluff up the down and fill it with the air pockets that actually keep you warm. One of these nights I must try it out.

Adjusting to suit the night

With experience (and I guess there's just no other way) you can usually gauge pretty accurately how much clothing, if any, you will need to wear in your sleeping bag. Or, in warmer weather, how tightly you need pull the hood drawstrings, and whether you should unzip the bag part way. But you will never get so good that you always hit the nail dead center.

In general, be a pessimist: if in doubt, wear that extra layer of clothing, and pull the drawstrings tight. Sleeping too hot is uncomfortable; but sleeping cold is murder. In any case, the night will usually, though not always, get progressively colder (the coldest time typically comes either at dawn or, even more often, in the last few minutes before sunrise).

But the main reason you do better by deliberately looking on the bleak side is that boosting the insulation is a major operation, reducing it a very simple one. When you wake up uncomfortably hot (and you will do so occasionally unless you consistently under-insulate, and then God help you) all you have to do is slacken off the drawstrings. At least, that usually lets out enough heat, especially if you flap the bag in a bellows effect a couple of times to introduce some cold air. But if you find that to establish the right balance you have to slacken the drawstrings until there is a gaping hole around your head, you will probably find that the upper part of your body gets too cold and the lower part stays too hot. If you are wearing heavy clothes, take off one layer. (A minor disadvantage of a close-fitting bag like the Slimline is that putting on or taking off socks and pants "indoors" is a struggle. But it can be done. At least, taking them off can be.) If you wake to find yourself too hot when you're wearing few or no clothes (which will mean that outside air temperatures are not too barbarously low) feel for the inside tab of the zipper and slide it part way or all the way down. Once again, only experience will tell you how far to go, and also how to tuck the opening under you, or to wriggle it around on top, or away from the wind, or whatever else achieves the balance you want. If you unzip, you may well have to re-zip as the night grows colder, and/or to tighten the drawstrings; but you soon learn to do so without coming more than about one eighth awake.

On really hot nights, the only comfortable way to use the bag may be as a cover—fully unzipped and just spread out loosely over your body. At such times it may be most comfortable to wear a shirt to keep your shoulders warm, and to tuck your feet part way into the foot of the bag. The advantage of the bag cover as opposed to a couple of layers of clothing is that as the night grows colder (and in hot weather it assuredly will) you can compensate, without really coming awake, by pulling the edges of the bag a little more firmly around you.

Dealing with a full bladder at night

See page 284.

Getting to sleep

An experienced outdoorsman has suggested that I include in this chapter "the ritual of getting to sleep in a bag," and as he is my editor I suppose I had better attempt the task.

My technique is to lie down, close my eyes, and go to sleep.

Clothes Closet

The best dress for walking is nakedness. But our sad though fascinating world rarely offers the right and necessary combination of weather and privacy, and even when it does the Utopia never seems to last for very long. So you always, dammit, have to worry about clothes.

The most sensible way to set about deciding what clothing to take on a trip and what to leave behind is to consult weather statistics (page 20) and your own experience and so arrive at an estimate of the most miserable conditions of temperature, wind, exposure, humidity, and precipitation that you can reasonably expect to suffer. The worst conditions recorded in, say, twenty years. Then, all you have to do is judge what you need take to keep you warm under daytime conditions when you are wearing everything and doing something, or at least are only sitting down and doing nothing for short intervals. If you hit this target around about center, you can feel reasonably sure that at night, with shelter and sleeping bags selected to match, you will sleep tolerably warm if you wrap yourself up in every stitch of clothing you have brought along. During the day, if you stop doing anything for any length of time and begin to feel cold, or even to think that you might soon feel cold, you simply pupate inside the sleeping bag.

This kind of calculation involves not so much a precise balancing of conditions and clothing as an exercise in extrapolating from experience. But it seems to work. I do not think I have been seriously cold for at least seven years now. Not, I mean, for more than the few minutes it takes me to do something about it. Mind you, I have never operated in bitterly cold conditions. Never below zero, in fact. But people who do so fairly often seem to apply much the same methods of choice and the same techniques.

Color

Generally speaking, it pays to choose clothes that are dark but bright. Dark, so that they will not advertise the inevitable dirt. And bright (especially red), because you can hardly walk away from camp and leave gaudy garments lying on the ground or hanging up to dry; because if you are brave enough to go out and walk during the hunting season, a plain-as-a-pikestaff exterior may save your life; because in case of accident, worn or waved clothing may attract rescuers' attention; and finally because a single spark of red or orange can electrify an otherwise lifeless color photograph.

On the other hand, it is worth having one set of outer garments in some obscurantist shade of brown or green or gray for those occasions when you don't want to be seen: fishing, photographing game, keeping out of people's way, trespassing.

Materials

Natural fibers tend to be a good deal more moisture-absorbent than synthetics but less resistant to wear and wind. So in general it pays to wear natural fibers such as wool or cotton next to the skin, and to use synthetics for outer garments. Synthetics are being improved so fast that the best for any particular function seems to change with every tide. At the moment, for most purposes, woven nylon rules the roost. Coated nylon is waterproof but in most cases does not "breathe." Treated nylon breathes but is only "water-repellent"—whatever you choose to take that to mean.

The distaff wardrobe

I have co-opted an experienced subcommittee to advise me on important differences. She mentions that in hot weather many women, like men, prefer to walk shirtless, and that to preserve the decencies they often carry a cotton sun- or swim-suit top (or halter). On a more fundamental level, she finds that by taking along one attractive garment ("something that makes me feel good"), she helps sustain her beleaguered sense of femininity. Otherwise, she says she can think of no mentionables worth mentioning.

Beyond these broad generalizations, choice of clothing is largely a matter of selecting each individual garment carefully for warmth in relation to weight, for toughness in wear, for versatility in use, and in some cases for water-resistance.

UNDERCLOTHING

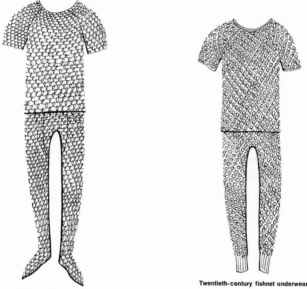

Medieval chain armor

Twentieth-century fishnet underwear

String (or fishnet) vests or shirts

These rather unlikely-looking garments are a lot of big holes tied together with string. At least, the original models were.* Today, the

---

* During World War II, I was for a time with a British unit that had been issued true fishnet vests as special mountaineering equipment. Eventually the unit was converted to cliff assault duty and moved to a Cornish fishing village. Our string vests astonished the fishermen and their wives. For several years they had, as experienced netmakers, been producing these strange devices for the war effort, in great secrecy, but they had never been able to guess what the peculiarly shaped nets were used for. No one, when sober, had seriously entertained the notion that they might be some kind of clothing.

string has been replaced by soft knitted cotton, but the holes are much the same—about ⅜ inch in diameter. And the holes are the important thing; they are what keep you warm when you want to keep warm and cool when you want to keep cool. To keep warm you button up all outer clothing and close neck and wrist openings. The holes of the fishnet weave then hold air in place close to your skin, and your body heat soon warms this air. The result is highly efficient insulation, much like that you get from down-filled sleeping bags.

To cool off, you simply loosen the neck opening of your outer garments and allow warm air to escape. Loosening wrist openings speeds up the process. If you really get too hot, simply unbutton jacket and shirt and allow all hot air to be replaced by cold. When you are unbuttoned like this, air circulates freely, and then a string vest is far cooler than conventional underwear.

Because of its dual efficiency, fishnet underwear is ideal when you are likely to work up a sweat while on the move, then cool off drastically the moment you stop, as when mountain climbing. It is also excellent when you get soaking wet: the wide fishnet weave holds little moisture and continues to provide good insulation.

To get full benefit from a string vest, wear outer clothing that unbuttons completely down the front, and carry a scarf so that you can block off the passage of air at your neck.

A string vest weighs about seven ounces and costs around $4. So do a pair of

String longs.

They are made on the same principle, and I understand they are excellent. But on such occasions as I feel the need for undercovering on my legs, I use old-fashioned

Long johns.

Some people wear long johns in relatively mild weather, little below freezing. I am not sure I have ever worn them on the march; but I occasionally take them when cold or wind threatens to be extreme, and have several times worn them in bed quite gratefully. Normally I wear ordinary cotton

Jockey briefs.

On longish trips, if weight is not too acute a problem, you may feel like taking along spare briefs, or at least lightweight substitutes, for the times you wash the first-line pair—in case it is too cool or unprivate to wander around naked while they are drying.

SHIRTS

The choice is almost unlimited. For cold weather, wool. In the West, the almost universally accepted name is Pendleton, and their shirts are certainly very good. For warm weather, any material that absorbs sweat will do: thin wool, cotton, or a combination. Avoid synthetics. I usually take a fairly thick shirt, and always one with long sleeves: except in quite cold weather I tend to walk without a shirt, and when I stop I want something comfortably warm. Otherwise, my only criteria are that the shirt shall unbutton all the way down the front, have at least one breast pocket and preferably two, not weigh too much, and be a bright color-photography red. Pockets with flaps and buttons are best. One friend of mine uses only shirts with zippered rather than buttoned fronts.

SWEATERS

In really cold weather, one or more thin sweaters between shirt and overclothing can make a lot of difference. Weight for warmth, there is supposed to be nothing quite like an old cashmere sweater.

On my California walk, the only really warm upper-body garment I took was a luxuriously thick Italian ski sweater that zipped down the front. Although it weighed two pounds, two ounces, and in a high wind needed some windbreaking outer garment such as a poncho, it filled the bill admirably. But I have since found a more efficient substitute (see "down-filled clothing," page 204).

PANTS

Whatever you wear on your behind, the material must be tough: you'll be using unpadded chairs. And choose a color that hides the dirt.

Shorts

I'm a whole-heartedly bigoted devotee of shorts—so much so that I often find myself wearing them until the temperature drops into the thirties or the wind develops a really keen cutting edge. At least once I have arrived at a 14,000-foot peak in shorts; but I hasten to add that there are not too many places and days you can do such a thing in comfort. A few months ago I wore shorts up 5000 feet of snow, on a cloudless day of icy winds, to the 12,000-foot rim of Fujiyama—and paid for my stupidity for the rest of the week every time I tried to force red, raw legs into the steaming hot baths that are the only form of ablution in Japanese inns, and which *noblesse* apparently obliges you to refrain from tempering with cold water. But I remain an unrepentant shorts man.

Shorts allow much more efficient ventilation than long pants do. Even more important, I find, is the freedom they give your legs. I've now reached the point at which I feel, or imagine I feel, dragged down by the restrictiveness of long pants. Fortunately, real cold seems to override the sensation. But several times I have started out on bitter mornings in longs and have realized later, after the day had warmed up, that I was making meager progress simply because I was still wearing them. A change to shorts has usually been enough to get me moving well again.

Really pesky insects might, I guess, drive even me to give up shorts for a while. See page 250.

Corduroy is the best material I know for shorts. It is warm and absorbent, washes well, and wears prodigiously. But it must be really good quality. The only way I've been able to get what I want is to have shorts made from material I've selected myself. Limited experience suggests that British corduroy may be the best.

Drill shorts are much lighter than corduroys and are worth considering if you'll be using them only occasionally, and they'll spend most of the time in your pack. They last a little while.

I like full ventilation on my shorts: the wider the leg openings the better, within the bounds of decency. And anyone whose midriff fluctuates in response to prolonged packing of heavy weights (and whose does not?) should make sure the waistband is adjustable (see belt, below). Pockets should be strong, numerous, and suited to your personal fancies. I like two hip pockets, two side pockets, and either one or two ticket pockets at the waistband (for book matches and fire-lighting waste paper). These requirements apply equally to

Long pants.

Even in the hottest weather, evenings are liable to be cool. So, except in low desert in high summer, I nearly always carry long pants. A stout whipcord pair, forest ranger style, all wool (1 pound, 10 ounces; $18.95), is the only kind I have used for some years. But the choice is wide. Many people take nothing but a pair of blue jeans for all uses. Others wear climbing knickers, tight-fitting below the knees. Take your pick.

For extreme cold, consider pants with instep straps.

Belt

If possible, buy pants with built-in waistbands and avoid this unnecessary item. It is not only a question of weight; any belt is uncomfortable under the waist belt of your pack. When you go off on packless sidetrips and need something around your waist to which you can attach a poncho-wrapped lunch and a cup and camera tripod and so on, simply use a few turns of nylon cord (see page 264).

Leg protectors

If you wear shorts, you may find that in certain kinds of country, especially desert, you need something to stop your bare and vulnerable lower legs from being savaged by scrub, thorn brush, and cacti. The best protection I've come across is a pair of Ace bandages (that I always carry anyway, see page 269), wrapped puttee-fashion from boots to just below the knees.

Gaiters

Something to seal off the gap between boots and long pants is essential in soft snow and profitable in cold winds. I have a pair of coated, water-repellent-nylon gaiters with elastic inserts top and bottom to grip pants and boots. Cords fit under the instep and stop the gaiters from riding upward. Side zippers make them easy to put on and take off. They work very well indeed. Height six inches (3½ ounces; $4.75).

DOWN-FILLED CLOTHING

When man woke up a few decades ago to the idea of taking a feather out of the birds' book and making down-filled clothing as well as sleeping bags, the result was so much more effective than anything he had used before that it revolutionized polar and high-altitude exploration. Men could operate with safety and even comfort where they once had to battle simply to exist. Even in much kinder environments it is well worth taking advantage of this breakthrough.

For my Grand Canyon trip, when I had to pare away every last half ounce, the one really warm upper garment I took was a

Lightweight down jacket.

Although snow fell twice during the early part of the trip and evenings were often decidedly chilly, I do not remember that I was ever cold. Now, I take the jacket on almost every trip, except in very cold weather (see below).

The nylon-shelled jacket is designed for use either as underwear or outerwear. Elastic knit cuffs effectively close off the wrist openings. There is an elastic ribbing collar too, but it's not very effective, and you need a small scarf. Five snap fasteners close the front fairly adequately. As sold, the jacket has a loose, floppy waist. I threaded a length of $\frac{7}{16}$-inch elastic tape through the double hem (using a big safety pin on the leading end) and stitched it back-center to prevent it from slipping out. This makeshift belt lasted four years, and has only recently needed replacing. Without it the jacket would lose half its efficiency.

Color: according to the catalogue, golden tan; to the eye, muck brown, (one pound, one ounce; $20).

A thick down jacket

Some such garment (often called a "down parka" if it has a hood, as it certainly should have) is essential if you are going to operate in real cold or in bitter winds. Such jackets come in various weights, qualities, and prices. One of the best is the French "Lionel Terray," used on several Himalayan expeditions. These beautifully made jackets, with overlapping tube construction in fine woven nylon, are astonishingly warm. So are similar American jackets. Weight, almost unbelievably, just two pounds even. Cost, quite understandably, $50 or more. (The Mount Everest Parka by Eddie Bauer of Seattle, Washington—as used by the 1963 U.S. Everest Expedition—weighs three pounds, two ounces, costs $100.)

In extremely cold weather you may also need

Down pants.

If, like me, you are one of those unfortunates whose upper and lower clothes layers tend to pull apart at the mid-section, make sure your pants come up high and have an effective built-in belt. Quality and warmth cover much the same range as for down jackets. Weights average about one pound, costs about $20 or $25.

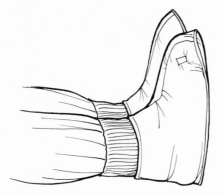

Down booties

Here is a new and engaging catalogue item that I have found highly practical. Once, they kept my feet totally warm—perhaps even a shade hot—in a Slimline bag, unprotected, at 11°F. (see page 187, footnote). On Kilimanjaro, when the temperature hardly fell below freezing but murkily miserable weather and the thin air at 16,000 feet made it seem colder, they kept my feet comfortable in a similar lightweight bag.

Booties—with light nylon shell and thick waterproof nylon sole padded with ¼-inch Ensolite—are also excellent for brief excursions from your tent out into the snow (see page 151), provided the snow is cold and dry (4 ounces; $7.50).

In really biting winds you may need a windproof jacket over your down clothing.

A windproof of this kind is often called a

Parka (or anorak).

"Parka" is an Aleutian word originally meaning "a fur jacket or heavy, long woolen shirt, often lined with pile or fleece, with attached hood." "Anorak" is the Greenland Eskimo word for a similar hooded garment, though it may be made of leather or cloth. In modern English the two words mean the same thing: a hooded jacket, windproof and waterproof to widely varying degrees. Anyone who has tried to operate without a hood in cold or very windy conditions will know why they are so popular.

A parka may be necessary over a down jacket not only in cutting winds but also when snow falls in temperatures only just below freezing. Under such conditions, escaping body heat melts snowflakes that come to rest on an unprotected down jacket and soon turn it into waterlogged and useless pulp. With the snow at lower temperatures and little body heat escaping, no such problem arises.

Most people seem to find, especially in the mountains, that a parka is about the most useful and versatile garment they own. Frankly, I don't have one that I'm well enough satisfied with to recommend unreservedly; but the choice is wide.

The fabric, it seems to me, is the vital matter. It should be strong. And it should allow your body to "breathe." Yet it must be not only windproof but also waterproof or, at the very least, strongly water-repellent. There is some doubt in my mind whether a fabric yet exists that will really fulfill all the necessary criteria under field conditions. Woven nylon seems the most popular material at present—in particular, a fabric called Reevair, which is supposed to keep out not only wind but also rain, yet to allow body moisture to escape. (It is called "microporous": although water cannot penetrate, water vapor in suspension can escape, more or less readily.) Opinion differs about whether the material is satisfactory as a waterproof, but it at least seems an improvement on earlier efforts.

The other requirements of a good parka are relatively simple. To shut out the wind you need drawstrings at hood and waist, and some effective closure at the wrists. The warmest "expedition" kind have crotch straps. Big pockets are a convenience. But the really important thing is size. Buy big. A size larger, perhaps, than the biggest you think you need. You'll be wearing the parka over many layers of other clothing, often including a bulky down jacket. And as every garment is essentially there to hold pockets of air in place, the whole object is defeated if you compress the layers. In any case, few parkas have front openings, and if you have never stood on a mountain ridge in a howling gale and tried to battle your way up and into a parka a size too small for you then I suggest you offer up a short prayer of thanks—and make every effort to avoid the experience.

Most parkas weigh around one pound. Cost can vary from $6 to $30.

As parkas become more waterproof and yet allow you to "breathe," so their usefulness as rainwear increases. In cold, very wet climates, waterproof parka and long pants (14 ounces; $5.95) may prove the most practical outer garments. The pants may also complete your protection in really biting winds.

On almost any trip, unless you're 99 per cent sure you'll escape without rain, you have to carry either a satisfactory waterproof parka (if you can find one) or some kind of a

Poncho.

A poncho is a waterproof sheet, four feet by seven feet or a little bigger, with a hood in the middle. In good backpacking ponchos the hood is displaced somewhat off-center, and the longer rear section covers your pack. At least, that's the theory; but if a wind is blowing don't expect too much overlap from theory into practice. The hood can be tightened flush around your face with a drawstring. The rest of the sheet hangs down like a shroud, but snap fasteners on the edges allow you to make rudimentary sleeves that help keep the poncho from flapping too wildly in a high wind. Some heavier models have a drawstring at the waist that not only cuts down the flappage but also holds in warmth—too efficiently sometimes. A length of nylon cord around your waist will do the job almost as well, though in time its rubbing may damage the waterproofing.

A poncho is one of the most versatile garments around. Those snap fasteners along its edges help, and so do the grommets sometimes put in at each corner. (I always have at least one other grommet —and probably three or four—inserted in the center of each long side; the short sides rarely have a wide enough hem to take even a small grommet.) With these simple fittings, a poncho can be much more than a waterproof garment. It can be a windbreaker—especially useful when a thin down jacket is the only warm garment you have with you. As we have seen (pages 160–3) the grommets allow you to turn it into a wild assortment of roofs and side-walls and cocoons that will ward off snow, rain, wind or sun. With two ponchos snapped together by their fasteners you can build a big ridge-backed shelter. Under certain conditions (pages 163 and 169) you may be forced to use your poncho as a groundsheet; but if you do, do not expect it to remain waterproof for long. On packless side trips or on short walks from home or car, a poncho makes a convenient envelope in which to wrap lunch and oddments, especially if there is a danger of rain. Finally, a poncho helps waterproof your pack contents during a river crossing (page 276).

Poncho materials include heavy-duty rubberized fabrics, coated nylon and other synthetic fabrics, and thin plastic (vinyl). Rubberized fabrics are heavy but very strong. Sometimes, when there is a danger of torrential or prolonged rain, I still carry a thick U.S. Army surplus model. Generally speaking, woven synthetic fabrics such as nylon are at present the best. They are very light, and are becoming progressively stronger and closer to waterproof, though no cheaper. Plastic ponchos are light, cheap, and wholly waterproof. But they do not breathe and so are extremely hot. Worst of all, they tear. They tear almost without provocation; and once started they don't stop. But they have short-term, shallow-pocket uses.

Weights run from around 2½ pounds for a rubberized poncho down to as little as ten ounces for a nylon or plastic one. A tough, coated nylon poncho that breathes may cost $16 or $17, though a less fancy and less durable one may run only $6. The plastic kind sell for as little as $1.25.

An alternative to a poncho is a

Cagoule.

The word is French and originally meant "monk's cloak" or "penitent's cowl." The modern outdoorsman's cagoule is a knee-length, sleeved cape with hood.

I recently bought one, made of waterproof-coated nylon, but

have not yet tried it out. It looks a practical wet-weather garment, though it may prove rather hot. Drawstrings at hood and hem allow them to be drawn tight. Elastic keeps the wrist openings closed. Excellent for camp use, I would guess; and good on the trail (11 ounces, $20.).

A cagoule cannot, like a poncho, serve as a roof. But it is designed for emergency bivouac use. You can if necessary draw your knees up inside the long "skirt," and seal yourself off by pulling the drawstring tight. If you carry a companion footsack-and-carrying-bag (6 ounces; $6.95) of the same material, you are in even better shape (see page 190).

Gloves

In big hiking parties, where heavy work such as digging and wood-gathering has to be expected, it is worth carrying a pair of leather work gloves. They're also useful in mild winds and cold. Some backpackers always take a pair—for firelighting, cooking, and protection against sunburn and insects (see, also, page 250) as well as the cold. Traveling on my own, I rarely carry them; but unless the weather is fairly sure to be consistently warm I usually take along a pair of light woolen gloves or mitts. For moderate cold, fleece-lined leather gloves or mitts are good. Mitts—which house all four fingers together and leave only the thumb on its own—are always warmer then gloves of similar construction.

For cold-weather mountaineering your hands need greater protection. One satisfactory pair of mitts I've used has leather palm and thumb, cotton twill backing with fur pad (mainly, I'm told, for wiping off that cold, dripping nose), and a long twill gauntlet with an elastic insert at the end that forms a good windproof seal, well above the wrist. These mitts also make excellent snow slippers for brief nature trips outside the tent (see page 151). I understand that for severe conditions, down-filled mitts are best. But even with them, as with any big mitts, you need inner gloves: you have to remove the outer layer for any task that needs fingers, from taking a photograph to lighting the stove, and bare hands can soon become frost-bitten. Wool inner gloves are warm but quickly develop holes. Thin silk inner gloves are now becoming popular. Although they look like something from a boudoir, they do not encumber your fingers at all, help a little in keeping them warm inside the mitts, wear better than wool, and are thick enough when worn alone to protect your hands for short periods and above all to keep the skin from sticking to cold metal. They are so extremely light and so reasonably cheap ($\frac{1}{4}$ ounce; $2.95) that on a long trip you can afford to take several pairs.

Scarf

The human neck is no doubt necessary, but it is a hell of a thing to keep warm. And it creates a weak point in almost any clothing system. Even in warm weather I always carry a small (one ounce) wool scarf to block off the escape of precious warm air from the main reservoir that clothing has created around my body. Unless you have tried it, you will find it difficult to believe how much difference this small detail can make, especially when your clothing is on the light side. In particular, a string vest unsupported by a scarf is only half-effective.

In really cold weather I used to carry a thick woolen scarf, but now take only a

Balaclava helmet.

A Balaclava rolls well down over the neck. Rolled up, it makes a warm hat that you can wear alone or under a parka or poncho hood (4 ounces; $2.75).

Down Balaclava

A new item (at least, it's new to me) by Sierra Designs. May be used as a hood with any garment, or worn under a parka hood, or folded into a hat—exactly like a wool Balaclava. Nylon shell, one ounce of down fill (2 ounces; $5.25).

Swimsuit

Where there's a chance of a swim, you may, unless you're reasonably sure of privacy, like to take along a thin nylon swimsuit (2½ ounces). On recent major river crossings with my pack (see page 279) in rough water and hot weather, I wore mine every time, so that in the unlikely event of being separated from the pack I would at least have some protection from the sun.

Bandanna

A large cotton bandanna or handkerchief, preferably bright-colored and therefore not easily lost, is your wardrobe's maid-of-all-work. It performs as potholder, napkin, dishcloth, washcloth, towel, emergency headgear, wet inside-the-hat cooling pad in hot weather, snooze mask, and even fig leaf (page 220).

Wash frequently. Dries quickly if tied on back of pack (2 feet square: 1¼ ounces; 65 cents).

Hat

Hikers wear about as many different kinds of headgear as you'll see in a fully fashioned Easter parade. But the only criteria that matter are lightness, protection afforded from heat, and ability to stand up to brutal treatment. (Rain resistance matters very little: you always have a poncho or parka hood.) Otherwise, suit your fancy. Naturally, the hat must stay on your head in a half hurricane, and the only way you can make it do so is with a chin strap. If the hat you like doesn't have one (and it probably won't) all you have to do is punch a hole in the brim on either side, close to the crown, grommet the holes or have a shoemaker do the job, and thread through the grommets a suitable length of braided nylon cord. (Red cord dirties less objectionably than white, and also helps color photography.) When not in use, the chin strap goes up into the crown. You soon get used to flicking it up without thought as you put the hat on.

My last three hiking hats have all been good-quality soft felts: Half Stetsons or reasonable facsimiles. Brims: about $2\frac{1}{2}$ inches wide, so that they give adequate shade but continue to stand out for themselves after being crushed, soaked, and trampled on. Crown: high enough to leave air space between bald pate and murderous sunshine. Color: brown or blue-gray, because they don't show the dirt and because I like the look of them (though I know that in theory a light-colored hat would reflect the heat better).

All these hats did their job well. But they took a continuous beating, and although each lasted several years, none looked pristine for very long. They not only got soaked and trampled on but spent long hours slung by their chin straps from my packframe. And occasionally they got stuffed into the packbag.

I bought one new hat just before the Grand Canyon trip. It soon reached maturity. At the halfway mark, when I met people for the first time since near the start, the month-old hat would hardly have done for church, and one bright girl asked, "But was it *ever* new?"

A few months ago I reluctantly pensioned off that worthy hat.*

---

* It now hangs on the wall of my office, a pleasing memento. I have just looked up at it and smiled happily.

After two years' hard labor its crown had worn through around the fold and was only held in place by about four inches of material at the back. This unintentional ventilation kept my head pleasantly cool in hot weather—and the bonus gave me an idea.

In hot weather you want all the ventilation you can get for your head; in the wet or cold, you want little or none. Straw hats, for example, are useless because although they ventilate your head well, they give no protection from wind or rain. (Nor do they stand up to more than a few days of the treatment any hiking hat must be able to absorb for months on end.) It seems to me that the obvious answer is an adjustable hat—a sort of stilt-roofed affair that you open up in hot weather and close down in cold:

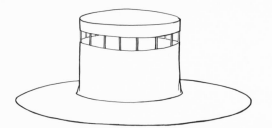

Generously, I fling this brilliant idea open to the public. All some ambitious man needs now is a little research into details. I will claim no more than a nominal 10 per cent rake-off.*

* I have just discovered that my idea is not quite as original as I had thought. By chance, I have happened on the following in a 130-year-old copy of an English publication, *The New Sporting Magazine* (Vol. 15, No. 87, July 1838, page 40):

How to make a ventilating hat for shooting, with a sliding shutter, better than any cap.
Probatum est.

Take any light beaver or felt hat, and make, with a wadding punch, four, six, or eight holes in its circumference, and about half an inch from the top. You need not use a hammer; let your punch be sharp, and then if you support the felt inside with the ends of the thumb and three fingers of your left hand, and hold the punch firmly and pretty low down with the thumb and forefinger-knuckle of the right, twisting it backwards and forewards, and pressing steadily all the while, the hat will speedily be cut through. So much for ventilation.

Failing some such modification, the way you wear the crown of your hat in hot weather can be critical. From force of city habit we tend to indent the top, "stylishly." But doing so in hot weather radically reduces the vital air-insulation barrier between the top of your head and the sun's rays. The thing to do is to push the crown out to its rounded maximum.

A rounded crown hardly helps you to look intelligent, but if appearance counts enough to force you to stay with a dented crown you had better confine your walking to the financial district.

Some sober and reliable people classify as pure myth the tradition that you need a hat in hot, sunny weather. Maybe they don't have liberal bald patches on their heads. Anyway, I know that if I go with-

---

Now for your shutter. Get an old hat of the same colour, as large or larger in the crown, and out of its circumference cut a ring or hoop, an inch and quarter, or so, in width. If it chances to fit *inside* the crown of your ventilator, so as just to slide up or down, your job is done; if not, and it be too large, cut it across, and place it in the ventilator's crown with its cut ends one overlapping the other, and while held firm in that position, mark with pen or pencil the extent of the overlapping—cut off the superfluous part, and then, if you have done your work well, it will exactly fit the *hat*-crown, and only wants the two ends joining—which you will effectively do by glueing a small piece of felt, or pasteboard, over the joint *inside*—to be as good a sliding shutter as if it had not been cut. Slipping it downwards you open your air-holes, either entirely or in part; slipping it upwards, you close them. You will meet sometimes a man whose wide-open eyes tell you plainly of bullets he supposes to have passed through your headgear; but *n'importe,* he will respect you "for the danger you have past," and your head will be cool with the thermometer at 100°.   *Thomas Trigger*

out a hat in any kind of hot sun I very soon feel dizzy. Or, at the least, I imagine I feel dizzy—and the two states are indistinguishable. So, to me, in summer desert, a hat is no joking matter.

On my California walk, when I rested for a day at the southern end of Death Valley, the temperature was 105° in the extremely rare shade. During the morning of that day I climbed up into some stark hills to photograph the gray trough that was the valley —the trough I would within twenty-four hours be walking through. All morning a strong west wind had been blowing. As I climbed, the wind increased. But the heat lost none of its intensity. By the time I reached the first summit ridge, the wind had risen to a half gale. On the ridge I stopped to take a photograph and used my hat to shield the camera lens from the sun. Afterward, in a careless moment, I forgot to slip the chin strap back under my chin. Before I could lift a hand, the wind had snatched the hat away and sent it soaring upward.

Suddenly the sun was battering down on my head like a bludgeon.

I cannot have stood there looking at the flying hat for more than two or three seconds. But I do not think I shall ever forget the feeling of helplessness as the twirling brown shape grew smaller and smaller. I stood still, watching it twist up and away into the hard blue sky.

Then the hat dived behind one of the fantastically colored ridges that stretched back and back as far as I could see.

Its disappearance snapped the spell. I broke into a run. As I ran I remembered how, only a couple of weeks before, a wise old desert rat had shown me a magazine picture of a corpse sprawled beside a bicycle out in the Mojave Desert. "No hat—not surprised," the old-timer had said. I raced on over bare rock. A makeshift hat in Death Valley? I might go days without seeing anyone. And I knew that I could hunt for hours among those endless ridges without finding the hat. I scrambled onto a chocolate-brown crest. And there, its strap neatly looped over a spike of rock, lay the hat.

I picked it up, chin-strapped it firmly onto my head, and then walked slowly back down the hill. Now the danger had passed, I felt

thankful that the desert had reminded me how fine a line divides
safety from tragedy—and how easily a moment of carelessness can
send you stumbling across it.*

Hat substitutes

Until a couple of months ago I had never lost a hat and been
forced to devise a substitute. Then, during a two-week trip beside the
Colorado River in lower Grand Canyon, with the temperature up
over 100° just about every day, I not only lost my hat (I think
it was plucked off by a mesquite thicket while hanging on the packframe during the cool of evening), but somehow succeeded in losing
as well both my bandanna, which had been acting as a wet-pad cooling system inside the hat and might have done as a river-soaked
substitute, and also, after they had done the job for a couple of days,
my jockey shorts. In summer, that part of Grand Canyon is a huge,
deep-cut, heat-reflecting oven of rock. Except in morning and evening, there is precious little shade, and I knew that I had to have some
kind of hat. My nylon swimsuit, I discovered, dried out too quickly
and was almost impossible to keep in place. But after a while I devised a method of folding the lightly inflated life vest (page 277) and
lashing it with nylon cord into such a conformation that, with its
web belt under my chin, it would stay on top of my head. This unlikely rig, immersed every hour in the river, and with the wet swim-
suit stuffed into its hollow center, turned out to be just about the

* From *The Thousand-Mile Summer,* pages 82–3.

coolest hat I've ever worn, even if not the most becoming. I had to hold my head fairly upright to keep it on, but that was probably good for my posture or something.

CARE OF CLOTHING

In the field

In civilized temperatures I generally try to wash most of my clothes at least once a week.* This works out well because I find— and I think most people find—that about once a week you need a day's more or less complete rest from walking. For most washing, use the kitchen detergent. For wool articles, see socks (page 35).

In back-of-beyond country, with virtually no chance of there being anyone just downstream, you can with a clear conscience wash clothes in creek or river. Your tiny contribution of soap or detergent won't harm even a small trout stream. But very little country remains in back-of-beyond. Someone is all too likely to be drinking from the creek just below you. And what is permissible practice when wilderness usage remains light becomes downright antisocial as soon as hikers and horsemen appear in numbers.

The solution is simple, cheap, compact—and light: a plastic or waxed-fabric bucket and bowl.

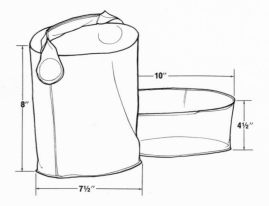

---

* In really cold weather you simply don't do any washing of clothes—or of yourself; which means that when you get back to civilization that first hot shower is not only sheer heaven but highly necessary.

You scoop up water in the bucket and wash clothes (and yourself) in the bowl. Dirty water can be ditched well back from the river and will filter clean as it seeps down through the soil. The plastic bucket-and-bowl set illustrated weighs eight ounces, costs $2, takes up almost no room in your pack, and is much more efficient than it looks.

To dry clothes, string them out on bushes or a nylon line. For shirts, if you're fussy about looks, it's easy to make a clothes hanger out of a piece of stick and some nylon line. For socks, see page 35.

In wet weather, the only answer to drying out clothes that have been ill-advisedly washed or have just plain got wet is a fire. Sometimes you're reduced to using the cooking stove inside your tent—if there's enough fuel. A tent with clothesline attachment—grommeted tabs at each end of the ridge for joining with nylon cord—may allow damp clothes to dry from a combination of stove and body heat. For final drying, take clothes to bed with you.

At home

Treat most articles of clothing like their everyday counterparts. For down-filled clothing, see sleeping bags (page 192).

THE WARDROBE IN ACTION

Sartorially (or, if you prefer it, clotheswise), hikers can be sub-divided into two distinct breeds: the "put it on and keep it on" school and the "keep adjusting your clothing all day long so that you're always comfortable" faction.

You undoubtedly save several minutes a day if you put on at the start what you judge is about right, and can then stick it out hour after hour without discomfort. But I belong, unreservedly, to the fussy, thermally responsive faction. With every variation of effort and environment I button and unbutton, unzipper and re-zipper, peel and restore, and then peel again. I find that in any but frigid weather it takes barely a mile of walking and a side glance of sunshine to strip me down to hat, underpants, shorts, socks, and boots. That, I find, is the way to walk. With air playing freely over your skin you feel twice as fresh as you did with a shirt on. And although you may lose precious body liquids more quickly this way, experience has convinced me that you walk so much more comfortably that you more than make up for any loss. At least, I do. Besides, I enjoy myself more.

On those rare but by no means unknown occasions when you are traveling beside a river or lake in very hot, low-humidity weather, you have a cooling system ready for use. It was only on that recent two-week trip in lower Grand Canyon, when I hiked day after day beside the Colorado River, that I learned to utilize this system to the full. I found that I could keep walking comfortably, even through the heat of the day, if at the end of each halt I dived into the river wearing my drill shorts and Dacron-wool shirt. For almost the whole of the next hour, the continuous evaporation from the rapidly drying clothes surrounded my body with a pleasantly cool "micro-climate." For the highly efficient hat that I used, quite by accident, see page 217.

Occasionally on that trip, because of a cut on one leg that I wanted to keep dry, I just soaked the clothes in the river. At other times, when the heat was not too ferocious, I simply draped the dripping wet shirt around my neck and kept resoaking it with barely a check in my stride by dropping it in the river and in one easy movement pushing it under and lifting it up with the tip of my walking staff.

It is not often that you meet the right and necessary combination of weather and privacy and so can carry the keep-adjusting-your-clothing-all-day-long-so-that-you're-always-comfortable system to its logical conclusion. The first time I did so for any length of time was on my long Grand Canyon journey. Of course, I exercised due care for a few days with the previously shielded sectors of my anatomy. In particular, I pressed the bandanna into service as a fig leaf. But soon I was walking almost all day long with nothing above my ankles except a hat.

Now nakedness is a delightful condition, and by walking naked you gain far more than coolness. You feel an unexpected sense of freedom from restraint. An uplifting and almost delirious sense of simplicity. In this new simplicity you soon find that you have become, in a new and surer sense, an integral part of the simple, complex world you are walking through. And then you are really walking.

Furniture and Appliances

No matter how grimly you pare away at the half ounces, you always seem to burden your house with an astonishing clutter of furniture and appliances. Each item, of course, is a necessary aid to some necessary activity. For example, there is the vital matter of

SEEING.

For night use I carry only a small

Flashlight.

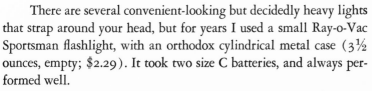

There are several convenient-looking but decidedly heavy lights that strap around your head, but for years I used a small Ray-o-Vac Sportsman flashlight, with an orthodox cylindrical metal case ($3\frac{1}{2}$ ounces, empty; $2.29). It took two size C batteries, and always performed well.

But a year or so ago I saw the much lighter Mallory flashlight ($1\frac{1}{2}$ ounces, empty; $1.98) that operates on two size AA Penlight batteries. It is reputed to throw a 250-foot beam, and certainly seems to give about as good a light as the heavier Sportsman.

At first, the flattened plastic case and flimsy innards of the Mallory inspired me with zero confidence, but people who had used it reported that it was astonishingly tough. So I tried it out. Now, I'm a convert.

The Mallory's chief advantage lies in saving weight. But it is impossible to understand comparative figures without first grasping the relative effectiveness of the different sizes and types of battery most often used in flashlights.

The standard (carbon-zinc or Leclanché) flashlight battery is entirely adequate for intermittent use. But if the light has to be kept switched on for long periods—as can happen in an emergency or through miscalculation or even by design on a long day—then the battery quickly loses energy and the light soon dims to a useless glow. An alkaline (or manganese) battery is far more efficient under such continuous-drain service. According to the makers, it may give up to ten times more service. For normal field use, this table probably gives a fair idea of what to expect:

Weights, continuous-service lives, and costs for
*PAIRS of various flashlight batteries**

Size:	AA	C	D
Name:	Penlight	¾-size	Regular
Diameter:	$\frac{9}{16}$ inch	$1\frac{1}{32}$ inch	$1\frac{11}{32}$ inch
Used in:	Mallory	Sportsman	Large flashlights
Bulb:	PR4 or 222	PR4	PR2
Standard:	1 oz. ½ hr. 20¢	3 oz. 1½ hrs. 20¢	6 oz. 2 hrs. 20¢
Alkaline:	1½ oz. 4 hrs. 50¢	4½ oz. 15 hrs. 60¢	9 oz. 12 hrs. 75¢

* The Union Carbide Corporation kindly supplied the facts and figures in this table and the paragraphs that follow—with one important exception.

That exception is the service life given for AA batteries in a Mallory flashlight. The Union Carbide figures were ¼ hour for standard batteries and three hours for alkaline batteries. It seemed to me that I remembered better service. So I did some experiments—and came up with the figures of ½ hour and four hours.

The difficulty, of course, is to decide when a battery is no longer giving useful light. This may be where Union Carbide and I differ. I tried to estimate, as well as I could in my garden, when I would no longer be able to find the way down a reasonably clear trail by flashlight alone. If anything, I tended to under-estimate service life.

Temperatures during the trial averaged 66°F. The tests were for continuous life: batteries were switched on and left on, with no rest periods. I did not warm the flashlights by holding them in the palm of my hand. Standard batteries soon dropped off peak performance and lost strength gradually, to the useful point and beyond. The alkaline batteries held close to their peak for about three hours, and after 4½ hours were still giving enough light to read this print by. Then, quite suddenly, they blacked out.

Tested again after 11 hours—with no heating or other coercion—the standard batteries lasted about five minutes with a rather poor light, the alkaline for rather more than half an hour. Tested four days later, the standards again lasted about five minutes (though more faintly than before), the alkalines for about twenty minutes.

For continuous-service use, then, alkaline batteries are by far the more efficient, ounce for hour.

Service-life figures for the kind of intermittent use a flashlight gets in camp are so subject to imponderables that they would be close to meaningless. But it seems that in the larger cell sizes alkaline batteries might deliver two to three times the service of their standard equivalents. In the AA size, you could expect much larger advantages from alkaline batteries.

Then there's the temperature question. Standard batteries are designed for use at 70°. At lower temperatures their efficiency falls sharply. At 32°, AA sizes will not function; C and D sizes give only poor light—for about one hour and two hours respectively. At 0° the figures are: AA — 0; C — forty minutes; D — sixty minutes. Exposed to temperatures above 125°, standard batteries rapidly disintegrate.

Alkaline batteries function quite efficiently at low temperatures. At 32° the continuous-service life of AA batteries is reduced from three to two hours, but there's little effect on C or D batteries. At 0° the figures are: AA — forty minutes; C — four hours; D — seven hours. Temperatures up to 130° have little effect on alkaline batteries, though prolonged exposure to such heat will shorten their "shelf-life." (Mercury batteries are very expensive, 30 per cent heavier than alkaline batteries, and last about 30 per cent longer—at 70°. But, although they work well in extreme heat, they're less than 10 per cent effective at freezing, barely 1 per cent at 0°.)

Because of all these factors, and also to keep the replacement situation simple, I nowadays carry only alkaline batteries. For a week's trip I take a reserve of two size C or four size AA. (I have found, rather to my surprise, that the first-line pair of AA batteries in the Mallory seems to last through a full week of normal use, with something to spare.)

We can now go ahead and compare the weights of the Sportsman and Mallory flashlights with alkaline batteries. Remember that the weights of the empty flashlights are: Sportsman, 3½ ounces; Mallory, 1½ ounces. And of the batteries: size C, 4½ ounces per pair; size AA, 1½ ounces per pair. So the comparative figures for the loaded flashlights plus a reserve of two batteries for the Sportsman and four for the Mallory (which is perhaps unnecessary) are:

$$\text{Sportsman:} \quad 3\tfrac{1}{2} + (4\tfrac{1}{2} \times 2) = 12\tfrac{1}{2} \text{ oz.}$$
$$\text{Mallory:} \quad 1\tfrac{1}{2} + (1\tfrac{1}{2} \times 3) = 6 \text{ oz.}$$

In weight, then, the Mallory wins hands down. And the margin grows even greater if you either rely on only one pair of batteries for spares or decide to take along an extra cushion of safety for both kinds of flashlight.

I am not yet finally convinced, but it may well be that the fragile-looking Mallory is actually tougher than the Sportsman. Certainly its plastic lens is less likely to break than the Sportsman's glass. It also has few metal parts that can corrode either from dead batteries or from dampness or from being dropped in water. And because of its shape and lightness and plastic case it is easy and reasonably comfortable to hold in the mouth, even in cold weather, while you use both hands to do something in its beam. What's more, all parts are easily get-at-able for drying, cleaning, or repair. In the Sportsman, as in any standard flashlight, the interior of the cylinder is virtually inaccessible, the switch mechanism totally so.

Accidental battery drainage

This far from minor mishap is all too likely to happen in your pack when something presses against the flashlight switch. The surest way to prevent it depends on the kind of flashlight you use. With the Sportsman, you simply reverse the lower battery. The Sportsman has a removable base, so this is a simple operation. You soon come to do it automatically every morning. Restoring the flashlight to working condition is something you most often do at dusk or after dark, but again it's all very simple. You just unscrew the base, shake out the bottom battery, replace it right way up, and screw the base back on. In wet weather you can do the job in a few seconds with the flashlight held out of rain and therefore out of sight under your poncho.

With the Mallory, such an operation is complicated, rough on the mechanism, and liable to send you down on hands and knees after dark looking for a wretched little screw that holds the two halves of the case together. But, fortunately, all you need do is put a piece of adhesive tape over the large-surfaced, rotating switch. With the tape in place, the switch cannot turn. At night, park the tape on a flat side of the flashlight. In the morning, replace it on the switch. A two-inch length of the one-inch tape from my first-aid kit does the job perfectly and lasts through a two-week trip.

Spare bulbs

Carry at least one spare. I carry two. They travel in a 35 mm. film can marked "odds and ends" (page 267). PR4's, or their equivalent, are the type for both Sportsman and Mallory. With the Mallory, a 222 bulb gives a somewhat brighter light but might be expected to have a rather shorter life.

Naturally, you must always know exactly where your flashlight is. During the day, mine goes into the inside pocket of the pack, where it is reasonably well protected and tolerably accessible. For use and storage at night, see page 194.

Candle lanterns

I have used candles on winter trips when the nights were long —though not for years now—but I have never tried one of those cute little catalogue items called candle lanterns. Some people say they work well. Others who have tried them seem to consider the game hardly worth the candle.

A catalogue now in front of me illustrates an almost irresistible little model with mica windows on three sides and a hinged door. It folds flat, opens up for use to 3 by 3 by 6½ inches. (Four ounces; $2.45.)

Stearene candles that can be shaved at the lower end to fit into the lantern measure ¾ inch by 4¾ inches, and burn about three hours (1 ounce each, 7¢).

Sunglasses

Dark glasses are a comfort and convenience just about anywhere, almost indispensable in deserts, totally so in snow.

For all-around use, G15 lenses (Bausch and Lomb) are generally recognized as best. I've had a pair for several months now and have found them excellent under widely differing conditions. Polaroids, even more than G15's, let you look through the surface glare of water—often a critical advantage in fishing. If you wear eyeglasses, either some or all of the time, prescription sunglasses are far better than either clip-on glasses or a large pair that will fit over your normal corrective glasses.

In snow, failure to take sunglasses may mean snow-blindness. I understand that in an emergency almost any opaque material with cross-slits or a small hole cut into it will let you see halfway adequately, and will ward off snow-blindness. Possibilities: cardboard from the office (page 256), Rip-stop tape (page 260), cover from a paperback book (page 255), part of a map or food wrapper.

Goggles

Goggles are essential for prolonged snow work, especially in high winds. The choice is wide.

A pair made by Sea and Ski that I bought recently has interchangeable lenses: smoke for sunglare, amber for overcast. The amber lens seems to help somewhat in bringing up muffled shapes from the deceptive flatness of a "whiteout," and the extra brightness it imparts to the outside world certainly helps keep you cheerful under what can all too easily become depressing conditions. These rather fancy goggles (2½ ounces) permit good side vision, and their ventilation is better than in most. (There's no real solution to the fogging problem; let in enough air, and you let in the snow.) But I am not sure they will stand up to much rough treatment. And they cost $7.50.

Smaller goggles, apparently quite serviceable, may weigh only one ounce, cost less than $1.

Even well-ventilated goggles will often cause

Misting (or fogging).

A glycerine-based anti-mist paste called Neva-Mist (made by the Tanosol Company of Berkeley, California) has a good local reputation and seems to work well. It comes in half-ounce tins, costs fifty cents.

A makeshift substitute is a wetted cake of soap. Apply a thin film to goggles or glasses and rub gently into invisibility. The effect lasts a surprisingly long time.

Your seeing—of all kinds—can be greatly amplified by

Binoculars.

I am always astonished that so few hikers carry them. It is not merely that a pair of binoculars can be extremely useful—that by leapfrogging your eyes out far ahead and disclosing the curve of a creek or the impassability of a rockwall they can save you hours of wasted effort. They are the key to many unexpected and therefore doubly delightful bonuses.

They lift you up so close to a planing hawk that you feel you could reach out and straighten a misplaced wing feather. They convert a small low-flying plane from an impersonal outline into a solid construction of panels and colors and markings, even of pilot and passengers with faces and lives of their own. They transform a deer on the far rim of a sunlit meadow from a motionless silhouette into a warm, breathing individual—alert, quivering, suspicious.

You can focus good binoculars down close, too—sometimes onto one of those unimportant, utterly fascinating little cameos that you are always liable to stumble on when you are in the right place and the right mood, with no stupidly important things to occupy your time and attention. You can even move over into the insect world. Last fall, on the slopes of a desert mountain, I sat idly watching with my naked eye as a clapper-rattle grasshopper made a series of noisy, stunted airborne journeys. In flight, with its wings beating furiously, it looked like a small and ungainly green butterfly. After one flight, the creature landed near the edge of a gravel road, eight feet in front of me, and rested. Squatting there beside a tiny tuft of grass, it was just a small, dark smudge, barely visible. I screwed my binocular focus adjustment fully out. The grasshopper crystalized into view: huge, green-armored, and apparently wingless, its front end tapering into the kind of chinless and no-brow head that to the human mind spells vacuity. Above the head towered a gigantic forest of grass blades. After a while the grasshopper moved. It advanced, bent-stilt leg slowly following bent-stilt leg, until it came to a small blade of grass on the edge of the forest. Dreamily, it reached out with one foreleg, pressed down on the blade, manipulated it, inserted the tip into its mouth, and clamped tight. Slowly it sidled around until its body and the grass blade formed a single straight line. And then, still unutterably dreamily, it proceeded to devour the grass blade as if it were a huge horizontal strand of spaghetti. It ate very slowly, moving forward from time to time with an almost imperceptible shuffle of its bent-stilt legs. All at once, when the blade of grass was about three-quarters gone, the grasshopper relinquished its grip and the truncated blade sprang back into place on the edge of the forest. The grasshopper moved jerkily away, skirting the enormous and overhanging green forest, traversing a tract of sun-beaten sand, then lumbering out over huge boulders of gravel. Suddenly, for no apparent reason, it launched once more into clapper-rattle flight and rocketed noisily and forever out of my vivid binocular world.

If you are going to carry binoculars as a matter of habit when you go walking you must be sure to get the right kind. They must be light. They must be tough enough to stand up to being banged around when hung on your packframe (see page 59). And they must not tire your eyes, even when used for long periods.

In choosing a pair of glasses, people tend to consider only magnification (indicated by the first of the two numbers stamped on the casing—the "6" in the average-power 6 × 30, for example). But powerful lenses magnify not only what you see but also the inevitable "jump" imparted by your hands. So, unless you can steady the glasses on something, magnification beyond a certain power—about 7 or 8 for most people—does not necessarily allow you to see more clearly. Generally speaking too, the greater the magnification, the narrower your field of view.

Again, if powerful glasses are not to darken what you see, they must have big end-lenses to let in adequate light. The second of the two numbers on the casing—the "30" in the 6 × 30—gives the diameter of the end-lenses in millimeters, and for daylight use there is no advantage, beyond a slight increase in field of view, to having that second figure more than five times as big as the first. Except at night, the average human eye cannot use the extra light that the big lenses let in. And big lenses mean cumbersome glasses that are too heavy for ordinary use. Once the first thrill of ownership has worn off they generally get left at home—ask anyone who has invested in a pair of those impressive looking naval-type binoculars. For average use, genuine 6 × 30's or 7 × 35's are probably best. My own 6 × 30's, with lightweight alloy casing, weigh just fourteen ounces. They are pre-World War II Zeiss, individual-focus type, and were used by the German army, from whom I appropriated them.

On some binoculars, a knurled wheel on the center post focuses both lenses, and any eye difference (except for very marked variation in long- or short-sightedness) is corrected with the right eyepiece. In other models, each eyepiece focuses independently. Both systems have advantages. For quick refocusing at short range, as in bird watching, you need center focus. But individual-focus glasses, more simply constructed, will stand up to rougher use.

A decade ago worthwhile binoculars were expensive luxuries. Then Japan began to produce good instruments at low prices. Today, fine-quality glasses need cost no more than $75. You can buy an adequate pair for less than $20.

Secondhand glasses are always a risk—unless you know exactly what you are doing. Even new ones should be bought only from reputable dealers who really understand their wares. New or old, make sure you test several pairs outside the store, in sunlight and shadow. Better still, insist on a cast-iron money-back guarantee in case you are not satisfied after, say, three days' trial. Misaligned or unsuitable binoculars can cause eyestrain, and they will probably, like too-heavy models, soon get left at home.

To get the most out of your binoculars, you must learn to use them automatically, almost without thought. First, set the barrels at the widest angle that gives you a circular field of view. Note the reading on the small center dial. Next, memorize the focus setting for *you* for long distance. Then, through practice, get used to looking through the glasses without strain. Some people tend to screw their eyes up just because they're looking through a strange instrument. Naturally, their eye muscles soon tire. If the binoculars' two barrels are properly aligned, anyone can look through them for protracted periods without strain. After all, seamen and bird watchers do, hours at a stretch. And there is never any reason for saying, "Oh, but my eyes are too old for binoculars." Given proper eyeglasses, age need make no difference.

If you wear eyeglasses you may have found that you see only a very restricted field of view when you look through binoculars. This is because normal eyepieces keep your eye too far back from the lens. Some manufacturers now supply special shallow eyepieces for eyeglass wearers. Others make adjustable cups that screw down out of the way. Some such device is a great advantage under snow-and-sunlight conditions, when you have to wear goggles all the time.

Some people experience difficulty at first in getting what they want into the field of view. One way is to draw your eyes back a few inches and align the center bar on the target; then, without moving the instrument, shift your eyes to the eyepieces. The target should be dead center in your field of view.

Once you are so used to your binoculars that you use them without a thought for technique, you will probably find yourself taking them along whenever you go walking. And they will always be opening up new possibilities. I still have a couple of unfulfilled wishes on my conscious waiting list. I want to examine a nearby rainbow's end. And one day I'd like to look from a respectful distance straight into the eye of an ill-humored rattlesnake.

Carrying binoculars

For many years now I have—except in rain and across very rough country—carried my binoculars slung by their leather or nylon harness over the projecting tubular top of one side of the packframe. (For bump pad to reduce noise, see page 59.) But my most recent packbag (see illustration, page 53) reaches almost to the top of each tube, and so little projection is left that the binoculars (and the camera, which hangs on the other side) are liable to bounce off at any marked jerk or forward lean. As a temporary measure I have knotted a length of nylon cord to the top securing ring bolt on each side of the packframe (for knots in nylon, see page 265). To the free ends of these cords I have tied belt clips (see page 267) that snap onto the carrying straps of binoculars and camera case. The cords are just long enough to let me bring the instruments forward in front of my eyes to the "use" position, but if either instrument jerks loose the cord normally prevents it from crashing down onto the ground. This device is clumsy, rather complicated, and not totally efficient; on very steep slopes or among big boulders, binoculars and camera can still fall far enough to be damaged. But until I come up with something better it will have to do.

It is less well known than it ought to be that binoculars can be used not only for seeing but as a worthwhile aid to

RECORDING YOUR MARVEL.

Nowadays, most of us tend to accept that we are failing in some kind of duty if we do not record our outdoor doings on film. Chalk up another victory to advertising. But, brainwashing aside, we all want on at least some occasions to carry back home a thin facsimile of the marvel we have discovered.

Movie cameras and their accessories are heavy, bulky, expensive, and a perishing nuisance, so most people record their backpacking highlights (not to mention the lowlights and midlights) by means of

Still photography.

The important thing is to choose equipment that is light, compact, light, simple, light, tough, and light.

The camera can be simple or fancy, as your pocket and inclinations dictate, but it must be small. For ten years I carried an Ansco Super Regent 35 mm. rangefinder model (one pound, ten ounces) that was tough as nails and had a gem of a lens. When tripod and camera blew over one gusty Grand Canyon afternoon and the faithful old Super Regent gave up the ghost, I replaced it, sadly, with a single-lens reflex Zeiss Contaflex that was a much finer instrument but weighed two pounds, seven ounces. Recently, taking advantage of a visit to Hong Kong, I bought a Japanese Pentax, with through-the-lens exposure meter, that weighs two pounds, six ounces, with case. (I'd previously carried a separate six-ounce exposure meter.)

The Pentax is a joy to use; once you've experienced the convenience and accuracy of a complete through-the-lens system, you're spoiled for other cameras. I don't yet know for sure how tough the Pentax is, but so far it has stood up well, and it has a good reputation.

A skylight (or UV) filter stays more or less permanently on the lens.

One advantage the Pentax holds over most cameras is the smallness and lightness of its lenses. My 150 mm. telephoto weighs only eleven ounces. For more on auxiliary lenses, see page 234.

For ways of carrying a camera, see page 231.

Ancillary photographic equipment should be as light and simple as your needs permit.

Tripod: At fourteen ounces, the lightest I can find. Folded: 8¾ inches long, 2½ inches wide. Telescopic legs extend to three feet, eight inches. The legs on such light models soon develop signs of palsy, but they'll work for several months, solid, before becoming seriously crippled.

Check that the feet of any tripod you buy have large rubber toes, not just little pimples of rubber that quickly wear out and leave you with metal tips that slip on any rocky surface.

My tripod travels, along with most of the photographic equipment, in the top left side pocket of my pack (see page 272). On packless side trips, its ball-and-socket screw fitting snaps into a belt clip (page 267).

You more or less have to carry a tripod if you walk alone: continuous shots of scenery without a human figure grow horribly monotonous. And it is quite amazing what you can learn to do in the way of running and positioning yourself in the ten seconds that elapse between pressing the self-timer and the shutter's action.

Camel-hair lens-cleaning brush: Screw-down metal-cased type that looks just like a lipstick and is always good for a laugh on that score (¾ ounce). Travels in pants ticket pocket. A pocket-clip type would be more convenient, but I've yet to find one that's strong or dirt-resistant enough.

Lens tissue: One virtually weightless packet, protected by the inevitable plastic bag, that goes into the flap pocket of the pack, where it won't get crushed.

Two close-up attachments (together, two ounces): Normally they live in a double plastic bag in a side pocket of the pack. If it seems likely they'll be needed, I transfer them either to the flap pocket of the pack or to a pants pocket.

Cable release: Useful both for "binophotography" (page 235) and for long-exposure shots in which the camera must be kept still. My eight-inch cable weighs ½ ounce. It travels—held in place by two or three rubber bands—tucked in beside the flange of the flash-fitting that I use for mating binoculars and camera (page 235; illustration, page 236).

Film: It pays, I think, to get used to one kind of film, so that you use it with very little thought. But it's good to experiment occasionally with new kinds, to make sure that your personal preferences, which are all that count, have not changed. These days, I rarely shoot black and white. In color, I used Anscochrome for many years but now prefer Kodachrome II. Kodachrome X is 1¼ stops faster and has its uses when speed becomes important in bad light or for high-power magnification; but this film gives you less latitude and definition. Agfachrome (one stop faster than Kodachrome II) is also good.

One truly objective criterion for judging film is its stability. Exposed color film is sensitive to high temperatures, especially when the humidity also runs high. And remember that even weak sunshine can soon raise the temperature in an outside pocket of your pack well above the possibly critical 75°F. mark. In anything but really cool weather take precautions. Replace exposed film in a can without delay and screw tight shut. Wrap all film cans in a plastic bag or in one of those insulated ice-cream bags that stores provide. Except in really cool weather, keep this bag deep in the center of the main section of your packbag, where the temperature changes less than anywhere else in the house. And get film processed as soon as possible.

You won't have trouble with heat damage to film very often; but if you do you won't forget it. One June, I spent a week in the bowels of Grand Canyon researching and shooting a photo story on assignment for a magazine. I used Kodachrome II, Kodachrome X (for close-up high-speed action shots), and Anscochrome (which perhaps penetrates shadow more effectively). Although humidity remained low all that week in Grand Canyon, the temperature exceeded 100°F. every day. High was 109°. These are shade readings and I was rarely photographing in the shade, so I took reasonable precautions. But not one frame of Anscochrome was usable: all had faded sadly and taken on a pale green overcast. The Kodachrome II and Kodachrome X came out perfectly.

Spare camera lenses are heavy, cumbersome, fragile, expensive, and dangerous. Their danger lies in temptation, for it seems to me that once you start carrying interchangable lenses it is fiendishly difficult to avoid becoming involved, far too often, in physical juggling and technical expertise.

For years I have shielded myself from such confusions and time-wasting by the simple device of not owning spare lenses, but when I bought my Pentax I was going game-viewing in Africa, and I knew it would be criminal to take only a standard lens. It remains to be seen whether I shall on future backpack trips be able to leave my one pound, three ounce telephoto lens behind—or whether I shall, conveniently, become a convert to multi-lensmanship.

Interchangeable lenses certainly feed the maggot inherent in all photography (see page 238), and I'm by no means convinced that, for the wilderness walker, they do not get in the way of the very best pictures. If you stick to a standard lens you will never have to stop and debate whether to fiddle about with a wide-angle or telephoto lens and will therefore always be ready to slip the camera off your packframe and capture, before the opportunity is lost, that superb but fleeting moment when a shaft of sunlight breaks through the storm clouds and arches a double rainbow across a somber mountain tarn; or ready to freeze for the future a pale but still evocative glimmer of the poetry that halts your breath when you look up from the rocky trail and see once again the always new and wonderful and calming and cooling magic of sunset on fiery desert hills.

On the other hand, there is no denying that a telephoto lens will record those vivid marvels—and especially the animal marvels—that you can see only through your binoculars.

The exit from this dilemma lies, logically enough, through your binoculars. It's called

Binophotography.

Now even the best pictures taken through binoculars are not quite as sharp as those taken with a telephoto lens. But if you do the job properly they can be effective close-ups—exact records of what you saw through the binoculars. My Grand Canyon trip was the first on which I tried binophotography in the field, and in the course of it I managed to capture presentable color bino shots of deer, wild horses, wild burros, beaver, and a bighorn sheep. The shots of wild burros and of the bighorn sheep were good enough to appear as black-and-whites in the book about that trip.

By far the most suitable camera for binophotography is a single-lens reflex: you look directly through camera and binocular lenses and see exactly what you photograph. But with practice, patience, determination, and luck it is possible to achieve tolerable results even with a rangefinder model. My Grand Canyon shots of wild horses and the bighorn sheep were taken with the old rangefinder-type Super Regent.

Ideally, the binoculars should be held rigidly in front of the camera, but the proper attachments are bulky and heavy, not to mention expensive. As a backpacking compromise I use the small and rather flimsy flash attachment shown on the next page (three ounces). Any good photographer would scoff at its inefficiency. But any backpacker would appreciate its lightness.

The binoculars are attached to the fitting by means of a clampocular—a small device, weighing a fraction of an ounce, that stays on the binoculars, folded down out of the way so that you almost never notice it.

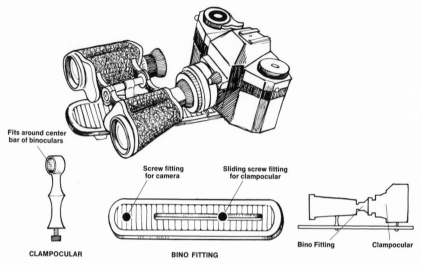

Fits around center
bar of binoculars

Screw fitting
for camera

Sliding screw fitting
for clampocular

Bino Fitting   Clampocular

CLAMPOCULAR   BINO FITTING

This is no place to go into the fine detail of binophotography with different kinds of cameras and binoculars.* But the fundamentals that you just have to grasp are focus and exposure.

With a single-lens reflex you can focus with either camera or binoculars, directly through the camera lens. In practice, I find it best to set the camera at minimum range, then focus with the binoculars. With viewfinder cameras, focusing is more complicated, but in general you set your camera at minimum range, then focus by eye through the free lens of the binoculars.

With a through-the-lens-exposure-meter camera, such as my new Pentax, exposure presents no problem: you simply open the aperture wide (i.e., set at the lowest f-stop number), then move the exposure indicator until the arrow stops in the right place. For other

* One source of information is *Binoculars and Scopes and Their Uses in Photography,* by Robert and Else Reichert—a paperback in The Modern Camera Guide Series, published in 1961 by the Chilton Book Company, Philadelphia ($1.95).

cameras (except subminiatures such as the Minox, and certain 8 mm. movie cameras) the formula for calculating exposure is:

$$\text{Exposure} = \frac{\text{Focal length of camera lens} \times \text{magnification of binoculars}}{\text{Diameter of objective aperture of binoculars.}}$$

Mercifully, this sum simplifies, with a standard 50 mm. focal length camera lens and 6 × 30 binoculars, into

$$\text{Exposure} = \frac{50 \times 6}{30} = 10.$$

In other words, you always shoot at f.10; and you change shutter speeds according to the light. (To remind myself of the constant f.10 setting, I scratched "10" on my clampocular with a pin.) But you do *not* set the camera aperture at f.10; you open it up as far as it will go (i.e., set it at the lowest possible f. number). Unless you do so you will subject your pictures to vignetting. That is, their edges will be blacked out, and the subject held within a circular black frame. (As a matter of fact, vignetting can sometimes be very effective, especially in animal photography, as it conveys the impression of looking through a telescope.)

Because of the long focal length of your combined instrument, the slightest vibration will blur your picture. Hand-holding rarely produces satisfactory results, though I've often got by with resting the rig on a rock and pressing the release manually. Where possible use a tripod and a cable release.

The most vital element in learning binophotography is practice. Before attempting to operate under the dirt, disorder and excitement of wilderness conditions I ran off several rolls on distant shots of my car (because it had easily focussed straight lines and could be moved into various lights), and I did not consider myself ready for action until I had successfully caught Willie Mays in the act of hitting a home run. (I like to say it was a home run. The way the ball is taking off, it could easily have been one. To be honest, it was just a long out.)

I have described in my other books some of the less obvious delights you can achieve with a camera.

Photography of any pretension at all eats up time at a rate that is rarely grasped by people who do no more than take snapshots of friends. And wilderness photography, even without interchangeable lenses, has its own special time-consuming idiosyncrasies. It is not just that exasperation and loving care have to fight their usual battles —first against each other, then as allies against form-balance, shadows, depth of focus, fluctuating light, parallax problems, and a wobbly tripod. You also have to cope with the irresistible beckonings of more and yet more brilliant wild flowers every time you move forward for a shot of an especially magnificent display; with the flimsy psyches of lizards; with the pathologically antisocial attitude of bighorn sheep; and with a fifty-pound pack that has to come off for almost every shot and then, by God, has to go back on again.

Now this kind of in-fighting has its merits. Up to a point it can be instructive, diverting, and satisfying. Up to a point.

Not until my Grand Canyon walk did I grasp, by sheer accident, that one of the great bonuses walking has to offer is

The delight of non-photography.

The accident that opened my eyes was the demise of that faithful old Super Regent camera.

At first, when I discovered that its shutter refused to function, I simmered with frustration. I was carrying only the one camera, and I knew that it would be at least a week before I could get word out that I urgently needed a replacement—a week in which I would walk through a spectacular, rarely visited landscape that I would almost certainly never visit again. It promised to be a bitter week. But within an hour I discovered that I had escaped from something I never quite knew existed: the tyranny of film. Photography, I suddenly understood, is not really compatible with contemplation. Its details are too insistent. They are always buzzing around your mind, clouding the fine focus of appreciation. You rarely realize this painful fact at the time, and you cannot do much about it even if you do. But that day in Grand Canyon, after the camera had broken, I found myself savoring in a new way everything around me. Instead of stopping briefly to photograph and forget, I stood and stared, fixing truer images on the emulsion of memory. And the week, set free, became a carnival.

I learned my lesson. Now, if I want a week of wilderness walking to be, above all, carefree and therapeutic, I often leave my camera at home—or at least restrict the quantity of film I carry. I find that, by and large, it works. Liberated, I have more time to stand and stare.

To nurture the holiday spirit on a minor trip I sometimes apply similar self-denial to another, much more necessary, activity:

ROUTE-FINDING.

I go without

Maps.

Or at least I take only rudimentary ones (see page 241). In part, this stratagem works; it injects into each day a steady stream of that titillating element, the unexpected. But sometimes I find that traveling without a map becomes so inefficient that it diminishes my freedom rather than amplifying it. For maps are indispensable to efficient walking—when it becomes important that you get to the right place at more or less the right time, and also as an aid in deciding what places you most want to see.

But maps are not merely for route-finding. They can radically influence many facets of your outdoor life. They act as aids not only to keeping going and to accurate estimating (see page 52), but in water logistics, foot comfort, warmth, and choice of campsites. Without a map to tell you where to find the next water—even though not always with certainty—you are liable to labor along under a quite unnecessary canteen load, or to walk for long, half-lived hours with your awareness clogged by the gray scum of thirst. If your feet are beginning to get sore you may be able to ward off real trouble by avoiding what the map shows is one of those steady, downhill, blister-sure routes. On a day lacerated by icy winds you can with luck and a map select trails that slink along in comparative coziness under the lee of a steep ridge. And with practice you can choose good campsites, hours or even days ahead—and in doing so may even collect one of walking's unexpected and delightful little bonuses (see page 168).

In the United States, the only maps that really convey much detailed information of the kind useful to a walker are the U.S. Geological Survey topographical series. These maps come in various sizes and scales, though most new ones are either fifteen-minute quadrangles (covering fifteen minutes of both latitude and longitude; scale, 1:62,500, or roughly one inch to one mile; contour interval usually eighty feet) or 7½-minute quadrangles (scale: 1:24,000; contour interval usually forty feet). Both kinds of "quad" are so detailed that you sometimes feel they would be adequate to guide you on a prowl around on hands and knees.

A selection of local quads is often available at retail outdoor equipment stores and in certain book stores. The price is likely to be around sixty cents. Direct from any U.S. Geological Survey map office, the quads are fifty cents each (20 per cent discount for orders $20 and over; 40 per cent discount for orders $100 and over).

The central distribution agency for maps covering areas east of the Mississippi River is: Distribution Section, USGS, Washington, D.C. 20242. For maps west of the Mississippi: Distribution Section, USGS, Federal Center, Denver, Colorado 80225. For Alaska: USGS, 520 Illinois Street, Fairbanks, Alaska.

There are subsidiary map distribution offices in Dallas, Texas; Salt Lake City, Utah; Spokane, Washington; Menlo Park and San Francisco, California; and Anchorage, Juneau, and Palmer, Alaska.

Any map office or distribution center will supply you, free, with an index map of your state or area. This map enables you to find the name of the quad or quads that cover the slice of country you are interested in. It also lists places within the state from which you can buy USGS topo maps.

In most big cities you can find out from the local USGS office (check in phone book) where to buy topo maps. Even if the office does not sell them itself, the staff will know the local retail outlets.

The Canadian equivalent of the USGS maps is the National Topographical Series, scale 1:63,360 (one inch to one mile). For these maps, and for information about their distribution, write: Map Distribution Office, Department of Mines and Technical Surveys, 615 Booth Street, Ottawa, Ontario, Canada.

U.S. Forest Service maps generally show roads, rivers and trails but little else. It's often worth picking one up from a ranger station to check that the details shown on a USGS topo map are up to date. And I sometimes use one on a minor trip when I want to know roughly where I'm going but also want to conserve that titillating element of the unexpected.

Another way to achieve that end is to take along only an ordinary road map of the kind you can pick up at any gas station. Between roads, these maps are mostly blank space. At the most, they have some rather speculative hachuring—a light shading that indicates the slope and direction of hill and valley. With such a map you can easily set yourself the vague sort of target that seems necessary to almost any kind of walk. (As someone has said, "Every journey must have a soul.") You just find a big blank space that intrigues you, drive to the edge of it, park the car, and walk in and find out what's there. Such an expedition can take an hour, an afternoon, a weekend, or a week. With a little experience, local knowledge, and luck, you may be able to burst clear not only of roads but of the last vestiges of any kind of a trail.*

Sometimes, lately, I've carried the map I was currently using in a light vinyl mapcase (1 ounce, 45 cents) that travels in my "yoke

---

* Do not underestimate the importance of such a bursting free. There is a cardinal rule of travel, all too often overlooked, that I call *The Law of Inverse Appreciation.*

It states: "The less there is between you and the environment, the more you appreciate that environment."

Every walker knows, even if he has not thought very much about it, the law's most obvious application: the bigger and more efficient your means of transportation, the further you become divorced from the reality through which you are traveling. A man learns a thousand times more about the sea from the *Kon Tiki* than from the *Queen Mary;* euphorically more about space at the end of a cord than from inside a capsule. On land, you remain in closer touch with office" (page 60) and not only protects the map from moisture and dirt and general wear and tear, but also seems to collect from time to time a pencil, a book of matches, camera lens tissue, and even (in rain) my notebook.

I've recently seen an intriguing catalogue item that looks as though it ought to work: transparent plastic sheeting, with adhesive on one side, that "will protect maps against damage from water or wear." I shall certainly try it. (With removable backing: 4 ounces per yard, 18 inches wide, 55 cents a yard.)

But mostly I just fold the map that I am using rather loosely and stuff it into my shirt pocket or the "yoke office." The practice often strikes me as dangerously slapdash, but the spring of the loosely folded map seems to hold it in place. I can remember only one occasion on which I lost a map, and that was when I needed just one small corner of a large map and had cut it down to postcard size so

---

the countryside in a slow-moving old open touring car than in a modern, air-conditioned, tinted-glass-window, eighty-miles-an-hour-and-never-notice-it behemoth. And you come in closer touch on a horse than in any car; in closer touch on foot than on any horse.

But the law has a second and less obvious application: your appreciation varies not only according to what you travel *in* but also according to what you travel *over*. Drive along a freeway in any kind of car and you are in almost zero contact with the country beyond the concrete. Turn off onto a minor highway and you move a notch closer. A narrow country road is better still. And when you bump slowly along a jeep trail you begin at last to sense those vital details that turn mere landscape into living countryside.

It is less obvious that these same discrepancies persist when you are traveling on foot. Any blacktop road holds the scrollwork of the country at arm's length: the road itself keeps stalking along on stilts or grubbing about in a trough, and your feet tread on harsh and sterile pavement. Turn off onto a dusty jeep trail and the detail moves closer. A foot trail is better still. But you do not really break free until you step off the trail and walk through waving grass or woodland undergrowth or across rock or smooth sand or (most beautiful and perfect of all) over virgin snow. Now you can read all the details, down to the finest print. Drifting snow crystals have barely begun to blur the four-footed signature of the marten that padded past this lodgepole pine. Or a long-legged lizard scurries for cover, kicking up little spurts of sand as it corners around a bush. Or wet, glistening granite supports an intricate mosaic of purple lichen. Or you stand in long, pale grass and watch the wave patterns of the wind until, quite suddenly, you feel seasick. And always, in snow or sand or rock or seascape grass, there is, as far as you can see in any direction, no sign of man.

That, I believe, is being in touch with the world.

that there was none of the usual fold-pressure to hold it in my pocket.

I tend to cut off all maps both the margins and also any areas that I know for sure I will not need, even for locating an escape route in an emergency. The actual weight saving may not amount to much, but with a really heavy load I find quite insupportable the knowledge that I'm carrying even one unnecessary dram.

Maps can furnish many bonuses that have nothing to do with efficiency. All you need to contribute is competence in using them and a certain quirky curiosity. At least, I think that is all I contribute, and I know I collect the bonuses. Map reading is one of the few arts I have been fairly competent at ever since I was a child—no doubt because I was fascinated from the very start by wriggling blue rivers and amoeboid blue lakes and rhombic green woods and, above all, by the harmony and mystery of patterned red contour lines. These fascinations have never withered. I would not like to say for sure that I ever walked twenty miles simply because I wanted to see the three-dimensional reality represented on my map by a dragon's-head peninsula or a perfect horseshoe river bend or an improbably vermiform labyrinth of contours. It is certainly many years since I did such a thing openly. For now that I am a man I have carefully put away such childish motives. In self-defense, I dig up more momentous reasons.

I am aware that, for many people, a map holds neither meaning nor mystery. I can only hope, compassionately, that the rest of their existence is not equally poverty-stricken.

Map measurer

A map measurer is a cunning little instrument with a tiny wheel that can follow any route, no matter how snaky, and which registers on its circular dial with many scales the mileage represented by the distance the wheel has rolled. Remember, though, that—except along absolutely straight roads or trails (come to think of it, who ever heard of an absolutely straight trail?)—your feet always slog a great deal further than the wheel indicates (see page 23). Still, a measurer can be a useful guide. I often use mine for planning, though I have never carried it in the pack. (1 ounce; $2.95.)

Guide books

I'm no devotee of guide books—to say the least of it—but they're undeniably useful if your time and opportunities for hiking are limited. I know none of the guide books to the eastern United States, but any good outdoor equipment store should stock a full local range. Several firms listed in Appendix II offer a good selection in their catalogues (see, especially, Camp and Trail Outfitters, New York). For the West, see western catalogues. The newly revised *Starr's Guide to the John Muir Trail and the High Sierra Region* (Sierra Club, 1934, 7 ounces; $2) has long been the standard for the Sierra Nevada. *Sierra North* and *Sierra South* by Karl Schwenke and Thomas Winnett (Wilderness Press, 1967 and 1968, 7 ounces and $2.95 each) are a new and highly successful concept. Each gives meticulous information for one hundred varied backpack trips.

I never walk far without

A compass.

Yet I can remember using mine only once for its primary emergency task: showing me which way to go when I'm unable to decide on or maintain direction by any other means. On that occasion I woke up one morning in broken hill country to find that a dense fog had settled down overnight, cutting visibility to about fifteen feet. I needed to get back to the car that day, I had no map, and there was no general slope to the ground to show me which way to go—only a confusion of huge rocky outcrops. And I could detect nothing that might help me hold whichever line I chose to take—not the slightest breeze, and no hint through the gray fog of where the sun lay. Fortunately I knew that only a couple of miles to the north there was a road running roughly east and west. So after breakfast I struck due north by the compass. Every hundred yards or so I had to change direction as another huge black outcrop of rock loomed up out of the fog. I doubt if I could have held any kind of course without the compass. But in little more than an hour I stepped onto the road.

Come to think of it, I suppose I use the compass quite rarely, but I would feel dangerously naked without it.

The one purpose I use it for at all often is siting a nightcamp so that it will catch—or avoid—the earliest sun (see page 167). It also serves, once in a while, to check my map orientation if I have not been following the detail closely enough. And I once made a pace-and-compass march—a surprisingly accurate method of hitting a target—out across the featureless salt flats of Death Valley to the genuinely lowest point in the Western Hemisphere.

My compass is an ex-U.S. Marine Corps model with a fold-over alloy cover built to withstand brutal treatment. It does. The instrument is not liquid-filled and therefore cannot develop that common and infuriating compass scourge, bubble trouble. But its dial stops oscillating within three seconds. It is fitted with a declination off-setting device. Weight: 4½ ounces. I have no idea how much it costs (it was given me) but catalogue equivalents seem to run about $15.

The catalogues often display a wide range of compasses, fancy and unfancy, from ½ ounce to five ounces, from ninety-eight cents to $15. Get one that's tough: it may lie around in your pack for months or even years, but it must be functioning perfectly when the testing time comes. If possible, get one that's well shielded from interference. (Check in the store to see if the needle swings when you pass near a large hunk of metal.) And get one that is designed to perform the fanciest function you want to use it for.

For these fancy uses, consult one of the little paperback how-to books on the subject. I am told that a good one is the 144-page handbook *Be Expert with Map and Compass,* by Bjorn Kjellstrom, sold by the compass makers Sibra Inc., 702 Ridgeway St., La Porte, Indiana ($2.95).

For the basic emergency use of holding a given line, simply see where the needle or north arrow points, then walk in the direction you have decided is the one to take. Base your decision about direction on the map, knowledge of the country, intuition, guesswork, or desperation, in that order of preference; but stick with it. In dense fog you must keep checking the compass, and hold dead on line. In good visibility, a quicker and much more accurate method is to pick out a distant and distinctive point that lies on the required line, put your compass away, and head for the distant point. Provided there is no danger of your losing track of the point, you can detour as widely and as often as you like.

I suppose I should have a lot more to say about route-finding. But, beyond map reading, it is mostly common sense, and I am not very conscious of any particular techniques. Once or twice I have been aware that I was not where I thought I was because the sun hung in the wrong place or the wind blew from the wrong direction, so I suppose I must take some vague cognizance of such direction checks. Otherwise, route-finding is largely a matter of obeying that sturdy old adage "Never lose elevation unnecessarily," and of getting to know the idiosyncrasies of the country you are in—the pattern its ridges tend to follow, or the way its southern slopes tend to be covered with impassable scrub, or the tendency of its northern slopes to drop away in unclimbable cliffs.

In time, you come to note without much thought the landmarks and the general lie of the land that will enable you to backtrack, should that become necessary, but I occasionally stop at points that may cause confusion—such as a junction of several valleys, or a watershed with diverging drainage systems—and look back in order to memorize the way I have come.

In certain kinds of country, the question of scale can become critical to route-finding. Among the repetitive rock patterns of Grand Canyon I at first found that it was often impossible to tell from a distance, even through binoculars, whether a sheer rockface was an inconsequential three or an unclimbable thirty feet high. But eventually I realized that the agaves or century plants that grew almost everywhere were a consistent three or four feet high, and from then on I used them as gauges.

Local knowledge can be an invaluable aid to route-finding, or at least to finding the most convenient route. But locals are not always crystal-pure sources of information, and if you are going to travel in strange country you must command a certain proficiency in the art of sifting fact from embroidery. The only reliable informant is the man who both knows what he is talking about and is not afraid to admit he doesn't know everything. You don't meet such men every day. The surest way of finding out if you have just met one is to ask questions to which you know the answers.

As I approached Death Valley on my summer-long California walk I passed through Baker, a populated road junction of the gasoline age. While I was there, one self-satisfied little man fixed me with beady eyes. "What's that?" he said. "Going through Death Valley? Huh, your feet must be stronger than your head. It'll be a hundred and ten up there by now. And climbing every day. I spent years right in the Valley, all summer too, so I know. I'm a real Desert Rat, I can tell you, a real Desert Rat."

"Oh, what sort of temperatures do they get on the floor of the Valley?" I asked—and waited.

I knew the Death Valley temperature position accurately. All-time high is a questionable 134°F., set in July 1913, that for many years held the world record. Later and more dependable readings have never risen above 127°. Most years, the limit is 124° or 125°.

The Baker Rat pounced on my bait. "Summer temperatures in the Valley?" he squeaked. "Well, I can't quote exact figures, but it gets hot, believe me. Here in Baker we have summer highs of a hundred and twenty-five or thirty. And sometimes"—he turned to his wife—". . . sometimes we run to a hundred thirty-five, don't we?"

"Oh, not very often, dear."

"No, not too often. But it happens. And you can add a good twenty degrees for the Valley. So you'd best get ready to sweat a bit, my lad."

I did not bother to ask the Baker Rat any of the other questions I had on my mind.*

A friend of mine who is a connoisseur of human foibles was

* If this bit of dialogue sounds familiar, and it worries you, see *The Thousand-Mile Summer*, p. 77.

quite delighted when I reported this conversation. "Now there's a beautiful example of the dedicated weather exaggerater at work," he said. "The real artist often uses that ploy—provoking something that seems close to dissent from one of his in-group so as to thicken the background."

It is not always so easy to winnow worthless information. Often, you have to fall back on mere confirmation of details from several sources. But this technique can backfire. Several years ago I was wandering in leisurely fashion across the Coast Range in central California, aiming broadly for the Pacific. One afternoon I emerged from forest into ranchland and almost at once met the rancher—a pleasant-faced man wearing a ten-gallon hat and a red shirt and driving a green pickup truck. We chatted cordially for some time, discussing how far it was down to the ocean, and what the best routes were. An hour later, far down the hill, I came to a cattle chute. A tall, baldheaded man wearing blue overalls was inoculating a herd of heifers. When he had finished he turned and walked toward me. Partly as an opening pleasantry, partly to confirm the figures and routes that the rancher in the green pickup had given me, I said, "Say, can you tell me how far it is down to the sea?" The man stopped and looked at me closely. Then, to my astonishment, he turned on his heel and walked back toward the chute. After a while I wandered away, wondering, through a belt of trees. Suddenly, beyond a small outbuilding, I almost walked into the green pickup. On its seat sat a familiar-looking ten-gallon hat.

Even now, six or seven years later, I still feel embarrassed whenever I remember that rancher.

KEEPING YOURSELF CLEAN
AND COMFORTABLE

Toilet gear

A highly personal department that every individual will stock differently, and which he will vary to meet varying conditions.

My list expands and contracts within rather wide limits, mostly in response to how crippling the load looks like being, but also according to whether I expect to touch civilization at all. The full selection includes:

Soap: A half or quarter bar, sometimes in a small plastic bag, sometimes in a light polyethylene container with built-in nailbrush (2 ounces; 79 cents)

Washcloth (or, sometimes, half a washcloth): Often doubles as towel.

Small towel: Occasionally taken when much swimming or washing expected and either the weather looks like being too cool or the privacy too faulty to let the sun do the drying.

Toothbrush: Often taken, sometimes used. I have a British one with a detachable brush that fits inside its own handle. (½ ounce. Cost: no idea.)

Toothpowder: Salt.

Deodorant, comb, even a brush: Taken when the social standards of a trip demand it.

Toilet roll: A roll, mark you, not one of those interleaved packs that in a high wind explode like bombs. For use, see, at some length, pages 282–4. I understand that some people, when they know that washing is going to be a problem, take along a few pads of "Tucks" —a medication-impregnated toilet paper.

Scissors: Kept protected in moleskin package, in "office" (page 256).

Items classifiable as "toilet gear" but discussed elsewhere:

Mirror: For signaling rather than primping (see page 289). If your hand falls on the mirror a few washless days out and, by reflex action, you look into it, you may get quite a shock. My mirror goes into the moleskin package, between the pads, where it protects the curved points of the scissors.

Foot powder and rubbing alcohol: See page 43.

Razors: Some people carry these barbarous instruments, but it is fifteen years now since I owned one.

Washing yourself is your business—except when it comes to dirtying the water. For factors to consider—and a solution in inhabited country—see Care of Clothing, page 218.

Occasionally you get quite sensuously delightful washing surprises. I particularly like to remember finding, a couple of hundred feet below the peak of Mount Shasta, at 14,000 feet, a bubbling hot spring. The sulphurous water smelled vile. But it was very hot. And, although the sun was already low, the air felt astonishingly warm for that elevation. So I filled both my cooking pots with snow and immersed them in the spring, which bubbles out of the ground over quite a large area. I waited until the snow had become hot water. Then I stripped off and poured both potfuls over my head. It was a lusciously hedonistic rite.

I learned later that John Muir, the Scot who around the turn of the century did so much for the conservation of wild California, was apparently saved by this spring when caught up there in a blizzard. By lying on the hot earth and moving his body from time to time, Muir was able to keep himself comfortably warm. Well, safely warm, anyway.

There are several additional items, not strictly speaking toilet gear, that you'll often need to keep yourself comfortable:

Fly dope: With luck you won't often have to use it, but once you have suffered helplessly from mosquitoes or their like you'll never travel without it. New and better formulas appear regularly. The best I know at present is the "Insect Repellent" accurately described by the makers, Cutter Laboratories, as "outlandishly expensive . . . incredibly effective and economic in use." A one-ounce plastic bottle costs $1.49.

Though I've never experienced trouble, I understand that prolonged use of insect repellent can irritate the skin. In such cases, if the insects become unbearable, it may be necessary to wear long pants, gloves, and a face-net.

Suntan lotion: Indispensable for those who sunburn easily, recommended for those who rather think they don't.

At high elevations, especially in windy weather, everyone needs some kind of skin protection, and it's as well to remember that many popular brands are ineffective up high. I find Glacier Cream good (1-ounce tube, 80 cents). Another good lotion is Sundare, made by the Texas Pharmaceutical Company. A lot of research work seems to have been done recently in the field of protection against ultra-violet rays, and several new and expensive creams are coming on the market. This is a department in which, even more than usual, you should try to ignore cost.

Lip salve: Some people need it in cold and windy or hot and dry weather. Just about everyone needs it for prolonged living above about 12,000 feet. Again, well known brands are often ineffective under bad conditions. A good salve is A-Fil, also made by Texas Pharmaceutical (98 cents a stick).

Hand lotion: For places the water is heavily alkaline. On the first half of the Grand Canyon trip my hands began to get raw from frequent use of Colorado water, and I was thankful to be able to get a tube of lotion at the halfway mark. Ignore jibes about effeminacy. I once heard a modern-day pioneer who ranched beside an almost untouched stretch of the Colorado River, and was about as masculine a man as you'll find anywhere, say to his wife as he pulled off his boots at the end of a long day, "Better throw over the hand lotion, honey. Had my arms in that damned river half the afternoon."

MEETING EMERGENCIES

First-aid kit

Contents depend on length of trip, terrain, and temperament. My somewhat variable list includes:

1 roll one-inch adhesive tape (outer cover discarded, to save weight).
1 roll three-inch gauze (or gauze compresses).
A dozen Band-aids.
½-ounce tube Bacitracin antibiotic ointment.
6 headache tablets. (You may need more at high elevations.)
2 segments chocolate laxatives. (Sometimes needed at the beginning of a trip, to combat radically altered routine and diet.)
Half a dozen needles (for removing thorns, breaking blisters, etc.). Kept with matches in waterproof matchsafe. (See also pages 103 and 261.)
Scissors: See page 249.

My first-aid kit travels in doubled plastic bags, averages around four or five ounces.

Mistrusting my judgment, I have just asked an Everest-climbing doctor his opinion on the adequacy of this list. To my surprise and relief he suggested only two additions.

The first was a safe but effective pain killer. He cited a recent occasion on which, coming down off a mountain, he twisted a knee rather badly. Without treatment he would have been able to keep going very slowly, if at all. But a shot of morphine killed almost all the pain, and he was able to get out to civilization without difficulty. Morphine may be a shade tricky for inexperienced laymen to use, but codeine tablets are almost as good. A dozen would be a reasonable stock. In getting a prescription, make sure that your doctor puts you wise to the pitfalls of usage.

The second suggested addition to my list was a dozen broad-spectrum antibiotic tablets—in case of general infection from an injury, or from some illness such as pneumonia. High-potency penicillin or Achromycin would be suitable. Again, check for pitfalls in usage when you get a prescription. And check for allergy.

First-aid instructions

Unless you're a competent first-aid man, you should probably carry some succinct lightweight instructions—the sort of thing you'll not look at for years on end, but might save your life in an emergency when you find you simply don't know what is the right thing to do. Any Red Cross chapter office (in the United States, see under American National Red Cross in phone book) will be pleased to supply you, free, with a useful advice sheet, "First Aid at a Glance." It is printed on both sides, weighs almost nothing, and gives some clear, basic information. A compact little 1¼-ounce, 35-page booklet called "Mountaineering Medicine," by Dr. Fred T. Darvill, Jr., an experienced outdoorsman, can be bought for $1 from Skagit Mountain Rescue Unit, Inc., P.O. Box 2, Mount Vernon, Washington 98273 (all profits are used to promote the rescue activities of the unit) or from some outdoor equipment suppliers. This booklet gives practical advice on everything from "Altitude sickness" through "Fish hooks, removal of" to "Ticks."

Snakebite kit

See page 303.

Signaling mirror

I now carry (with my moleskins; see page 249) an ordinary 3-by-3¾-inch metal mirror, the kind you can pick up for thirty cents in any variety store (1 ounce). In an emergency it could attract the attention of people on the ground or in the air by reflecting sunlight. For use in rescues or airdrops, see page 289.

Smoke bomb or flare

Also for airdrops. See page 291, footnote.

Whistle

"A must for safety in the mountains," say some catalogues. And maybe they're right. I must get one. (½ ounce, 30 cents).

Flint stick

For emergency fire-lighting. (See page 104.)

Emergency fishing tackle

The only living off the land that I normally do is fishing, and in almost any country I carry a tiny survival kit that weighs about ¼ ounce and contains:

> 1 spool (60 feet) six-pound nylon.
> Half dozen hooks, assorted sizes.
> Half dozen lead shot.
> Half dozen trout flies.

The whole kit wraps into a small, tough, polyethylene dried-fruit bag.

Such a kit could help keep you alive, and it can often augment and vary a dehydrated diet.

In Grand Canyon I took along a 35 mm. film can of salmon eggs. They worked well. Using my staff as rod, I caught many small catfish and one carp of about 1½ pounds. Small fish of any kind demand considerable cooking effort for rather little sustenance, but bigger fish are rewarding. Carp need only be laid on hot embers, as their thick skins act as aluminum foil. Come to think of it, a little aluminum foil might just be worth taking along for less obliging species.

In trout country, the best rod is a switch cut from the riverbank.

For more elaborate fishing tackle, see "Enjoying Extra-Perambulatory Activities" (page 262).

Nylon rope

In really rough country, when there are two or more of you, a rope is often worth carrying as a safety measure. Alone, you'll rarely find much use for it, unless you expect to rappel down a cliff (that is, to pass the rope around your body in such a way that you can lower yourself at any desired speed by controlling with one hand the friction the rope creates on your body as you descend). You need at least two people for a belay (that is, for tying yourself to rock or tree so that should your partner fall you can hold him with the rope)—or for a rescue.

The only time I have carried a rope was in Grand Canyon. I knew that for weeks on end I would be walking two or three thousand feet above the river, with my way down to it barred by a series of sheer cliffs. But there were places where most of the cliffs had eroded nearly through, and it seemed to me that in dire emergency a rope might just allow me to rappel down an otherwise impassable barrier to the lifesaving water of the river. On short rappels I might be able to retrieve the rope for re-use by doubling it and pulling it down after me through some form of loop. (Rather than carry the orthodox carabiner—or metal spring loop—for this unlikely eventuality, I decided to rely on a multiple loop of nylon cord, or perhaps a convenient tree. On long rappels I would have to use the rope single and leave it behind.) After much balancing of usefulness against weight,

I took a 100-foot length of ¼-inch laid nylon rope, about 1900 pounds test (1 pound, 14 ounces; $6).

No dire water emergency arose. But once, reconnoitering a tricky route, I found a rather steep ten-foot rockface that I knew I could get down but did not feel sure I could reclimb should the way ahead prove impassable. So I fastened the rope to a convenient rock pillar and handlined down. The route proved impassable all right, and I duly and thankfully handlined back up again.

I also used the rope several times to lower the pack down pitches I could manage quite confidently unladen but didn't fancy tackling with a pack. Nylon cord (see page 264) will do this job, but rope is easier on the hands and waist or shoulders, which should be used for braking. Rope also gives you a better chance of pulling a pack up—though once you have tried this game with a sixty-pound pack and seen how adept the frame ends are at grabbing the rock, you will go to some lengths to avoid a replay.

IMPROVING THE MIND

Reading matter

For me, the book should be light in weight and not too leaden in content. If your natural-history knowledge is as sketchy as mine, one of those little identification books on trees or reptiles or mammals or such would seem a good choice—though I have now accepted that I am simply not a namer of things, and have given up the struggle. Generally, I find myself taking books that are relevant to some aspect of my journey but which do not deal too closely with the detail around me. On the California walk I browsed slowly through a five-book paperback Mentor series on philosophy (the books were mailed ahead singly to post offices along the route). In Grand Canyon I extracted many seminal thoughts from a paperback that dealt discursively rather than didactically with present geologic knowledge (*The Crust of the Earth,* edited by Samuel Rapport and Helen Wright, Signet Science Library, 1955—5 ounces, 60 cents). Poetry is good too: wilderness can open new windows into old lines.

Notebook

If you intend to take notes of some sort on a trip but have not yet tried it, I sound a warning: time is the trouble (see table, page 24). Notewriting always seems to be among the activities that get consistently crowded out. I used to imagine that this was a personal inefficiency, but I understand that it's an occupational hazard among geologists, naturalists, and others committed to wilderness note-taking. I offer no solution other than determination. Don't kid yourself, as I used to, that you will just jot down a word or two for each thought, more or less as you go, and will spend the evening—or the long midday halt—expanding it. The expansion just doesn't happen. At least, not regularly. Not if you're having to push at all hard, physically. The best I've been able to do is to jot down as much as I can in my notebook *at the time* and then attack the fuller and more discursive stuff as opportunity offers. Mostly, that means on rest days.

I generally use a plastic-cover, spiral-back, loose-leaf notebook that fits conveniently into shirt pocket or "yoke office" (see page 60). One nineteen-cent book lasts at least a week. The spirals should be at the top rather than the side, so that they do not catch in pocket or office.

Pens and pencils

Ballpoint pens, with refills. Pencils with pocket clips. Don't sharpen pencils too fine, they'll only break. And sharp points can savage you.

Onion-skin paper

I take onion-skin paper for fuller, more discursive notes—and back them with a rectangle of stiff cardboard, to which I secure the paper, top and bottom, with rubber bands.

The office

My office is a specially made 12 by 16-inch envelope of coated nylon fabric, zippered at the top (four ounces). Designed primarily for the cardboard-backed onion-skin paper (see above), it has become the home of many items that need to be kept flat or otherwise protected: spare pens and pencils, paperback book, stove-nozzle cleaner (taped to cardboard), Rip-stop patching material, moleskins with mirror and scissors, spare flashlight batteries, miniature can opener, rubber bands, maps not in use, car key, spare sunglasses, and survival fishing tackle.

But I imagine that few backpackers feel the need of a special office.

FIGURING

It would seem reasonable to suppose that you can escape from the man-world more easily if you walk out into wilderness without a

Watch.

But the stratagem may backfire. Without a watch (as can happen if you go without maps), you may find yourself operating so inefficiently that ways and means begin to obscure the things that matter. It is not simply a question of knowing the time of day. (Provided the sun shines, you can gauge that kind of time accurately enough—though in dank or snow-clogged weather or in country so precipitous that the sun sets soon after noon even that may prove a problem.) But you have lost the sharp instrument that keeps prodding you forward. That is what I find, anyway, because I have fallen into the useful habit of marking on my map (see page 52) the time I stop for each halt—or at least of noting it mentally. Without a watch, too, I cannot work out times and distances for the way ahead. And that, for me, means a loss rather than a gain in freedom. Some people may find the precise opposite. But the fact remains that after one week-long trip without a watch I have gone back to wearing one.

If you decide to take a watch it is probably a good thing if it bears the words "waterproof and shock-resistant" or some other encouraging legend. And check before you go on a trip that the crystal, or glass, is in first-class condition. Also that the strap (assuming you wear a wrist watch) is not only in good repair but of a suitable kind. Plastic is useless: under wilderness conditions, even more

quickly than at home, sunlight and cold and wear will cause dangerous cracks. Leather is better, though sweat may rot the stitching.
For some reason I do not like metal straps: I have an idea, possibly
erroneous, that they can get uncomfortably hot and cold; and the
links certainly catch the hairs on my wrist. Woven nylon straps, I
find, are ideal: they do not rot; it takes years for them to show any
appreciable wear; and, although they tend to reek of sweat, they can
be easily washed and dried. The only safe strap, of any material, is
the one-piece kind that passes under your watch.

No matter how much faith you choose to put in the word
"waterproof," I think it is always worth taking precautions when you
have to swim across a river, or feel that you may fall in—such as
when you wade deep or venture out on a narrow log. A safe waterproofing method, I'm told, is to tie your watch into a condom. For
swimming across a river with a pack, my watch goes into the safe
sanctum sanctorum (see page 276).

A cruder kind of time-figuring is almost always essential:

Keeping check on the days.

Even if you have no vital commitments to meet in the outside
world, you should certainly have given somebody a time and a date
beyond which it can be assumed that, if you have not shown up, you
are in trouble (see page 25). Or you may have arranged an airdrop,
or a meeting with packers. In any of these cases, a mistake in the
day can cost you dearly.

I always prepare a table on a page near the end of my notebook
(not the last page, because it may pull out). I block out the days and
leave room for writing in the name, actual or fancied, of the place
at which I camp each night. This detail, I find, is the one that my
mind distinguishes most clearly in identifying the days. Without my
calendar table I would often—perhaps most often—not know what
day it was. The table also makes it much easier to figure out, days
ahead, whether I really need to hurry or can afford to amble luxuriously along.

Pedometer

Theoretically this instrument is a valuable item (two ounces; $6.95). But although I own one, I've never got past the finicky job of trying to calibrate it to my normal stride. Perhaps that's because I question how useful such calibration would be over any but smooth, level ground—and because I regard wilderness mileage figures as being, in most cases, singularly meaningless (see page 23).

Thermometer

It is five years now since I began taking a thermometer on walks, and I still have no reasoned explanation of why it makes such a beguiling toy. I have to admit, I suppose, that it is primarily a toy. It has taught me any number of interesting facts: the remarkably tenuous relationship that exists between air temperature and what the human body feels (see page 183); the astonishingly hot surfaces your boots often have to walk on and can sometimes avoid (see page 45); and the actual temperature of a river I had to swim in (the body is a miserable judge here too, and the temperature can be critical if you have to swim far [see page 281]). But the sort of information my thermometer has given me has more often been interesting than practical.

A couple of years ago, in early February, I took a three-day hike along Point Reyes National Seashore, just north of San Francisco. On the last day a cold, damp wind blew in from offshore fogbanks. At lunchtime I sheltered from the wind in a little hollow on the edge of the sand dunes bordering the beach. Down in the hollow, the wind barely rustled the thin, tough blades of beach grass. And the sun beat up genially from pale sand. After a few minutes I felt sweat beginning to trickle down my face. Idly, I checked the temperature in the shady depths of the densest grass: 64°. Then I moved the thermometer out into the sun, on open sand. The mercury finally stopped at 112°.

For no clear or logical reason, I'm always checking and noting temperature readings: in shade and sun; in the air, on and below the surface; above, on, and below different neighboring surfaces; in rivers and hot springs. Once, I found myself delighted by the singularly useless information that it was still 55° in my boots half an hour after I had taken them off, when the ground temperature had already fallen close to freezing.

I suppose I gradually gain from such readings, in an untidy and diffuse sort of way, some new and rather tangential understandings of how our fascinating world works, but I doubt that this is really why I go on with the measuring and figuring. Mostly, I think, it's just that I enjoy my thermometer. I never think of leaving it behind.

It is an ordinary mercury thermometer that comes in a pencil-size (⅜ by 6¼ inches) metal case with a good strong pocket clip and a carrying ring at the top. Range: −30°F. to 120°F. (which is really too low if you want to play) (1½ ounces; $2.98). These thermometers are reasonably tough; but I assure you that they'll break if you drop them far enough.

Practical hints: Always calibrate a new thermometer against a reliable and preferably official one. For a quick "shade" reading when there is no shade, twirl the thermometer around on the end of a length of string or nylon cord that you leave knotted to the carrying loop; but check the knot first (see knots, nylon cord, page 265). In hot weather, be careful where you leave the thermometer; in the sun, surface temperatures can easily exceed 130°F., and much beyond that you may find yourself with an empty glass stem and a blob of free-lance mercury.

MENDING

Rip-stop repair tape

For repairing sleeping bags, tents or pack bags—in fact, almost any kind of equipment—there is nothing I know of to compare with this strong, lightweight, self-adhesive nylon fabric that comes in two-inch by 25-foot rolls in red, blue, and green (5 ounces; $2.50 per roll; 15 cents per foot). You simply peel off the protective paper from its adhesive side and press the fabric in place. No heating, no nothing. And it sticks. The repair seems to withstand any amount of washing too, though not dry cleaning. I always carry a length of it in my office (page 256)—up to two feet, according to the length of the trip. Unexpected recent uses include repairing the split lens of a pair of snow goggles, binding the splintering end of my staff (page 38), and stopping the reek of butane gas from the empty cartridge of a Bluet stove by simply sealing off the hole (page 113).

Needle and thread

For reinstating buttons and repairing anything from tent tabs to "yoke office." (They also puncture blisters. See page 47.) Half a dozen needles travel in my matchsafe (page 103). Short lengths of strong thread are threaded through three or four of these needles, and are wrapped around them like pythons. A longer reserve of thread, wrapped around a small piece of paper, goes into the "Odds and Ends" can (page 267).

Spare parts for pack

Every pack has certain small attachments which, if lost or damaged, could disrupt a trip. In the "Odds and Ends" can (page 267) I carry a spare end-button for the frame (page 59), and three of the aluminum eyebolts that hold packbag to frame (see page 62)—though I must admit I've never had to use one. Into a separate small plastic bag goes a spare set of the buckles that attach the yoke to the foot of the packframe (see illustration, page 53).

Makeshift repairs

Substitutes for Rip-stop tape include adhesive medical tape (page 251) and moleskins (pages 36 and 46).

Occasionally, for such unexpected tasks as tying on a wrenched-off zipper tab, I've used nylon fishing line (page 253).

For Epoxy, see page 171.

ENJOYING EXTRA-PERAMBULATORY
ACTIVITIES

For many people, perhaps for most, a walk is rarely a self-fulfilling operation, whether it lasts an hour or a summer. Alone, with an agreeable companion, or in a group, they walk as a means to some such specific end as hunting, fishing, photography, bird watching, sex, or geology.

Generally speaking, the equipment for such activities lies outside the scope of this book. The exception is

Fishing.

An orthodox two- or three-piece rod is a perishing nuisance on a backpack trip. (I am thinking primarily of trout fishing, because that is what you usually find in the wilder areas still left for backpacking. And I am thinking above all of fly fishing, because in most remote areas that is the way to get the most pleasure from your fishing—and sometimes to catch the most trout. But what I have to say applies to most kinds of rods.)

If you lash an orthodox rod to your packframe—the best place for it—the risk of damage is high. If you tote along an aluminum rod case, the wretched thing tends to get in the way. When fishing is your overriding object, the inconvenience may be worth it; but if fishing is really an excuse for escape, and even more if it is just a possible bonus, the solution lies in a portmanteau rod. Mine goes on all backpacking trips that have a hint of fishing in them.

My four-piece, 4¼-ounce, 7½-foot glass fly rod breaks down to 23½ inches. It fits snugly into the packbag, down one side, close against the packframe. With no protection except a flimsy cloth cover, it has never come to any harm.

The difficulty with this kind of rod is always its action: the perfect rod is a one-piecer, and every ferrule marks another step down from perfection. (Each ferrule also used to add critically to the weight, but new alloys have pretty well solved that problem.) So with a four-piece rod you must test the action carefully, not forgetting that there may be marked differences between half a dozen shop samples of the same model. Try them all. My little rod (a Model #175 by Shoff of Kent, Washington) comes as close to a good action as any portmanteau rod I've tried—which, come to think of it, is precious few.

The rest of my backpack fly-fishing tackle fits into a small leather reel bag: the reel itself, six spools of nylon (2-, 3-, 4-, 6-, 8- and 10-pound test), a small can of flies, and line grease. Total: eleven ounces.

Anyone with enough wit to resist the widespread fallacy that you go fishing mainly in order to catch fish will understand that spinning is a barbarous way to catch trout. But I have to admit that there are places, such as high mountain lakes, where fly fishing may often be useless. And there are times, of course, when you'll want to fish purely for food. For such occasions I have once or twice carried a little closed-faced abomination of a spinning reel (nine ounces) that takes most of the pleasure out of fishing but does not need a large butt ring and can therefore be used with a fly rod. Into the abomination's little bag went some lead shot and weights, a few lures and bait hooks, and a bobber.

There are times when fly fishing is plainly impossible. (Often, for example, when the fish are not trout.) So I have a four-piece, four-ounce, six-foot spinning rod that breaks down to twenty inches. It was made to my specifications from a hollow-glass blank that I selected from stock. It cost $12, a dozen years ago. My other spinning tackle is standard.

You can fish purely for fun—and get it—with emergency tackle (page 253) and a light switch.

The remaining activities you're likely to indulge in can be conveniently classified under such headings as:

ALWAYS-COMING-IN-USEFUL-
AND-IN-FACT-QUITE-INDISPENSABLE
DEPARTMENT

Nylon cord,

Braided nylon cord, usually called "parachute cord" (⅛-inch diameter, 550-pound breaking strain), is to a backpacker what adhesive tape is to a doctor: an indispensable maid-of-all-work. I always carry half a dozen hanks, in lengths from two to about fifteen feet; and occasionally a full 100-foot hank (6 ounces; $1.50).

No matter what lengths you find it best to carry, remember that cut cord always frays at the ends. To prevent fraying simply fuse the ends into unravelable blobs by holding them briefly in the flame of match or stove. Hanks should travel, easily available, in an outside pocket of your pack.

Among their proven uses:

1. Rigging tents and allied shelters (pages 152–65)
2. Clotheslines
3. Fish stringers
4. Measuring lengths of fish and snakes, for later conversion to figures (mark with a knot)
5. Tying socks to pack for drying (page 36)
6. Securing camera and binoculars to pack by clip spring, so that if dislodged they cannot fall far (page 230)
7. Belt for pants (page 203) or for flapping poncho in high wind (page 208)
8. Lowering pack down difficult places (page 255)
9. Replacement binocular strap
10. Chin band for hat (page 213)
11. Lashing tent poles to packframe (page 147)
12. Hanging cooking pots over a fire, from a tree, for melting snow for water. (This way you can build up a really big fire and keep warm at the same time. You do so, of course, in the uneasy knowledge that the cord may burn; but in practice it doesn't seem to)

13. Wrapping around camera case screw fitting, pulling, and so un-jamming the screw for film changing
14. On packless sidetrips, tying poncho into lunch bundle (food, photo accessories, compass, etc.) and securing around waist (page 209)
15. On river crossings:
    (a) Lashing air mattress to pack (page 278)
    (b) Lashing plastic sheet into virtually watertight bundle for protection of valuables, either as sanctum sanctorum of pack (page 278) or as lone floating bundle to be pushed ahead or towed on packless crossings (page 275), and
    (c) Towing walking staff along behind.

Among uses I've often had in mind but have not yet had occasion to try:

1. Spare bootlaces
2. Lifting water from well
3. Attaching flashlight to self at night (page 194)
4. Doubled or tripled or quadrupled, as "carabiner-type" loop for ensuring that doubled climbing rope used for rappelling (or roping down) can be recovered from below (page 254)
5. As main rope for roping down cliff (in extreme emergency only, as cord might be weakened to danger point by knotting at top and by possible wear, and would in any case be viciously uncomfortable even if used doubled or quadrupled), and
6. In river work, for pulling yourself back up against slow-to-medium river current—in case you find it necessary to float a short way past a blind headland to see if a safe land route lies ahead around dangerous rapids.

Most ordinary knots in nylon eventually slip. The only safe knot I know—and it is less difficult to tie and less bulky than it looks—is the fisherman's blood knot:

Rubber bands

For sheer all-round usefulness, rubber bands rank second only to nylon cord. Their most vital function in my regimen is as weak and nonrestrictive garters for my turned-down socks, to keep stones and dirt out of the boots. Other uses: resealing opened food packages; closing food bags that are too full to be knotted at the neck; holding sugar-container lid firm; battening down the moleskin package with its added contents of nail scissors and metal mirror (page 249); securing camera cable release conveniently to binophotography bracket to prevent damage in the pack, and also for attaching the bracket to waist belt on packless sidetrips; holding onion-skin paper (for notes) to its rectangle of stiffening cardboard; and keeping notebook instantly openable at the current page.

Rubber bands have a habit of breaking and also of getting lost, and I recommend that you wrap as many as you think you need ready for immediate use around the protruding arms of your packframe. Then add the same number again. Then put into a small plastic bag about ten times as many as are on your packframe, and put this reserve safely away inside the pack.

Plastic bags

I sometimes wonder what backpackers used as the interior walls of their houses before the days of plastic freezer bags. I use them, in various sizes, not only for almost every food item (page 121) but also, copiously and often double-thickness, for wrapping many other things: camp moccasins, underclothes, dirty socks, cooking pots, frying pan, book, rubber bands, stove, matches, toilet gear, first-aid kit, film, camera accessories, toilet paper, spare flashlight cells, signal flare, fishing tackle, certain spare pack attachments, Visklamps and rubber balls for plastic shelter, car key, and unburnable garbage. Also, sometimes, as a wallet. I always take along a few spare bags.

For details of sizes and uses, and hints on packing, see pages 121–2.

35 mm. film cans

These cans are the best containers I know for salt tablets, water purifying tablets, salmon eggs for bait, and coconut oil for lube jobs on hair and beard and even boots, not to mention for cooking. I also carry one can for odds and ends: spare plastic end-button and three spare aluminum eyebolts for packframe; two spare flashlight bulbs; and some strong button thread wound around a small piece of paper. At one time I also carried, with what struck me as a masterly stroke of foresight, several small screws for repairing separated boot soles; but the only time a loose sole did develop, the screws proved starkly ineffective.

Belt clips

Swivel-mounted snap hooks (1 ounce; 70 cents) on small leather or nylon loops are useful for carrying certain items suspended from your belt or the built-in waistband of your pants: a cup, in good drinking country (page 101); occasionally, your hat; the camera tripod or other light equipment on packless sidetrips.

If you use a belt clip while carrying the pack (for a cup, say), make sure you pass the belt *inside* the clip; otherwise the belt's pressure may force the clip open. After a little while you find yourself flipping the cup outside automatically every time you put the pack on.

At the moment, I'm using two belt clips on makeshift safety lines for both binoculars and camera (see page 230).

LINKS-WITH-CIVILIZATION DEPARTMENT

Generally, the last thing you want to do out in wild country is to carry any item that helps maintain a link with civilization. But there are exceptions. For example, it is sometimes more convenient and even cheaper to fly rather than drive to and from your chosen wilderness. And then you have to carry, all the way, some kind of

Wallet.

The simplest and lightest is a small plastic food bag. Into it you may want to put, according to the needs of the moment, some form of identification (driver's license is best, in case you need to drive), fishing license, and fire permit. Also some money (although it's the most useless commodity imaginable once you're actually out in the wilderness). Consider both ready cash and traveler's checks, and perhaps one or two bank checks as reserve. A gasoline credit card may be worthwhile too: quite recently I used one to pay in advance for a short charter flight that put me down on a remote dirt road, and also for an airdrop of food that was to follow a week later.

A little cash may be worth taking along even when you are coming back to your car: last fall, after a week in the mountains that ended with a fast, steep, 10,000-foot descent, I emerged with very sore feet onto a road fifty miles from my car, quickly hitched a ride in the right direction, and managed to persuade my benefactor that it was worth $5 for him to drive me several miles up a steep mountain road to where my car was parked.

Nowadays I always carry a dime taped to the cardboard stiffener of my office (page 256): few things are more frustrating than to emerge into man-country at last with a message heavy on your chest and find yourself at a remote telephone booth, dimeless and therefore mute.

Car key

The obvious place to leave your car key is at the car—taped or magnet-attached to some secret corner of it, or simply hidden close by. But I once came back from a winter mountain trip and found the rear bumper of my car, with the key craftily magnet-attached inside it, buried under a ten-foot snowdrift. Fortunately, a freak of the wind had left a convenient alley along one side of the car and I was able to get at the key without too much difficulty. But since then I find, rather to my surprise, that I tend to avoid vague worries about snow and torrential rain and landslides and thieves (human and other) by packing the key along with me. Cached or carried, the key gets wrapped in the inevitable plastic bag.

Radio

Believe it or not, I am regularly asked, "But don't you carry a transistor radio . . . so that you can keep in touch . . . or for the weather . . . or anyway for company?" You're allowed one guess.

STRICTLY-PERSONAL-BUT-YOU'LL-PROBABLY-HAVE-YOUR-OWN DEPARTMENT

Everyone, I imagine, has one or two little personal items that go along. They'll vary according to individual interests and frailties. Two very experienced friends of mine always carry small pliers. In addition to items I've already mentioned, such as office and prospector's magnifying glass, my list includes spare eyeglasses (sometimes), and two Ace bandages (always). The bandages are primarily for a troublesome knee and for emergency use in case of a sprained ankle but they have seen most use in thornbush and cactus country, wrapped puttee-fashion around my bare and vulnerable lower legs (page 203).

Housekeeping and Other Matters

ORGANIZING THE PACK

The best way to stow your gear into your pack is to pursue, all the time, a reasonable compromise between convenience and efficient weight distribution.

For the main considerations in weight distribution—loading high and close to the back—see pages 58 and 59. Common sense and a lick or two of experience will soon teach you the necessary refinements: after some angular item such as the stove has gouged into your back a couple of times you'll make sure, almost without thinking, that flat or soft articles pad the forward surface of the packbag's main compartment; and once you've put both the full canteens that you're carrying on the same side of the bag and then found that the load rides like a one-armed gorilla, you're unlikely to repeat the mistake.

The most convenient way to stow gear varies from trip to trip, from day to day, from morning to evening. Obviously, the things you'll want first at the next halt should go in last. So the groundsheet will normally travel on top. In dry country, so will one canteen (though in sunny weather it should be covered with a down jacket or some other insulator). And the balance of the week's ration bag, the signal flare, reserve or empty canteens, and refill cartridges for the Bluet stove should—on the score of sheer convenience—languish down in the basement. Otherwise, the really important thing is not where each item goes but that you always know where it is.

There will be variations of course. If rain threatens, the poncho must be on top and perhaps even sticking out, ready to be plucked into use. On cold evenings, have your heavy clothing ready to put on even before you start to make camp. If it looks as though you are going to have a long, torrid, midday halt, make sure you don't have to dig down to the bottom of the packbag for plastic sheet or poncho before you can rig up an awning. But all this is just plain common sense.

So are the compromises you are always making between maximum convenience and fully efficient weight distribution. In time, every backpacker works out a way of stowing things that suits him best. But the inexperienced may be able to find some guidelines in the solutions that I have evolved. (A good deal of this information has been scattered around in earlier chapters, but it seems worthwhile to summarize it here.)

I always pad the forward side of my packbag with the office, and sometimes with camp moccasins (soles facing out). A scarf and the spare plastic bags also go into the inside pocket and so increase the padding effect. The flashlight travels there too—safe from being pulled out accidentally, well protected against damage, and so situated that even after dark I can reach in and find it without fumbling. Put in at the right angle, it never gouges my back, though I can't quite understand why. In one forward corner of the main sack, fitting snugly against the packframe, go the gasoline container and, on top of it, the stove. If I'm carrying a portmanteau fishing rod or a cloth stove screen or both, they fit into the opposite and similar corner.

There are few other firm rules for the main sack. Cooking pots and the food-for-the-day bag normally go side by side on the same level, because when I want one I want the other, but otherwise the packing arrangements depend largely on what items I expect to need next. Generally, though, I try to pack heavy articles close to the packframe. (See pages 58 and 59).

Because I always use large packbags (main compartment of present one: 10 by 14 by 25 inches), the space problem rarely becomes acute. Even on snow trips, with heavy clothing and tent, I get comfortably by. So in the past I have rarely used stuff bags (see page 191). But I've recently begun to accept that lightweight nylon stuff bags with drawstring enclosures make it simpler to fit everything in, save sleeping bags and down clothing from unnecessary wear and tear, and provide additional protection from rain and snow. (But see page 58.)

My present pack has six outside pockets: one on the flap, two on each side, and one amidships, aft. (See page 62, and illustration, page 53.)

Into the shallow flap pocket—which is the easiest of all to get at—go spare clean socks, or damp or dirty socks (in plastic bags) when for some reason such as rain or grabbing thorns it is inadvisable to leave them airing on the outside of the pack. Also camera lens tissue, camera close-up attachments (when it seems likely they'll be needed in a hurry), and (when they're in regular use) water-purifying tablets in a 35 mm. film can.

The upper starboard pocket is the "nibble" pocket—the most often used of all. Into it go beef jerky, the day's energy bar, and the day's allowance of mintcake and raisins—the quick-boost foods I nibble at almost every halt. One meat bar lives there too, so that if there's no time to stop for a regular lunch I need not unpack the main food. Sometimes the semisweet chocolate goes in as well, and the canister of salt tablets.

The lower starboard pocket always holds footpowder and rubbing alcohol (page 44), and sometimes the small plastic baby bottle canteen (see page 98), and one package of fruit-drink mix. Also, when they're carried, fly dope, suntan lotion, and hand lotion.

The upper port pocket is the photography room: tripod, close-up attachments, binophotography bracket, cable release, strap extension for camera case (the camera hangs on a short strap; the extension is needed for slinging camera over shoulder on packless jaunts), and in really cool weather, film (see page 233).

The lower port pocket is for other miscellaneous items that must be get-at-able in a hurry or are too small and losable to travel in the main sack: first-aid kit, compass, belt clip, carborundum stone, gasoline funnel, stove-cover handle (from Svea), odds-and-ends can, and spare pack fittings.

Into the big central pocket go toilet paper, sheath knife, hanks of nylon cord, and unburnable garbage (in plastic bag).

Tent poles, when carried, are lashed to the packframe (page 147).

The only radical changes in organizing the pack come at

RIVER CROSSINGS.

Simple crossings raise no problems. Failing a natural log bridge or steppingstones, you just take off your boots and wade. At least, I do. Some people keep their boots on, but I mistrust the effect on boots and feet. Or perhaps I just mean that I abhor the idea of squelching along afterwards. On easy crossings, carry your boots, with socks pushed inside. Knot the laces together and twist them around one wrist. On deeper crossings, hang the lace-linked boots on the packframe. In really difficult places it's safer to stuff them inside the packbag.

A friend has very recently suggested a method he uses regularly and which, for fast and rocky rivers, sounds obvious enough and well worth a trial: take off socks, replace boots, wade river with well-protected feet, replace socks, and go on your happy and reputedly unsquelching way.

Provided you choose the right places, you can wade surprisingly large rivers. (Fast rivers, that is, where the depth and character vary; slow, channeled rivers are normally unwadable.) It often pays to make an extensive reconnaissance along the bank in order to select a good crossing point. You may even need to detour for a mile or more. Generally, the safest places are the widest and, up to a point, the fastest. Most promising of all, provided the water is shallow enough and not too fierce, tend to be the fanned-out tails of wide pools. Boulders or large stones, protruding or submerged, in fairly shallow water may also indicate a good crossing place: they break the full force of racing water, and you can ease across the most dangerous places on little mounds of stone and gravel that have been deposited by the slack water behind each boulder. But always, before you start across, pick out in detail, with coldly cynical eyes, a route that looks tolerably safe—all the way. And don't get into a position you can't retreat from.

Experience is by far the most important aid to safe wading (I wish I had a lot more), but there are a few simple rules. Use a staff—particularly with a heavy pack. (It turns you, even more critically than on dry land, from an insecure biped into a confident triped. Those who don't normally carry a staff should cut one whenever faced by a major wading challenge.) The safest route for wading, other things being equal, is one that angles down and across the current. The faster and deeper the water, the more sharply downstream you should angle. The next best attack is up and across. Most hazardous of all—because the current can most easily sweep you off balance—is a directly-across route.

Unless you are afraid of being swept off your feet (and in that case you'd almost certainly do better to swim across a deep, slow section), wading does not call for any change in the way you pack. But before you start across you should certainly undo your waistbelt. Always. The pack (at least until it fills with water) is much more buoyant than your body and should you fall in, it will, if held in place by the belt, force you under. It is easy enough to wriggle out of a shoulder yoke, particularly if it's slung over only one shoulder. At least, I like to imagine so.

The only other precaution I sometimes take when wading, and then only at difficult crossings, is to unhitch camera and binoculars from the packframe and put them inside the pack.

But if you have to swim a river you must reorganize the pack's contents.

The first time I tried swimming with a pack was on my Grand Canyon journey. Because of the new Glen Canyon Dam, a hundred miles upriver, the Colorado was then running at only 1,200 cubic feet per second—far below its normal low water level. Even for someone who, like me, is a poor and nervous swimmer, it seemed comparatively easy to swim across a slow, deep stretch with little danger of being swept down over the next rapids. I adopted the technique developed by the one man who had been able to help me with much information about hiking in remote parts of the Canyon. He was a math professor at Arizona State College in Flagstaff; and he was also, his wife said, "like a seal in the water." He had found that by lying across his air mattress with the pack slung over one shoulder, half-floating, he could, even at high water, dog-paddle across the Colorado—which is the third-longest river in the United States, and is muscled accordingly. I tried his method out on several same-side detours, when sheer cliffs blocked my way, and by degrees I gained confidence in it.

The air mattress made a good raft. Inflated not too firmly, it formed a reassuring V when I lay with my chest across it. I used it first on a packless reconnaissance. Remembering how during World War II we had crossed rivers by wrapping all our gear in waterproof anti-gas capes and making bundles that floated so well we could just hang on to them and kick our way forward, I wrapped the few clothes and stores I needed into the white plastic sheet and lashed it firmly

with nylon cord. It floated well. I found that by wrapping a loose end of cord around one arm I could tow it along beside me and dog-paddle fairly freely.

With the pack, dog-paddling turned out to be a little more restricted, but still reasonably effective. The pack, slung over my left shoulder and half-floating, tended at first to keel over. But I soon found that I could hold it steady by light pressure on the lower and upper ends of the packframe with buttocks and bald patch. It sounds awkward but worked fine.

My staff floated along behind at the end of three feet of nylon cord tied to the packframe. Everything else went into the pack. I had waterproofed the seams of the packbag rather hurriedly, and I found that water still seeped through. So into the bottom of the bag went bulky and buoyant articles that water could not damage: canteens, cooking pots, and white-gas container. Things better kept dry went in next, wrapped in the white plastic sheet. Items that just had to stay dry went on top, in what I thought of as the sanctum sanctorum: camera and accessories, flashlight and spare batteries, binoculars, watch, writing materials, and toilet paper. I tied each of these items into a plastic bag, rolled them all inside the sleeping bag, and stuffed it into the big, tough plastic bag that usually went around the cooking pots. Then I wrapped the lot in my poncho. Before strapping the packbag shut I tied the ends of the poncho *outside* the white plastic sheet with nylon cord. (On one trial run the pack had keeled over and water had run down inside the plastic sheet, though the sanctum had remained inviolate.) On the one complete river crossing that I had to make, nothing got even damp.

This system, or some variation of it, should prove adequate for crossing almost any river, provided you do not have to go through heavy rapids. I am more than half-scared of water and a very poor swimmer, so if I can do it, almost anyone can. The great practical advantage of this method is that you do not have to carry any special equipment. All you need is an air mattress, a poncho and a plastic sheet or a groundsheet.

Heavy rapids present a different problem. Not long ago I took a two-week hike-and-swim trip down seventy miles of the Colorado, in lower Grand Canyon. Although many people have run the Colorado by boat, everyone had until then had the sense to avoid attempting this very enclosed stretch on foot, but I knew from boatmen's reports that even if the route proved possible I would almost certainly have to make several river crossings. I also knew that, with the reservoir now part-filled behind Glen Canyon Dam, the river was racing down at an average of about 16,000 cubic feet per second—more than twelve times its volume on my earlier trip. That meant I would almost certainly be carried far downstream each time I attempted a crossing. Even the calmer stretches would be swirling, whirlpooled horrors, and I would probably be carried through at least some minor rapids. Under such conditions I wasn't willing to risk the lying-across-an-air-mattress technique, and I evolved a new method, more suitable for a timid swimmer.

Just before the trip I bought an inflatable life vest. (Stebco Industries Inc., Model LP 31; 1 pound, 2 ounces; $11.50.) It is made of bright yellow rubberized cotton fabric, and there is a valve for inflation by mouth and also a small metal cartridge that in an emergency fills the vest with carbon dioxide the instant you pull a toggled cord. The vest yokes comfortably around the neck so that when you float on your back your mouth is held clear of the water. When I tried it out in a sidecreek as soon as I reached the Colorado, I found that I could also swim very comfortably in the normal position. From the start, I felt safe and confident.

I had already decided that, rather than lie across the air mattress, I would this time rely solely on the life vest to keep me afloat—partly because I was afraid the vest's metal cartridge or its securing wire might puncture the mattress, but even more because I did not fancy my chances of staying on the mattress in swirling water. (A young fellow crossing the Colorado on a trip with my math professor friend had been swept off his mattress by a whirlpool and had drowned.) It seemed quite clear to me that the trick was to make the pack buoyant in its own right, and just pull or push it along with me.

The coated nylon fabric of the packbag was fully waterproof but, although I had applied seam sealant, water still seeped in. So I decided to try to keep the pack as upright as I could in the water and protect the really vital gear, up near the top. First, for extra buoyancy high up, I put one empty plastic quart-size canteen in each of the upper sidepockets. Into the bottom of the bag as ballast went the two cooking pots and two half-gallon canteens, all filled with water. Next I lined the remaining space in the main sack with my transparent polyethylene groundsheet and left the unused portion hanging outside. Like all groundsheets, mine had developed many small holes, but I figured it would ward off the worst of any water that might seep in from the upper seams or under the flap, and that what little did get through would collect harmlessly in the bottom of the pack. The items that water couldn't damage (see page 276) went in first. Next, those preferably kept dry. Then I made the sanctum sanctorum. Into the white plastic sheet (because rain was unlikely, I carried no poncho this trip) went all the things that just had to stay dry (also page 276). Most of them were additionally protected inside an assortment of plastic bags. I lashed the white bundle firmly with nylon cord, put it on top of everything else, then folded over the unused portion of the groundsheet that was still hanging outside, and carefully tucked it in between the main portion of the groundsheet and the packbag itself. I knotted down the pack flap, tight. Then I partially inflated my air mattress and lashed it securely with nylon cord to the upper half of the pack, taking care to keep it central. Finally I took the four-foot agave-stem walking staff that I had cut at the start of the

trip (page 39) and wedged it down into the cross-webbing of the packframe, close beside one upright.

I held the pack upright in the water for several minutes, forcing it down so that water seeped in and filled the bottom seven or eight inches—thereby helping, I hoped, to keep the pack upright. Then I slid down into the river beside it. With my left hand I grasped the lowest cross-rung of the packframe and pulled downward. Provided I maintained a slight downward pressure (see illustration) the pack floated fairly upright, though tending to lean away from me, and I was free to swim in any position with one arm and both legs.

Besides the inflatable vest, I wore my ultralightweight nylon swimming trunks (page 212). I'd brought them because at the start, at the sidecreek in which I practiced, there was a possibility of meeting people. But I found that I actually wore the trunks on all crossings, so that I would have at least some protection from the sun if I became separated from the pack. And so that I could still light a fire in that unlikely event, I tied the waterproof matchsafe (page 103) onto the vest.

The whole rig worked magnificently. I made four crossings. The white plastic sheet hardly ever got damp, even on the outside, and the sanctum remained bone dry, every time. So, mostly, did all other items stowed near the top of the pack. Because I could swim freely, I got across the river quite fast. Each time I could have landed

within half a mile of my launch site; but twice I allowed myself to be carried a little farther down to good landing places. (And as I floated down the calmer stretches on my back, with both feet resting on the packframe in front of me—my mind and body utterly relaxed, and an integral part of the huge, silent, flowing river—I found that I had discovered a new and serene and superbly included way of experiencing the Grand Canyon of the Colorado.)

I also made two same-side river detours around impassable cliffs. And one of these detours was the high point of the trip.

For the first fifty feet of the rapids I had to go through, the racing water battered on its left flank into a jagged rockwall. I knew that the one thing I absolutely had to do was to keep an eye on this rockwall and make sure that if I swung close I fended off in time with arm or pack or legs. From the bank, the steep waves in the heart of the rapids didn't look too terrifying: not more than three or four feet high at the most. But throughout the double eternity during which I swirled and wallowed through those waves—able to think of nothing except "Is it safe to grab a breath now, before I go in under that next one?"—I knew vividly and for sure that not one of them was less than fifty-seven and a half feet high. And all I saw of the rockwall was a couple of split-second glimpses—like those near-subliminal inner-thought flashes they use in the new movies.

I missed the rockwall, though—through no effort of mine— and came safely through the rapids. A belch or two in mid-river cleared the soggy feeling that came from the few mouthfuls of Colorado that I had shipped; and once I got into calmer water and had time to take a look at the pack it seemed serenely shipshape. (In the rapids, frankly, I hadn't even known that I was still hanging on to it.)

The only problem now, in the fast water below the rapids, was getting back to the bank. It took me a full mile to do so.

At first I had to stay in mid-river to avoid protruding rocks at the edge of some more and only slightly less tumultuous rapids. Then, after I'd worked my way quite close to the bank, I was swept out again by tailwash from a big, barely submerged boulder. Almost at once I saw a smooth, sinister gray wave ahead, rising up out of the middle of the river. I knew at once what it was. Furiously, I swam toward the bank. A few strokes and I looked downstream once more. The wave was five times closer now, ten times bigger. And I knew I could not avoid it. Just in time, I got into position with the pack held off to one side and my legs out in front of me, high in the water and slightly bent. Then I was rising up, sickeningly, onto the crest of the wave. And then I was plummeting down. As I fell, my feet brushed, very gently, over the smooth, hard surface of the hidden boulder. Then a white turmoil engulfed me. But almost instantly my head was out in the air again and I was floating along in calmer water. For a moment or two the pack looked rather waterlogged; but long before I made landfall, a couple of hundred yards downstream, it was once more floating high. When I unpacked, I found the contents even drier than on some of the earlier and calmer crossings.

After those rapids and that boulder, I feel I can say with some confidence that my new river-crossing technique works.

That trip was something of a special case, but it has taught me a useful lesson: if you have to swim a river, and have no air mattress and no inflatable vest, rig your pack somewhat after the manner I did. It will float buoyantly, and vital items will travel safely in the sanctum sanctorum. All you do is pull down on the bottom crossbar of the frame and swim alongside or in front or behind (in swirling water you'll do all three within seconds). A fair swimmer would have no difficulty, I imagine, in any reasonably unbroken water. And if, like me, you are a weak swimmer, you could almost certainly keep yourself afloat and moving across the current by just hanging onto the pack and kicking.

For crossings of any but the widest rivers, parties of hikers have it easier than a man on his own—provided they are carrying enough rope or cord. Only one man need swim across under his own power. The others, after paying out a cord or rope attached to his body, can be pulled across by him. At least, I guess so.

Don't forget that water temperature can be treacherous in river crossings. Even when you're wading, really cold water can numb your feet and legs to danger point with quite astonishing speed. And no one can swim for long in liquid ice—cannot even live in it for very

long. Yet your body will work efficiently for a long time in 50°
water. On that recent hike-and-swim trip down the Colorado, river
temperature averaged about 57°, and although the water always felt
perishing cold when I first got into it (which was hardly surprising,
with shade temperatures rising each day to over 100°, and precious
little shade anywhere), I was never once, even on the longest swims,
at all conscious of being cold.

SANITATION

Sanitation is not a pleasant topic, but every camper must for the
sake of others consider it openly, with his mind unblurred by prudery.

Decent and hygienic disposal of feces in the outdoors is largely
a matter of common sense. What is acceptable at one time and place
may be disgusting and dangerous at another. In most cases the
differences boil down to differing densities of human use.

At one extreme there is the situation in which permanent johns
have been built. Always use them. If they exist, it means that the
human population, at least at certain times of year, is too dense for
any other healthy solution.

A big party camping in any kind of country, no matter how
wild, automatically imposes a dense population on a limited area.
They should always dig deep latrine holes and, if possible, carry lime
or some similar disinfectant that will counteract odor, keep flies away,
and hasten decomposition. And they must fill holes carefully before
leaving.

A party of two or three in a remote area—and, even more certainly, a man on his own—must make simpler arrangements. But
with proper "cat sanitation" and due care and consideration in
choice of sites, no problem need arise.

Cat sanitation means doing what a cat does, though more
efficiently: scraping a hole, and covering up the feces afterward. The
hole need not be deep; but it must be a hole, at least four or five inches
deep, rather than a mere scratch on the surface. In many soils you

can dig easily enough with your boots or a stick. I carry my sheath knife along whenever I go looking for a cat-john site, and use it if necessary for digging. I always carry a book of matches in the double plastic bags that hold my roll of toilet paper. I tear one match off ready beforehand and leave it protruding from the book, so that I need handle the book very little; and when I have finished I burn all the used paper (unless there is a fire hazard). The flames not only destroy the paper but char the feces and discourage flies. Afterward I carefully refill the hole. Unless the water situation is critical, I have a piece of soap and an opened canteen waiting in camp for immediate hand washing.

Choice of site is largely a matter of considering other people. Wherever possible, select tucked-away places that no one is likely to use for any purpose. But do not appropriate a place so neatly tucked away that someone may want to camp there. A little thoughtful common sense will be an adequate guide.

In deep snow there is unfortunately little you can do except dig a hole, burn the paper, cover the hole and afterward refuse to think about what will happen come hot weather. There is not much you can do, either, about having to expose your fundamentals to the elements. Actually, even in temperatures well below freezing, it turns out to be a surprisingly undistressing business for the brief interval necessary, especially if you have a tent to crawl back into. Obviously, blizzard conditions and biting cold may make the world outside your tent unlivable, even for brief intervals, but a cookhole in the tent floor (see page 145) would solve this problem.

It is horrifying how many people, even under conditions in which cat sanitation is easy, fail to observe the simple, basic rules. Failure to bury feces is not only barbaric; it is a danger to others. Flies are everywhere. And the barbarism is compounded by thoughtless choice of sites. I still remember the disgust I felt when, late one rainy mountain evening, several years ago, I found at last what looked like an ideal campsite under a small overhanging rockface— and then saw, dead center, a cluster of filthy toilet paper and a naked human turd.

That rockledge was in a fairly remote area. The problem can be magnified when previously remote countryside is opened up to people unfit to use it. Power boats now cruise far and wide over Lake Powell, which is backing up fast behind the Colorado's new Glen Canyon Dam, and the boats' occupants are able to visit with almost no effort many ancient and fascinating Indian cliff dwellings. Previously, these dwellings could be reached only by extensive foot or fast-water journeys. Now people who have made such demanding journeys have usually (though not always) learned, through close contact with the earth, to treat it with respect—and power boats do not bring you in close contact with the earth. I hear that most of the cliff dwellings near Lake Powell have already been used as toilets.

Urination is a much less serious matter. But dense and undisciplined human populations can eventually create a smell, and although this problem normally arises only in camping areas so crowded that you might as well be on Main Street, it can also do so with locally concentrated use, especially in hot weather and when the ground is impervious to liquids. During my first Grand Canyon journey I camped on one open rockledge for four days. As the days passed, the temperature rose. On the fourth day, with the thermometer reaching 80° in the shade—and 120° in my unshaded camp—I several times detected whiffs of a stale odor that made me suspect I was near the lair of a large animal. I was actually hunting around for the lair when I realized that only one large animal was living on that rockledge.

But urination is usually no more than a minor inconvenience—even for those who, like me, were in the back row when bladders were given out. An obvious precaution is to cut down on drinking at night. No tea for me, thank you, with dinner. But I rarely manage to get through a night undisturbed. Fortunately, it is surprising how little you get chilled when you stand up for a few moments on quite cold nights, even naked. I go no farther than the foot of my sleeping bag, and just aim at the night. Hence the "animal lair" at that rocky Grand Canyon campsite.

For footwear when scrambling out of a tent at night, see page 151. For the cookhole alternative, see page 145.

REPLENISHING SUPPLIES

On extended trips you always face the problem of how to replenish your supplies. Generally speaking, you can't carry food for more than a week or so (page 19). Other items need replacement too: powder and rubbing alcohol for your feet, toilet paper, other toilet articles. You'll probably need additional film as well, and new maps, and replacement equipment, and perhaps special gear for certain sections of the trip.

Outposts of civilization

On my six-month California walk I was able to plan my route so that I called in every week or ten days at remote country post offices. Before I started the trip I had mailed ahead to each of these post offices not only a batch of maps for the stretch of country ahead but also items of special gear, such as warm clothing for the first high mountain beyond the desert. At each post office I mailed to my regular outdoor equipment suppliers back in Berkeley a list of the food and equipment I wanted to pick up two weeks later; and a list of film and personal requirements went to a reliable friend. So at each post-office call-in I found waiting for me everything I needed for the next leg of the journey.

These calls at outposts of civilization provided a change of diet too: there was always a store near the post office, and usually a cafe— and a motel. I often stayed a day or two in the motel to write and mail a series of newspaper articles (and also to soak in several hot showers and cold beers). Exposed film went out in the mails, and completed notes, and sometimes equipment I no longer needed. All in all, the system worked very well. It could probably be adapted, with modifications to suit the needs of the moment, for many kinds of walking trip.

In wild areas you have to replenish by other means. One way is to make

Caches.

On the California walk I put out several water caches at critical points and at one or two of them I also left a few cans of food. Later I realized that I should have left a store of dehydrated food as well, and cut down my load.

I was able to put those caches out by car, on little-used dirt roads, but on most wilderness trips you have to pack the stuff in ahead of time. On the two-month Grand Canyon trip I put out two caches of water, food, and other supplies. From the purely logistic standpoint I should have carried these caches far down into the Canyon so that on the trip itself I would not have to detour. But there is, thank God, more to walking than logistics. I had been dreaming about the Canyon for a year, and one of the prime concerns in all my planning was to shield the dream from familiarity—that sly and deadly anesthetic. As I wrote in *The Man Who Walked Through Time,* "I knew that if I packed stores down into the Canyon I would be 'trespassing' in what I wanted to be unknown country; but I also knew that if I planted the caches outside the Rim I would in picking them up break both the real and symbolic continuity of my journey. In the end I solved the dilemma by siting each cache a few feet below the Rim."

Such delicate precautions should, I think, always be borne in mind when one of the aims of a backpacking trip, recognized or submerged, is to explore and immerse yourself in unknown country. You must avoid any kind of preview. Before my Grand Canyon trip, several people said, "Why not fly over beforehand, low? That's the way to choose a safe route." But I resisted the temptation—and in the end was profoundly thankful I had done so.

The best way to make, mark, and protect a cache will depend on local conditions. Rain and animals pose the most obvious threats. But extreme heat has to be avoided if there is film in the cache, and extreme cold if there is water. (For the protection and re-finding of water caches, and the best containers, see page 95. For precautions when caching dehydrated food in damp climates, see page 79.)

A cave or overhanging rockledge is probably the best protection against rain. Burying is the simplest and surest protection, especially in sandy desert, against temperature extremes and also against animals. For animals that can read, leave a note. On the California walk I put one with each cache: "If you find this cache, please leave it. I am passing through *on foot* in April or May, and am depending on it." Similar notes went on the Grand Canyon caches. But I doubt if any of them were ever read.

At each Grand Canyon cache, all food and supplies went into a metal five-gallon can. These cans are ideal for the job. Provided the lid is pressed firmly home, the cans are watertight, something close to airtight, and probably proof against all animals except bears and humans. I find that by packing the cans very carefully I can just squeeze in a full week's supply of everything. They are useful, too, for packing water ahead (see page 96). They are also excellent for airdrops—and having them interchangeably available for caches or airdrops may help keep your plans conveniently fluid until the last possible moment.

Airdrops

Prearranged parachute airdrops are a highly efficient means of replenishment. They are noisy, of course, and I am by no means happy about their being used extensively in remote areas. Once they became anything more than a very exceptional incursion, they could easily disturb the solitude that is the whole point of wilderness. As with sanitation, it is a matter of density.

A minor disadvantage of airdrops is that they tie you down to being at a certain place at a certain time. Although they are more dependable than most people imagine, uncertainties do exist—above all, the uncertainty of weather—and I am not sure I would rely on an airdrop if there were any considerable danger that the plane might be delayed more than a day or two by storms or fog.

Airdrops have one important advantage over other means of supply: they act as a safety check. Once you've signaled "All's well" to the plane everyone concerned soon knows you are safe up to that point. And if the pilot fails to locate you or sees a prearranged "in trouble—need help" signal, then rescue operations can get under immediate and well-directed way. (See page 312.)

Airdrops are not cheap—but neither are they ruinous. Most small rural charter outfits seem to charge between $25 and $30 for each hour of actual flying. If the base airport is within, say, fifty miles of the drop site, you ought to get by on about 1¼ hours flying time, or less than $40—provided the pilot has no trouble locating you. But you may have to add the cost of the parachute.

Establishing contact is the crux of an airdrop operation.

First, make sure you've got hold of a good pilot. Unless there was no alternative, I'd hesitate to depend on a man who had never done a drop before. It is essential too that he can map-read efficiently. (I suppose all pilots are more or less competent for the conditions they're used to; but that does not mean they can all pinpoint an agreed drop zone accurately enough in roadless wilderness.) Above all, satisfy yourself that you've got a careful and reliable man. Make local inquiries. And try to assess his qualities when you talk to him. Distrust a slapdash type whose refrain is "Just say where and when, and leave the rest to me." Feel reassured if he wants to cross all t's meticulously and to dot every last i and to have clear in his mind all alternative actions in case of delay for weather, failure to make contact with you, or some such snafu as supplies falling into a river or smashing to pulp on rock because the parachute failed. I admit that it's a problem to know what to do if you decide, after discussing the minutest details with a pilot, that you just don't trust him. It's not easy to extricate yourself without gashing the poor fellow's feelings. The solution is probably to approach him first on a conditional basis: "Look, I find that I *may* need an airdrop at—" But perhaps you can dream up a better gambit.

Success in making contact depends only in part on the pilot. The man on the ground has a lot to do with it too. So make sure you know what the hell you are doing.

The first time I arranged an airdrop I was very conscious that I had no idea at all what the hell. The occasion* was the long Grand

* Described in rather different detail in *The Man Who Walked Through Time*, pages 81–4.

Canyon trip. I wanted three airdrops. Talking over details with the pilot beforehand, we decided that, under expected conditions, the surest ground-to-air signal was mirror-flashing. I would carry a little circular mirror, about two inches in diameter—the kind you can pick up for fifteen cents in any variety store. The pilot, who had been an Air Force survival instructor, assured me that such a mirror was just as good as specially made signal mirrors with cross-slits. (It was also appreciably lighter: less than one ounce.) The trick was to practice beforehand. I soon picked up the idea. You hold the mirror as close to one eye as you can and shut the other eye. Then you extend the free hand and aim the tip of the thumb at a point (representing the plane) that is not more than about a hundred yards away. You move the mirror until the sun's reflection, appearing as a bright, ir-regular patch of light, hits the top of your thumb. Then you tilt the mirror up a bit until only the lowest part of the patch of light re-mains on your thumb. The rest of it should then show up exactly on the object that represents the plane. If it does not, keep practicing with fractional adjustments of mirror and thumb until you know exactly where to hold both so as to hit your target. You are now ready for the real thing. Ready, that is, to flash sunlight into the pilot's eyes.

"It's the surest way I know," said my Grand Canyon pilot. "On survival exercises I've located guys that had nothing to flash with except penknife blades or even just sunglasses. When that flash hits my eye, just once, the job's done. That's all I need to know: where to look. But without something to start me off, the expanse of ground I can see, especially in broken country like the Canyon, is just too damned big."

After a few minutes' practice I had complete confidence in the mirror routine; but we also arranged that I should spread out my bright orange sleeping bag as a marker, and would have a fire and some water ready so that when the plane had located me and came over low on a trial run I could send up a plume of smoke to indicate wind direction.

Because I was not sure how far I could travel across very rough country in a week, and because I did not want to be held back if I found I could move fast, we arranged primary and alternate sites for the first drop. We set zero hour at ten a.m. on the eighth morning after I left an Indian village that would be my last contact with civilization. The chances were good that at ten o'clock no clouds would obscure the sun and that the day's desert winds would not yet have sprung up.

I made the alternate site in time and, with complete confidence in the mirror signaling technique, decided for various reasons to take the drop about two miles from the prearranged place, out on a flat red rock-terrace. The plane arrived dead on schedule. But it failed to see my frantic flashings, and after an hour's fruitless search around the prime site and back along the way I'd come was heading for home and passing not too far from me when I poured water on the waiting fire and sent a column of smoke spiraling up into the clear air. Almost at once, the plane banked toward me, and within minutes my supplies were sailing safely down, suspended from a big orange parachute.

Later, a park ranger in the plane told me that he'd seen the smoke the moment it rose in the air. "But we didn't see the flashing until we were almost on top of you. At a guess, I'd say you didn't shake the mirror enough. You've got to do that to set up a good flashing. Oh, and your orange sleeping bag didn't show up at all against that red rock. We could hardly see it, even on the drop run."

So my first airdrop taught me a valuable lesson: unless it is absolutely unavoidable, don't change your prearranged drop site, even by a short distance. For the two later drops on that trip we had picked only one site, and each time I was in exactly the right place. I also had the white eight-by-nine-foot plastic sheet (page 155) in my pack, and I spread it out beside the sleeping bag. Each time, the pilot saw the white patch as soon as he came within range, and although I had begun to flash with the mirror, the plane rocked its wings in recognition and stopped me before there was time to assess the mirror's worth. Both these later drops went off without a hitch.

I didn't have a chance to test the mirror technique again on the only other airdrop I have taken. That was on the seventeen-day hike-and-swim trip down the Colorado. The pilot this time was a young man named Jack Westcott whose father before him had flown the whole Grand Canyon region. The drop had to be down in the Inner Gorge, between rockwalls more than two thousand feet high and, at their foot, barely two hundred yards apart. From the map we selected a clearly defined ledge for the drop site; but, because my route was untried, there was no certainty I could make it that far down in time. So we agreed that if Jack did not see me at the appointed place he would fly on upriver to the point at which I started and then would return, still low. He would come between five thirty and six in the morning, before any wind was likely to spring up. At that hour there would be no sun to reflect with a mirror, but I would have a fire ready and would signal with smoke. If Jack missed me on the upriver flight, I would on his return sortie signal not only with natural smoke but also with the "day" end of a day-and-night signal flare.*

In spite of pushing as fast as I could, I failed to reach the drop site in time. At dusk the day before our scheduled rendezvous, I was still three miles upriver. In that country, three miles meant three or four hours' hard slogging, even in daylight—and night travel is just about impossible. So I camped on the most obvious and open ledge I could find—though it was neither very obvious nor very open. Before cooking dinner I collected a healthy pile of dry driftwood (working at the end by flashlight). I set two full canteens beside the wood and spread out my white plastic sheet and weighted down its corners with stones.

In the morning I had the fire alight by five twenty-five. The minutes ticked past. Five forty-five . . . five fifty-five . . . six o'clock. A couple of centuries later my watch read six thirty. A millennium more, and it was seven o'clock. Now I should warn you that if you are waiting for an airdrop and the plane is late, your mind conjures up the most dire explanations. At least, mine does. (The same thing happened when the plane was late for one of the earlier Grand Can-

---

* Each end of this flare burns for forty-five seconds—one as a red flame for night use, the other in dense orange smoke. (Weight, 7 ounces; cost unknown —it was a naval flare, given to the man who gave it to me.) The flare I'd recommend for purely daytime use was not available at that particular time. It also gives off orange smoke but burns for one minute (1½ by 5 inches; 3 ounces; $2.50).

yon drops.) By seven twenty-five, the only doubt left was whether the failure was due to Jack Westcott's having crashed or to the beginning of World War III. The plane came at seven thirty. It came low, so that the sound of its motor gave me little warning, but I managed to pour the contents of both canteens onto the fire just as it appeared. Now desert driftwood burns very quickly and you can't keep a big blaze going for two hours without a truckload of logs, so the fire had burned pretty low and when I poured the water on all it produced was a feeble little puff of smoke that rose barely six feet. The plane passed slowly by, way out over the river, with no sign of having seen me. (By this time, sunlight was streaming obliquely across the gorge just above my camp, and Jack told me later that as he flew upriver it shone directly into his eyes. It was all he could do to see the rockwalls, he said, let alone shadowy details down beside the river.)

By the time the plane came back downriver I had the fire blazing again, and plenty of water ready. The signal flare lay beside the waiting canteens and cooking pots. The moment I heard the plane's motor I emptied both cooking pots onto the fire. A column of dense smoke rose high into the air. I picked up the signal flare and tugged at the metal loop of the friction igniter at the "day" end. For a moment nothing happened. I pulled harder. Suddenly the tab pulled free and dense orange smoke gushed out and up. And then, before this smoke had risen more than a few feet, the plane was thundering directly overhead, very low. It did not rock its wings in recognition, but I felt fairly confident from the angle at which it came that it had turned in toward me from out over the river. And when it somehow managed to turn, deep within the gorge, just a few hundred yards downriver, I knew that Jack had seen me. The plane came back somewhat higher—perhaps three hundred feet up—with the motor running very slowly. As it passed overhead a dark blob dropped clear. Almost at once, the parachute opened. It was a makeshift parachute that Jack, to save me unnecessary expense, had made by stitching together two plastic windsocks. It worked perfectly. The unprotected metal can landed about fifty feet from my white marker. It landed, rather heavily, among some angular rocks. One corner of the can was dented, but when I had cut free the nylon cords and had pried off the lid, everything looked fine. Above all, there was no smell of butane from the two refill cartridges for the Bluet stove (page 111). Before I had checked all the can's contents the plane came by again, heading back downriver. I butterflied "All's well" with my arms. The plane vanished. In the suddenly very silent silence, I finished my check. The damage was minor: a couple of food bags had burst, with no serious effects.

Later, Jack told me that on his second run he had seen the smoke from the fire, clear and unmistakable, from far upriver. It rose well above the rocks and trees that hemmed in my little ledge. He did not think he had seen the orange smoke on that run (probably because the flare had only just begun to burn); but on the drop run, when he was once more heading into the blinding sun, the big orange cloud, which persisted very effectively, had shown up well.

So from my limited experience with airdrops I have come to the following tentative conclusions: The easiest and surest way to attract a pilot's attention under suitable conditions is by a fire-and-water smoke column. A good day flare may be even better, but is perhaps too valuable in an emergency (see page 312) to be used in supply drops except when other methods have failed. Obviously, there are conditions under which any smoke signal may be ineffective: among very tall trees (where you'd hardly choose to take a parachute drop anyway), and probably in very high winds. For me, mirror-flashing remains an unproven but potentially valuable method. (I always carry a mirror nowadays, mainly for emergency use.) As for markers, I suspect that white is better than orange on most backgrounds other than snow. Finally, I grant now that it is dangerous to change your drop site unilaterally; but if you are going to be somewhere along an unmistakable line, such as a river, and the pilot is prepared to search along it, you can with reasonable safety leave a lot of latitude.

Helicopter

Although often physically feasible, supply by helicopter is expensive. Average charter rates for a small helicopter operating no higher than about five thousand feet run around $60 an hour. Supercharged 'copters for mountain work may cost $100 an hour. (Comparable rates for small conventional plane: $25–$30.)

Most wilderness rescue work is now carried out by helicopter. It's therefore worth knowing that helicopters cannot put down just anywhere. A slope of more than about ten degrees is not a feasible landing place for even a small machine. In good conditions, though, on a clear surface, an expert pilot may be able to hover with one skid on a steeper slope long enough to pick up a casualty. But even for this method the slope cannot be more than about twenty-five degrees.

Pack animal or support backpacker

I have never tried replenishing supplies by either of these methods. Obviously, though, you must make cast-iron arrangements about the meeting place—and hardened-steel arrangements if someone else is going to plant your cache.

AUXILIARY PACK ANIMAL

Indoorsmen often ask why I never use a pack animal on any of my long walks. They always seem to mean a burro, and blame for the thought probably lies with Robert Louis Stevenson and his *Travels with a Donkey.*

Frankly, I've never even been tempted to try. For one thing, I can go places a burro can't. And I blench at the prospect of looking after a burro's food and water supply. Also, although I know nothing at firsthand about managing the beasts, I mistrust their dispositions. Come to think of it, I do not seem to be alone in my mistrust. Precious few people use burros these days. It is perhaps significant that on the one occasion I can remember coming across the man-beast combination, the man was on one side of a small creek pulling furiously and vainly at the halter of the burro, and the burro was planted on the far bank with heels dug resolutely in.

Should you decide to use a pack animal, note that The Smilie Company of San Francisco (Appendix II) offers mulepacking as well as backpacking equipment.

DANGERS, REAL AND IMAGINED

For cross-country walkers, no single source of fear quite compares with that stirred up by

Rattlesnakes.*

Every year, an almost morbid terror of the creatures ruins or at least tarnishes countless otherwise delightful hikes all over the United States and Canada. This terror is based largely on folklore and myth, hardly at all on fact.

Now rattlesnakes can be dangerous, but they are not what so many people fancy them to be: vicious and cunning brutes with a deep-seated hatred of man. In solid fact, rattlers are timid and retiring. They are highly developed reptiles, but they simply do not have the brain capacity for cunning in our human sense. And although they react to man as they would to any big and threatening creature, they could hardly have built up a deep-seated hatred: the first man that one of them sees is usually the last. In addition, the risk of being bitten by a rattler is slight, and the danger that a bite will prove fatal to a healthy adult is small.†

---

* Only two distinct kinds of poisonous snakes occur in the United States: the coral snakes and the pit vipers—a group that includes rattlesnakes, cottonmouths (or water moccasins), and copperheads.

Coral snakes, though highly poisonous, rarely bite humans; and they are restricted to the southeast corner of the country and to one part of Arizona.

† In the United States, more people are killed and injured in their bathtubs than by snakebite. Of 190 million Americans, perhaps 1,100 will be bitten this year. Eleven of these (or 1 per cent) may die; but this figure includes people who have been badly frightened, those with weak hearts, and small children whose bodies cannot absorb the venom. Even without treatment, odds on survival are long.

In other words, ignorance as usual has bred deep and unreasoning fear—a fear that may even cause more harm than snakebite. Not long ago, near San Diego, California, a hunter who was spiked by barbed wire thought he had been struck by a rattler—and very nearly died of shock.

The surest antidote to fear is knowledge. When I began my California walk I knew nothing about rattlesnakes, and the first one I met scared me purple. Killing it seemed a human duty. But by the end of the summer I no longer felt this unreasoning fear, and as a result I no longer killed rattlers—unless they lived close to places frequented by people.

Later I grew interested enough to write a magazine article about rattlesnakes, and in researching it I read the entire 1,500-odd pages of the last-word bible on the subject. As I read, the fear sank even further away. Gradually I came to accept rattlesnakes as fellow creatures with a niche in the web of life.

The book I read was *Rattlesnakes: Their Habits, Life Histories and Influence on Mankind* by Laurence M. Klauber (2 vols.; University of California Press, 1956; $22.50). Dr. Klauber is the world's leading authority on rattlesnakes, and he sets out in detail all the known biological facts. But he does more. He examines and exposes the dense cloud of fancy and folklore that swirls around his subject. I heartily recommend this fascinating book to anyone who finds that his peace of mind is sometimes disturbed by a blind fear of rattlesnakes—and also to anyone interested in widening the fields in which he can observe and understand when he goes walking. The book should be found in any university library, and in any medium-size or large public library.

Among the many folklore fables Dr. Klauber punctures is the classic "boot story." I first heard this one down in the Colorado Desert of Southern California—and believed it. "There was this rancher," the old-timer told me, "who lived not far from here. One day he wore some kneeboots belonging to his father, who had died ten years before. Next day, the rancher's leg began to swell. It grew rapidly worse. Eventually he went to a doctor—just in time to avoid amputation from rattlesnake poisoning. Then he remembered that his father had been struck when wearing the same boots a year before he died. One of the snake's fangs had broken off and lodged in an eyehole. Eleven years later, it scratched the son."

Essentially the same story was read before the Royal Society of London by a New World traveler on January 7, 1714. That version told how the boot killed three successive husbands of a Virginia woman. Today the incident may take place anywhere, coast to coast, and the boot is sometimes modernized into a struck and punctured tire that proves fatal to successive garagemen who repair it. Actually, the amount of dried venom on the point of a fang is negligible. And venom exposed to air quickly loses its potency.

Then there is the legend of the "avenging mate": Kill one rattler, and its mate will vengefully seek you out. Pliny, the Roman naturalist who died in A.D. 79, told this story of European snakes, and it's still going strong over here. In 1954, after a rattlesnake had been killed in a downtown Los Angeles apartment, the occupant refused to go back because a search had failed to unearth the inevitably waiting mate.

The legend probably arose because it seems as though a male may occasionally court a freshly killed female. Some years ago, a geographer friend of mine and a zoologist companion, looking for specimens for research, killed a rattler high in California's Sierra Nevada. The zoologist carried the snake two hundred yards to a log and began skinning it. My friend sat facing him. Suddenly he saw another rattler crawling toward them. "It was barely four yards away," he told me later, "and heading directly for the dead snake; but it was taking its time and seemed quite unaware of our presence. We killed it before it even rattled. It was a male. The first was a female." An untrained observer might well have seen this incident as proof positive that the second snake was bent on revenge.

Recently, toward the end of my seventeen-day trip down the Colorado, I saw with my own eyes just how another myth could have arisen. I was running very short of food, and after meeting four rattlers within four days I reluctantly decided that if I met another I would kill and cook it. I duly met one. It was maybe three feet long— about as big as they grow in that country. I promptly hit it with my staff a little forward of the tail, breaking its back and immobilizing it; but before I could put it out of its pain by crushing its head, it began striking wildly about in all directions. Soon—and apparently quite by accident—it struck itself halfway down the body. It was a perfect demonstration of how the myth arose that wounded rattlers will strike themselves to commit suicide. (Quite apart from the question of whether snakes can comprehend the idea of a future death, rattlesnakes are little affected by rattlesnake venom.)

After I had killed that snake I cut off the head, wrapped the body in a plastic bag, and put it in my pack; but I could not for the life of me remember what Dr. Klauber had said about eating rattlers that had struck themselves. As I walked on, thinking of the venom that was probably still circulating through the snake's blood system, I grew less and less hungry. After half an hour, feeling decidedly guilty about the unnecessary killing, I discarded the corpse.

Later, I found that although people are often warned against eating a rattler that has bitten itself there is in fact no danger. The poisonous quality of snake venom is destroyed by heat. It's as well to cut out the bitten part, though, just as you cut away damaged meat in an animal that has been shot. Back in the 1870's, one experimenter got a big rattler to bite itself three or four times. It lived nineteen hours and seemed unhurt. He then cooked and ate it without ill effect!

According to Dr. Klauber, rattler meat has been compared with chicken, veal, frog, tortoise, quail, fish, canned tuna, and rabbit. It is, as he points out, useful as an emergency ration because it is easily hunted down and killed, even by people weakened by starvation. But there's only one pound of meat on a four-foot rattler, $2\frac{1}{2}$ pounds on a five-footer, and $4\frac{1}{2}$ on a six-footer.

Even straightforward information about rattlesnakes often gets hopelessly garbled in the popular imagination. For example, the only facts about rattlers that many people know for sure are that they grow an extra rattle every year, revel in blistering heat, and are fast and unfailingly deadly. Not one of these "facts" is true. Number of rattles is almost no indication of age. A rattler soon dies if the temperature around it rises much over 100°. It crawls so slowly that the only dangerous rattler is the one you don't see. Even the strike is not nearly as fast as was once thought. Tests prove it to be rather slower than a trained man's punching fist. If you move first —as fast as you can, and clean out of range—you may get away with it, though avoiding the strike, even if you're waiting for it, borders on the impossible.

Accurate knowledge will not only help dispel many unreasoning fears (it is nearly always the unknown that we fear the most), but can materially reduce the chances that you will be bitten.

Take the matter of heat and cold, for example. Rattlesnakes, like all reptiles, lack an efficient mechanism such as we have for keeping body temperature constant, so they are wholly dependent on the temperature around them. In cold climates they can hibernate indefinitely at a few degrees above freezing, and have fully recovered after four hours in a deep freeze at $4°$F. Yet they can hardly move at $45°$F., and they rarely choose to prowl in temperatures below $65°$. Their "best" range is $80-90°$F. But at $100°$ they're in danger, and at $110°$ they die of heat stroke. But these, remember, are *their* temperatures—that is, the temperatures their bodies attain through contact with the ground over which they are moving and with the air around them. These temperatures may differ markedly from official weather readings taken in the shade, five feet above ground level. When such a reading is $60°$, for example, a thermometer down on sunlit sand may record $100°$, and in the lowest inch of air about $80°$. (See pages 45 and 259.) In other words, a rattler may feel snugly comfortable in a weather temperature of $60°$. On the other hand, in a desert temperature of $80°$ in the shade the sunlit sand might be over $130°$ and the lowest inch of air around $110°$, and any rattler staying for long in such a place would die.

Once you know a few such facts, you find after a little practice that your mind almost automatically tells you when to be especially watchful, and even where to avoid placing your feet. In cool early-season weather, for example, when rattlers like to bask, you will tend to keep a sharp lookout, if the sun is shining but a cold wind is blowing, in sunlit places that are sheltered from the wind. And in hot desert weather you will know that there is absolutely no danger out on open sand where there is no shade. On the other hand, the prime feeding time for rattlers in warm weather is two hours before and after sunset, when the small mammals that are their main prey tend to be on the move; so if you figure that the ground temperature during that time is likely to be around 80° or 90°, you keep your eyes skinned.

You'll be safer, too, once you understand how rattlesnakes receive their impressions of the world around them. Their sight is poor, and they are totally deaf. But they're well equipped with other senses. Two small facial pits contain nerves so sensitive to heat that a rattler can strike accurately at warm-blooded prey in complete darkness. (Many species hunt mainly at night.) They're highly sensitive to vibration too, and have rattled at men passing out of sight 150 feet away. (Moral: in bad rattler country, at bad times, tread heavily.) Two nostrils just above a rattler's mouth furnish a sense of smell very like ours. And that's not all. A sure sign that a snake has been alerted is a flickering of its forked tongue: it is "smelling" the outside world. The tongue's moist surface picks up tiny particles floating in the air and at each flicker transfers them to two small cavities in the roof of the mouth. These cavities, called "Jacobson's Organs," interpret the particles to the brain in terms of smell, much as do the moist membranes inside our noses.

In Biblical times, people wrongly associated snakes' tongues with their poison. Nothing has changed. Stand at the rattlesnake cage in any zoo and the chances are you'll soon hear somebody say, "There, did you see its stinger?" or even, "Look at it stick out its fangs!" It is true, though, that an alarmed snake will sometimes use its tongue to intimidate enemies. When it does, the forked tips quiver pugnaciously out at their limit, arching first up, then down. It's a chillingly effective display. But primarily, of course, a snake reacts to enemies with that unique rattle. Harmless in itself, it warns and intimidates, like the growl of a dog.

The rattle is a chain of hollow, interlocking segments made of the same hard and transparent keratin as human nails. The myth that each segment represents a year of the snake's age first appeared in print as early as 1615. Actually, a new segment is left each time the snake sheds its skin. Young rattlers shed frequently, and adults an average of one to three times each year. In any case, the fragile rattles rarely remain complete for very long.

In action, the rattles shake so fast that they blur like the wings of a hummingbird. Small snakes merely buzz like a fly, but big specimens sound off with a strident hiss that rises to a spine-chilling crescendo. Someone once said that it was "like a pressure cooker with the safety valve open." Once you've heard the sound, you'll never forget it.

The biggest rattlers are eastern diamondbacks: outsize specimens may weigh thirty pounds and measure almost eight feet. But most of the thirty different species grow to no more than three or four feet.

People often believe that rattlers will strike only when coiled, and never upward. It is true that they can strike most effectively from the alert, raised-spiral position; but they are capable of striking from any position and in any direction.

Rattlers are astonishingly tenacious of life. One old saying warns "They're dangerous even after they're dead"—and it is true. Lab tests have shown that severed heads can bite a stick and discharge venom for up to forty-three minutes. The tests even produced some support for the old notion that "rattlers never die till sundown." Decapitated bodies squirmed for as long as 7½ hours, moved when pinched for even longer. And the hearts almost always went on beating for a day, often for two days. One was still pulsating after fifty-nine hours.

A rattlesnake's enemies include other snakes (especially king snakes and racers), birds, mammals, and even fish. In Grand Canyon I found a three-foot rattler apparently trampled to death by wild burros. Torpid captive rattlers have been killed and part eaten by mice put in their cages for food! Not long ago, a California fisherman caught a big rainbow trout with a nine-inch rattler in its stomach. But only one species of animal makes appreciable inroads on the rattlesnake population. That species is man—to whom the warning rattle is an invitation to attack. If man had existed when rattlesnakes began to evolve, perhaps six million years ago, it is unlikely the newfangled rattlebearers would have succeeded and flourished.

In spite of stories to the contrary, a rattlesnake meeting a large animal such as man does not attack so long as the potential enemy stays outside its striking range. (Very rarely, when courting, it may just possibly attack; but then, so will a deer or even a rabbit.) It may move toward you, but that will be for other reasons, such as the slope of the ground. Its first reaction is most likely to lie still and escape attention. Then it may crawl slowly for safety. Detected or alarmed, it will probably rattle and rise into its menacing defensive coil—a vibrant, open-spiral quite distinct from the tightly wound pancake resting position. It may also hiss. Finally, it may strike. Usually, though by no means always, it will rattle before striking. Of course, none of these comments necessarily applies if a man treads on it or comes suddenly and alarmingly within its restricted little world. Then, not unnaturally, it will often strike without warning.

But it's important to remember that rattlesnakes are as moody as men, as unpredictable as women. A man who for many years was rattlesnake control officer of South Dakota concluded that they simply "are not to be trusted, for some will violate all rules." Certain individuals, even whole species, seem to be always "on the prod." A few habitually strike without warning. Others seem almost amiable.

Defense is not, of course, the main purpose of a rattler's venom and fangs. Primarily, they're for securing food.

The fangs, regularly replaced, are precision instruments. One slender, curving tooth on each side of the snake's upper jaw grows almost five times longer than its fellows. In large rattlers it may measure ¾ inch. A cunning pivot-and-lever bone structure ensures that when the mouth is closed these fierce barbs lie flat; but as the jaws open wide to strike they pivot erect. Each fang is hollow. Its cavity connects with a venom sac beneath the eye, equivalent to our salivary gland. When the fangs stab into a prey, the snake injects a controlled dose of venom through the cavity and out of an aperture just above the fang's point. In the small mammals that rattlers mostly feed on, the venom causes almost instant paralysis and rapid death.

A rattlesnake's venom—present from birth—is as unpredictable as its temperament. Quantity and toxicity seem to vary widely from species to species, from individual to individual. In general, though, the bigger the snake the greater the danger: a big snake stabs deeper with its fangs and injects more venom. But there are other, quite unpredictable, factors in any case of snakebite. It's not just that a rattler can control, at least to some degree, the amount of venom it injects; the quantity in its sacs will vary markedly according to whether it has or has not expended venom recently in killing prey.

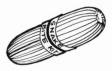

Treatment of snakebite

The greatest danger is probably hysteria; people bitten by harmless snakes have come close to dying from fright. What many snakebite patients need most, in fact, is rest and reassurance. But there is no doubt that in genuine cases of snakebite *quick* physical treatment can save lives.

Some doctors hold that the only emergency treatment worth a damn is cryotherapy: making the site of the bite so cold that the body absorbs the venom slowly enough to neutralize the most serious effects. For use in the field, where more elaborate treatment will not normally be available, they recommend carrying ethyl chloride. Applied to the skin, it evaporates quickly and cools the immediate area.

This method enjoyed a recent vogue but seems to be losing favor. Many doctors now recommend the old cut-and-suck method: removing as much venom as you can, *as soon as possible.* The first few seconds and minutes are the critical time, before the bulk of the venom has a chance to circulate. I find myself inclined to believe the cut-and-suck experts—possibly because theirs was the first method I learned. Anyway, I always carry a Cutter Compak Suction Kit in my pocket: One of these neat little devices (1 ounce; $2.98) is no bigger than a 12-gauge shell. It includes three rubber suction cups. Two of these cups form the kit's outer shell and are indented on the outside so that they grip the bottom of your pants pocket. I have never had one even hint that it might fall out. The interlocking suction cups contain a small, very sharp blade, a vial of sterilizing liquid, a tourniquet, and full instructions. Memorize at least the essence of the instructions. And always remember that in the unlikely event of your being bitten it's the first few seconds and minutes that count.

The "cryotherapists" tend to decry the effectiveness of cut-and-suck. "Cut-and-suckers" reciprocate. This is known as human nature. It may well be that the practical answer is to do the best you can with both methods. Meanwhile, I shall continue to carry my little rubber lozenge. There may be some element of doubt about its effectiveness, but I can assure you that in snake country its presence in your pants pocket is highly reassuring. A less purely psychological consideration is that, unlike ethyl chloride, it is always with you—unless you take off your pants.

The one emergency treatment that everyone now agrees is not merely useless but positively dangerous—because it stimulates your metabolism and therefore spreads the venom more quickly—is the old-timers' "snakebite cure": alcohol.

Any snakebite kit you carry (unless it contains an antivenin, and that can be dangerous for an inexperienced layman to use) is essentially an emergency measure. Whenever possible, get the patient (whether yourself or a companion) to a doctor as quickly as possible. He will be able to administer one of the modern, highly efficient antivenins. But the advantages of medical treatment have to be balanced against the dangers of rapid movement that will spread the venom quickly. If you are many miles from the nearest help, particularly if alone, the safest thing to do after applying suction treatment may be to rest in a cool place, keep the site of the bite as cold as possible (perhaps with creek water), immobilize that part of the body, and prepare for a forty-eight-hour siege—during which you are likely to vomit and retch and feel feverish and generally pretty damned bad.

I must accent that what I have said applies only to rattlesnakes and the other pit vipers of the United States and Canada (see footnote, page 295). All have comparatively low-toxicity venom. Where the snakes are much more deadly—such as in Africa and, I understand, Central and South America—the only worthwhile snakebite kit is antivenin and a syringe.

I hope this rather long discourse has convinced you that rattlesnakes, although dangerous, are not the vicious and deadly brutes of legend. If you have in the past felt, as so many people do, a deep and unreasoning fear of them, then I hope I have helped just a little in dispelling that fear—and have left you free to walk anywhere with enjoyment.

You may even find that your understanding of rattlesnakes passes at length beyond mere factual knowledge. I have described in *The Man Who Walked Through Time* (page 166) how I was sitting one afternoon on a sandbar at the edge of a willow thicket when I saw a pale-pink rattlesnake come gliding over the sand, barely six feet away from me, clearly unaware of my presence. Sitting there watching it, I found that I felt curiosity rather than fear. Slowly, gracefully, the snake threaded its way through a forest of willow shoots. As its flank pushed past each stem I could see the individual scales tilt under the stem's pressure, then move back flush. Four feet from my left buttock the snake stopped, its head in a sun-dappled patch of sand beside a cluster of roots. Unhurriedly, it drew its body forward and curled into a flat resting coil. Then it stretched and yawned. It yawned a long and unmistakable yawn. A yawn so uninhibited that for many slow seconds I seemed to see nothing but the pale lining of its mouth and two matching arcs of small, sharp teeth. When the yawn was over at last the snake raised its head and twisted it slowly and luxuriously from side to side, as a man or a woman will do in anticipation of rest and comfort to come. Finally, with such obvious contentment that I do not think I would have been altogether surprised to hear the creature purr, it laid its head gently on the pillow of its clean and beautifully marked body.

And all at once, for the first time in my life, I found that I had moved "inside" a rattlesnake. Quite unexpectedly, I had shared its sleepiness and anticipation and contentment. And as I sat looking down at the sleeping snake coiled in its patch of sun-dappled shade, I found myself feeling for it something remarkably close to affection.

Frankly, the feeling has not lasted. I am still no rattlesnake *aficionado*. But my fear, helped by the moment of understanding, has now contracted to vanishing point. Recently, on my trip down lower Grand Canyon, I met five rattlesnakes in five days. One small specimen even struck from under a stone and hit my boot (no damage done). Yet even at that moment I do not think I felt fear—only interest and curiosity. But—and it may be a very big "but"—the rattlesnakes of Grand Canyon do not grow more than about three feet long. Whether I would have been so consistently calm in country thick with big diamondbacks, I just don't know.

Scorpions

A friend of mine who does a great deal of hiking in Arizona once told me that he worried more about scorpions than about rattlesnakes. "You can see the rattlers," he said.

In Arizona there is good reason for respecting scorpions: the sting of two quite small, sand-colored species that are found in that state—and only there—is always serious and can prove fatal. But the sting of other scorpions found in North America (except Mexico) is rarely much more serious than a beesting. (Remember, though, that some people react violently to almost any venom. For them, even a bee sting may be fatal.)

But unless you go around turning up stones you are not very likely to see a scorpion. I have only come across one; and that, rather surprisingly, was at an elevation of over 10,000 feet.

There is a well-known desert tradition that in scorpion country you always turn out your boots before putting them on in the morning. Before I went down into Grand Canyon I asked an experienced park ranger about it. "Oh, it always sounds to me like an old wives' tale," he said. Then a smile leaked slowly out over his face, and he added, "But I still do it."

Tarantulas and black widows

The chance of being bitten by either of these spiders is small. And the tarantulas that occur in the United States do not, in spite of their evil aspect and matching reputation, inflict a serious bite. No more serious, again, than a bee sting.

But black widows are dangerous. Although they're very much smaller, their bites are always serious and can prove fatal, even to adults. Cut-and-suck treatment is ineffective: there's simply not enough venom (which is of a neurotoxic type). Cryotherapy or cooling of the site (see page 303) is the best first aid. Keep the patient (whether you or non-you) quiet, and if possible get him to a doctor as soon as possible. At first, the only sensation may be as of a pin-prick—though the spider may still be adhering to the skin. But after a few hours the pain may become severe.

Black widows have spherical bodies about the size of a marble. They do not have particularly noticeable legs. They are entirely black except for a red patch on the underside, shaped like an hourglass.

Other animals

Contrary to popular indoor opinion, there is almost no danger from such large and reputedly ferocious mammals as mountain lions and bobcats. Mountain lions (also called cougars) may follow you at a safe distance out of curiosity, but they will not attack—unless, possibly, you have a dog with you. I have woken up to find fresh bobcat tracks within six feet of my sleeping bag.

It is fairly safe to say that no healthy animal will attack you unless provoked. But it can be provoked unintentionally. If you stumble on almost any animal and surprise and frighten it, it may react ferociously in self-defense. Again, thirst or hunger or the sex urge or mother love may turn a normally peaceful beast into a potentially dangerous one. The best known example is probably the black bear mother with cubs. But even rabbits, when courting, have been known to attack an interfering intruder.

Another possible but extremely slight risk is from attack by rabid animals. I have seen only one animal that I assumed was rabid: a jackal that in broad daylight walked openly across a wheat field we were harvesting in Kenya. It seemed to be walking in a self-contained little world of its own, and it took no notice at all of either a combine or several people standing alongside. As it walked it kept twitching its head in a regular and demented fashion. It was, in other words, "acting contrary to general behavior patterns"—which is what rabid animals are described as habitually doing.

Naturally, you just have to take your chance over these very slight risks from attack by wild animals. Provided you behave sensibly, the danger is probably a great deal less than that involved in getting to the wilderness, when some unprovoked animal traveling rapidly in the opposite direction may fall asleep or suffer a heart attack or a burst tire and slew across the dividing line and write an abrupt "finis" to your little game.

There seems to be some doubt about how far you can trust grizzly bears; but grizzly bear country is now pretty accurately defined, so you can take precautions:

1. Stay away; or
2. Accept the risk (knowing that it's likely to be less in really remote areas than in places the bears have been harassed by humans); or
3. Walk alertly and carry a big gun. (Except in rare cases, this is a poor solution that could turn out to be the most dangerous of the lot.)

There is one animal, though, that puts the fear of God into me: *Homo sapiens nimrodamericanus,* the red-breasted, red-blooded, North American hunter. Every year, in the fall, the woods are alive with hunters, and every year a few more hunters fall dead. I am aware that some of the massacre stories are probably apocryphal, but I play it safe: when the calendar springs the hunters loose, I stay at home.

Outside North America, the general animal situation can be less reassuring. In East Africa, for example, many rhinos and some elephants and buffalo will charge without apparent provocation. (Or does trespass on another animal's territory constitute provocation? Remember Cuba.) Lions, if surprised, may also attack. See also page 145.

Lightning

Lightning is a low-risk danger worth learning something about: knowledge can reduce the hazard to the vanishing point.

Mountains are the dangerous places. American Alpine Club statistics show that in the past eleven years there have been seven lightning accidents on U.S. mountains. Seventeen people were involved. Seven died.

If you are caught up high in a storm, the first thing to remember is the old mountaineering maxim: "In a storm, get off peaks and ridges." Avoid steep inclines (where the current flows fastest) and seek out flat ledges or gentle slopes. If possible, get near a pinnacle that will act as a lightning rod. Stay a little way out from its base but not farther away than its height. Crouch low, touching the ground only with your feet, or sit on some insulator such as a coiled climbing rope. A cave, although the obvious shelter, is probably the most dangerous place of all, unless it is very deep and high-roofed. Stay resolutely clear of shallow, low-roofed caves that are really no more than overhanging ledges. On August 4, 1948, a party of four California climbers was surprised by a storm near the summit of Bugaboo Spire in British Columbia and took shelter in just such a "cave." Almost at once, a bolt of lightning struck outside the entrance. Two of the party died; the other two, dazed and burned, barely managed to make their way down safely.

No matter how careful you are, of course, the element of luck remains. On Bugaboo Spire, it was the chance positioning of the four members of the party at the moment of the strike that determined who would live and who would die. Remember, though, that near-strikes such as the Bugaboo party suffered are not always serious. That day, three other parties of the same expedition were all "hit," out in the open, with no ill effects. And mountains are by no means the only dangerous places. On the same day as the Bugaboo accident, two children were killed by lightning in an open field in Oklahoma.

Many experienced outdoorsmen—and all responsible hiking organizations—contend that the greatest danger in wilderness travel is one that permeates this book:

Walking alone.

They may have something too. But once you have discovered solitude—the gigantic, enveloping, including, renewing solitude of wild and silent places—and have learned to put it to creative use, you are likely to accept without a second thought such small additional dangers as the solitude imposes. Naturally, you are careful. You make darned sure that someone always knows where you are, and when you will be "out." You leave broad margins of safety in everything you do: hurrying (or not hurrying) over rough country to make up time; crossing (or not crossing) the creek on that narrow log; inching past (or not inching past) that perilously perched boulder. And when it comes to the all-important matter of luck, you keep firmly in mind the Persian proverb I have already quoted: "Fortune is infatuated with the efficient."

But if you judge safety to be the paramount consideration in life you should never, under any circumstances, go on long hikes alone. Don't take short hikes alone either—or, for that matter, go anywhere alone. And avoid at all costs such foolhardy activities as driving, falling in love, or inhaling air that is almost certainly riddled with deadly germs. Wear wool next to the skin. Insure every good and chattel you possess against every conceivable contingency the future might bring, even if the premiums half-cripple the present. Never cross an intersection against a red light, even when you can see that all roads are clear for miles. And never, of course, explore the guts of an idea that seems as if it might threaten one of your more cherished beliefs. In your wisdom you will probably live to a ripe old age. But you may discover, just before you die, that you have been dead for a long, long time.

A book like this should obviously have something to say about

SURVIVAL.

But I find to my surprise that I can rake up precious little—and that I've never really given the matter the thought it seems to deserve.

Hoping to fill this awkward and humiliating gap in my knowledge, I asked a friend of mine—an experienced hiker, a cross-country skier of repute, and an expert climber who has been on Alaskan and Himalayan expeditions—for suggestions about books to read. "Oh, I dunno," he said. "I never read them. And I guess I never give the matter much thought."

Somewhat relieved but still uneasy, I turned for counsel to a practical outdoorsman who is in heavy demand as an instructor of survival and associated crafts. We talked for some time, but with each subject he brought up—water sources, signal flares, first-aid and snakebite kits, loosening waistbelt when wading rivers, and so on —I found myself saying, "Oh, but I've discussed that in the book as part of normal operating procedure."

After four or five such answers my counselor paused. "Yes," he said slowly. "Come to think of it, I guess you could say, really, that if you know how to operate properly in wilderness, then you know most of what there is to know about survival.

"What it generally amounts to, anyway, with inexperienced people, is simply not giving in to terror. That's what usually happens: ignorance—then panic. If your partner breaks a leg, for instance, you're in bad shape if you start thinking, "Is it safe to leave him here, with all these wild animals around?" Of course it's safe —provided he's warm and comfortable. But if you don't know that, and feel suddenly overwhelmed and alone, you're liable to give way to panic. Naturally, you must be able to find your way out to civilization, or the nearest help, and then guide rescuers back unerringly to the right place . . . but here we're back with plain competence in operating. And this is the kind of survival problem that's most likely to arise with walkers in the United States. Almost anywhere, outside of Alaska, you can get out to civilization—if you can walk—within two days at most. The old idea of survival as the problem of having to look after yourself for six months, completely cut off, when you're in good physical shape, just doesn't apply here any more. And the rest amounts in most cases to medical knowledge and common sense."

Living off the land (see page 66) poses a different problem. It's a real one all right, but the answers are specifically local. Knowing what to eat and what not to eat in the Sierra Nevada will get you nowhere in the Adirondacks, and even less place in the Mojave Desert. In each kind of country you have to learn it all again. Sometimes there are local books or pamphlets—often listed in equipment makers' catalogues (Appendix II). Useful sources include Explorer Scouts, hiking and mountaineering clubs (Appendix III), and universities (forestry departments might be good places to start).

If you want reassurance on the broader questions of survival, and if you're a reader of books on such matters (and I guess you are if you've come 300 pages with me), there's plenty of material. Some of the best-known books are by Bradford Angier (*Living Off the Country,* Stackpole, 1956, $5, with a paperback version called *How to Stay Alive in the Woods,* by Macmillan, Collier Books, 95 cents; *How to Go Live in the Woods,* Stackpole, 1959, $5; and *Free for the Eating, Stackpole,* 1966, $4.95), but the survival sections are apparently oriented toward the north woods and the problem of being cut off for months on end, far from help. Another and perhaps more applicable book is *Getting Out of Outdoor Trouble* by W. K. Merrill, Stackpole, 1965, $2.95. *How to Survive on Land and Sea* by Frank C. and John J. Craighead (published by the U.S. Naval Institute, Physical Education Series, Annapolis, 1943, $4) has for years been the survival bible. I understand, though, that it's now regarded as the old testament—and that the new testament does not yet seem to have been written.

But perhaps, like me, you're lazy or a touch skeptical about such reading. If so, just remember, comfortably, that survival is 80 per cent competence, 20 per cent local knowledge, and 100 per cent keeping your cool.

Emergency signals

These days, almost any search operation for people believed lost in wild country is carried out, at least at first, from the air. So it pays to carry something that will enable you to signal to a search plane even if you are injured and can move very little or not at all. A mirror and a smoke flare are obvious candidates. But if you are able to build a fire and have water available, natural smoke may be the best bet. For use and usefulness of mirror, flares, and smoke, see pages 289–93. The same signals can, of course, be used for establishing contact with search parties on the ground. So can a whistle (page 253). For places a helicopter can and cannot land, see page 293.

PRESERVING THE WILDERNESS

Once you become a walker, you become a conservationist: no one can walk for days on end through wild and unspoiled country and then stumble on some man-perpetrated horror without having his blood start to boil.

Please do not misunderstand me. On balance, I am in favor of man. But there have been moments when my vote might have gone the other way—and such moments have mostly come when I have stumbled on the atrocities of the feeble-minded. I still remember vividly, from almost a decade ago, walking across a secluded forest glade and all at once finding myself standing stock still beside an old campsite that was a carnage of beer cans and cardboard boxes and torn plastic sheeting and dirty aluminum foil plates and crumpled, soggy newspapers. Recently, deep in a sidecanyon that led to the Inner Gorge of the Colorado River, I passed half a dozen pale pink boulders that the ages had worn into smooth and sensuous sculpture but which had recently been overprinted with crude black drawings and the timeless legend "Batman." Such droppings of bat-witted individuals are bad enough, but it angers me far more when a whole segment of society goes in for large-scale desecration. A dozen years ago, for two long and satisfying summers, I walked the virgin forests of western Vancouver Island, British Columbia, prospecting and staking claims for a mining company (and hoping, with some confidence, that the claims would never be developed). All through those two summers, with increasing and appalling frequency, I would emerge without warning from the coolness and cloistered calm of huge trees and green undergrowth into the glare and heat and desolation of gouged earth and splintered wood. (I have never recovered from those summers: logging is still the one provocation that I acknowledge might drive me to murder.) But most of all, now, I fear the deadly tentacles of the engineering mind. More and more, it seems, the engineers are gathering up the reins of power. And they are little men, most of them, with no concept at all of what their projects are doing to the face of the earth. They will, if it serves any half-baked economic purpose, slash a freeway through irreplaceable redwood groves. Driven by an undeniable and quite understandable professional challenge, and by an equally understandable desire to have plenty of work in the years ahead (and also driven, even less consciously, by the built-in self-aggrandizement mechanism that rots into the structure of almost all our human institutions) they will concoct plans for gigantic and quite unnecessary dams. If they have their way, every yard of the Colorado River that I followed on my recent trip in lower Grand Canyon will be drowned by a ninety-three-mile reservoir that will form behind "the tallest dam in the Western Hemisphere." That inundation would be only a preliminary in the slow destruction of the glory that is Grand Canyon. And after that would come Alaska and the huge and horrendous Rampart Dam.

But I said that these things would happen if the engineers had their way—and there are plenty of signs that they will not always have their way.* Of course, they have not always had their way in the past. You cannot help but feel hopeful of real progress when you cease to take for granted the vast and in some cases still unspoiled national parks and wilderness areas that man has had the wisdom to shield from progress. And it is comforting to reflect that even as the menace and arrogance grow, so does the wisdom. It looks as though sanity may still . . .

But wait a minute. I did not mean to write these last two paragraphs. After all, I had made my point: once you become a walker, you become a conservationist. The rest follows. And I had intended to move on without delay to a warning. But I think I shall let the intruding paragraphs stand. It's not just that I needed to get them off my chest. Much more importantly, they are a shining example

* Since I wrote the above, it has begun to look, thank God, as though we have really saved Grand Canyon—for the present.

of what I wanted to sound a warning about. They are self-righteous. And self-righteousness is an occupational hazard for conservationists.

Now it does not matter much that self-righteousness begets crashing bores—the sort of people you're always slipping away from at cocktail parties. What does matter is that as soon as we raise our self-righteous banners we lose our effectiveness. The Sierra Club, of which I am a member and a strong supporter, is probably today's most effective conservationist voice in the United States. It has, for example, fought more stoutly than anyone in the battle to save Grand Canyon. But, like cooperative societies and organized religious bodies, it tends to be a holier-than-thou organization. The maggot is built in. As a result, the words "Sierra Club" are liable to raise, in certain neutral circles, a chorus of groans. A recent meeting of suburban housewives became thoroughly aroused to the dangers of blind industrial "progress" by a conservationist slide show; but then a Sierra Club member, in an uninvited "speech from the floor," laid the line on too thickly. It was as if a fog had blanketed the hall. The audience, which had been asking keen and probing questions, began to subside. First the mood changed to apathy. Soon it became a resentful and almost tangible hostility. The same kind of reaction occurs, I think, when we who are rabid anti-litter fiends forget that we are human (see, pointedly, page 122) and start throwing our holy weights around. The result may well be a hostile group strewing their every last can and food wrapper about the landscape, deliberately and gleefully.

Now the last thing I want to do is condone such barbarism. The point is that incidents of this kind have happened—and are desperately understandable. The lesson to be learned from them is that we conservationists must strive to suppress our self-righteousness. It is difficult, I know. I too am pretty damned sure that we *are* holier than the litter louts and the engineers. But we must not let the conviction show. Not because it is bad for our souls or something, but because it reduces the chances that we will achieve what we desperately want and need to achieve.

LEARN OF THE GREEN WORLD

Learn of the green world what can be thy place.
Ezra Pound

When I began this book it was my intention to examine, here at the end, the delights of walking in different kinds of country. For I was afraid that in the course of 300 fundamentally how-to pages we might have forgotten the feel-how—that the ways and means might have masked the joys and insights that can come, in the end, from the simple act of walking. I am still afraid that such an eclipse may have occurred. But I see now that the delights of different places are not what I must write about. They too are only means to an end.

Now I am the last person to deny that each kind of country— and also each season of the year and each hour of day—has its own very special enchantments.

Mountains offer the slow unfolding of panoramas and the ex- hilaration of high places. Their summits, even the humble ones, are nearly always pinnacles of experience. And afterward you come back down. You ease back, step by step, from stark rock and snow into the world of seething life: first, a single tuft of vegetation in a wind- swept saddle; then the tracks of a small mammal; two hours later, the first tree; then the first tree that can stand upright against the wind; then the tracks of a large two-footed animal that was wearing cleated boots; then undeniable soil; soon, trees that would be trees in any company; finally, thick undergrowth beneath the trees—and you pat your pocket to make sure the snakebite kit is still there.

In the desert you rediscover, every time you go back, the cleanness that exists in spite of the dust, the complexity that underlies the apparent openness, and the intricate web of life that stretches over the apparent barrenness; but above all you rediscover the echoing silence that you had thought you would never forget.

Then there is untrodden snow country, silent with its own kind of silence. And the surging seashore. And other dominions too, each with its own signature: estuaries, the river worlds, marshland, farmlands, moors, and the open plain.

But in the course of time the memories meld. For they come, all of them, from the green world.

When I open my own mind and let the memories spill out, I find a many-hued mosaic. I remember the odd excitement and the restricted yet infinitely open world I have moved through several times when I have clambered up—very late at night, and following the little pool from my flashlight beam—to the flat, grassy summit of the hill on which I wrote at last the opening chapter of this book. I remember a three-day walk along an unspoiled beach with the wind always barreling in from the Pacific and the sand dunes always humping up on my left; and I remember the ceaseless surging and drawing back of the sea, with its final, curving excursions into smooth sand—excursions that sometimes left stranded, high and almost dry, little fragments of transparent protoplasm (which set me thinking, "This is the stuff we came from") and sometimes cast up a bottle that I could peer at (laughing at myself for being so childlike) in the hope that it might contain a message. I remember standing on snowshoes outside my half-buried tent after a four-day storm, in a newly gleaming white world, and watching the guilty, cloud-bearing southwest wind trying to reassert itself; I remember feeling a northeast breeze spring up, and almost hearing it take a deep breath and say "They shall not pass," and then begin to blow in earnest; and I remember watching, thankfully, as the line of dark clouds was held along a front, horizon to horizon, and then was driven back, slowly but inexorably, until at last it retreated behind the peaks and the sky was left to the triumphant northeast wind and the warm and welcome sun. I remember trying to clamber up a steep woodland bank after dark, somewhere in the deep South (I think it was in Alabama), and finding myself in an enchanted world of fireflies and twisted tree roots and fireflies and clumps of grass and fireflies and wildflowers and fireflies and fireflies and fireflies—a world suddenly filled with a magic that I had not glimpsed since I was ten, and had almost come to disbelieve in. I remember striding down a desert road as dusk fell, with the wind catching my pack and billowing out the poncho like a sail and carrying me almost effortlessly along before it; and I remember how, when the rain came, it stung my bare legs, refreshing without hurting. I remember, in a different, sagebrush desert, coming to the edge of a village and passing a wooden building with three cars and a truck parked outside, and a battered sign that said PENTECOSTAL CHURCH OF GOD, EVERYONE WELCOME; I remember that the church door stood open to the warm evening, and that I could hear a piano and the congregation following along, with only a hint of exasperation, a half-beat behind a contralto whom nature had endowed with the volume, tempo, rigidity, and determination of a brass band. In another desert village—a long-dead ghost town, this one—I remember a clump of wild blue irises growing inside the worn wooden threshhold of a once busy home. I remember red, red sunsets in a small desert valley when I was not alone. I remember, further back, a dead native cow in a clearing in the dry African bush; and, in the blood-softened soil beside its torn-out entrails, a single huge paw mark. I remember the small, round furry heads of the hyraxes that would solemnly examine us from the boulders just behind our 13,000-foot camp, up near Lewis Glacier on Mount Kenya. Further back still, I remember three otters cavorting across a moonlit Devonshire meadow; and a stag on a Scottish moor, silhouetted, elemental; and a shoal of small fish swimming slowly over a sloping bed of brown gravel that I can still see, stone fitting into stone, down the tunnel of thirty-five years. And now, vaulting back into yesterday, I find I am remembering an elk that stands regally among redwood trees and the last tendrils of morning mist, and a surprised beaver that crouches almost at my feet and eyes me for clues, and a solitary evening primrose that has prospered in a desolation of desert talus, and a rainbow that arches over a dark mountain tarn, and the huge and solemn silence that encompasses, always, the buttes and mesas and cliffs and hanging terraces of the Grand Canyon of the Colorado.

Everyone who walks has his own floodlit memories—his own fluttering windwheel of scenes and sounds and scents. (It is often the scents that linger longest, though you do not know it until they come again.) But no matter what the hue of the individual memories, they all come from the green world. And in the end, when you have learned to connect—only to connect—you understand that it is simply the green world that you seek.

I suppose you could say that going out into this older world is rather like going to church. I know that it is in my case, anyway. For me, praying is no good: my god is not interested in what happens to me personally. But by walking out alone into wilderness I can elude the pressures of the pounding modern world, and in the sanctity of silence and solitude—the solitude seems to be a very important part of it—I can after a while begin to see and to hear and to think and in the end to feel with a new and exciting accuracy. And that, it seems to me, is just the kind of vision you should be hoping to find when you go to church.

Now I do not want to suggest that out in the wilderness my mind—or, I suspect, anyone else's mind—is always soaring. Most of the time it operates on a mundanely down-to-earth level. A few months ago, during a four-day hike taken primarily so that I could sort out ideas and directions for the second half of this book, I tried to write down before they had faded away the thoughts that had run through my head while I was climbing one afternoon up a long and fairly steep hill. What I scribbled down was, in part: "Wonder how far now, over top and down to next creek. Maybe should have half-filled canteen from that last spring. . . . Oh hell, left heel again! Hope it's not a blister. Moleskin? No, not yet. Oh, look at that squirrel!

Sun caught it beautifully, coming in from behind at an angle. Hm, horse tracks. Wonder how old. . . . Phew! Pretty damned hot for January. Better take off shirt at next halt. Almost time for rest anyway. Only five minutes. That should just get me to top of hill. . . . Hey, what's that on my leg? Oh, just water dripping off wet socks, on pack. . . . Oh my God, look! It'll be at least ten or fifteen minutes to top of bloody hill. Maybe more. . . . Say, your thoughts really do run on, don't they? Normally, don't notice it much, but . . . wait a minute, better jot down what I've been thinking, as accurately and as far back as I can. Might just be worth using in the walking book. Yes, out notebook right now . . ."

Twice more on that four-day trip I jotted down odd islets of thought that jutted up from what was no doubt a continuous stream. Once, on a slightly less mundane but still distinctly unsoaring level, I found that as I walked I had concocted a mnemonic sentence ("King Philip, come out, for God's sake!") for a sequence that often leaves me groping: the hierarchy of categories into which biologists divide the living world (kingdom, phylum, class, order, family, genus, species). And one evening I was warming myself by a camp-fire and looking up at the tops of dark pine trees silhouetted against a quarter moon and beginning to think of beauty and life and death (or so my notes assure me) when I realized with some surprise that I was at the same time singing quietly to myself the soulful and almost immortal refrain from a song that was implanted in my mind somewhere deep in half-forgotten childhood: "And the captain sat in the captain's chair, and he played his ukulele as the ship went down."

But in trying to remove a false impression, I must not overcompensate. There are, of course, times when your mind soars or floats or hangs free and impartial—or dives into the depths.

For even in wilderness you may, very occasionally, plunge into despair—into the blackness that exists, I suppose, deep down in all our lives, waiting to blot out the underpinnings and so keep us honest. I remember a desert canyon in which, as I lay quiet beneath the stars, man was a pointless impostor on the bleak and ancient surface of the earth, and I knew I would never hope again. And I remember a night on a mountain when all that existed out in the blackness beyond my campfire was a small hemlock, and even the hemlock only flickered into and out of existence at the mercy of the fickle firelight; a night on which, for an endless, empty span, that little tree with its dark, stark needles was more lasting and more real than I was, and so claimed a crushing victory; a night on which, above all, the blackness beyond the tree was tragically and incontestably more real than the fragile tree, and therefore claimed the final, aching, desolate victory. Such interludes—in which the keepers of the void ensnare you and all, all is vanity—come very rarely in the wilderness. But they come. And, although I would like to deny it, they are worse than in the city. While they last, the blackness is blacker, more hopeless, more desolately victorious. This time, you cannot appeal to a more profound reality.

But, far more often than despair, you find elation. A squirrel leaps across a gap in the trees, a hundred feet above your head, and your mind, caught by the beauty, leaps too—across the gap between the dragging everyday world and the universals. Two swallows, bound head to tail in tight and perfect formation, bank up and away from a cliff face in a joyous arc of freedom. A quartet of beavers browses by the margin of a backwater, silent and serene, a tableau from a calmer age. Or you sit, triumphant, on a rocky peak and look and look at the whole world spread out below; and for a while, though still a man, you are no longer merely a man.

At such moments you do not "commune with nature" (a trite phrase that seems to classify nature as something outside and separate from us men). At such moments you know, deep down in your fabric, with a certainty far more secure than intellect can offer, that you are a part of the web of life, and that the web of life is a part of the rock and air and water of pre-life. You know the wholeness of the universe, the great unity. And if you keep walking long enough—for several weeks or for several months—you may with care and good fortune experience whole days or even series of days during which you exist in this happy, included state.

They do not last, of course, these rich cadenzas. But their echoes linger. When you first return to the world of man there is a period of readjustment, just as there was when you left it and went out into the wilderness. After that first glorious hot shower (which is always, quite unfailingly but always rather surprisingly, a great experience in itself) you live for a day, or perhaps three days, or even a week, an unreal, cut-off-by-a-screen-of-gauze sort of existence. But once you have readjusted to hot showers and radios and orthodox beds and automobiles and parking meters and sidewalks and elevators and other people and other people's points of view, you begin to find that you have regained thrust and direction and hope and wonder and other such vital intangibles whose presence or absence color so indelibly the tenor of our lives, but which are very difficult to discuss without sententiousness. You find yourself refreshed, that is, for the eternal struggle of trying to see things as you more or less know they are, not merely as other people tell you they are. Above all, you find that you have re-comprehended—totally, so that it is there behind every thought—the knowledge that we have arisen from everything that has gone before. You know, steadily, that we are more than just a fascinating and deadly and richly promising species that has begun to take over the face of the earth. You know again, fully, that this species you belong to is the current spearhead of life—and that your personal meaning is that you are a part of the spearhead. And so you find that you can take up once more the struggle we all have to make in our own several and quirky ways if we are to succeed in living lives that are truly human—the struggle to discern some glimmering of sense in the extraordinary phenomenon that is man.

And that, I guess, is quite a lot to get out of such a simple thing as walking.

Check List of Equipment

Everyone should in the end develop his own check list (see page 22), but this may be a useful starter.

Suggestion: photostat the following list of items, draw columns in each margin, and before a trip check off each item as you put it on one side, as you pack it at home, and again when you finally strike out and away from civilization.

This is an exhaustive list, including just about everything—except the strictly-personal-but-you'll-probably-have-your-own department (page 269)—that a backpacker will want to consider taking along on any kind of trip. What he actually takes will always, of course, be a great deal less. For samples of gear that the author carried under specific conditions, see *The Thousand-Mile Summer,* photographs between pages 32 and 33, and *The Man Who Walked Through Time,* Appendix, page 235.

Weights are for author's own equipment or, where no such item is owned, an average.

Foundations

Page		lbs.	oz.
28	Boots	5	12
34	Socks (3 pairs)	0	15
36	Moccasins	0	15½
37	Staff	1	0
40	Ice ax	2	6
40	Crampons	1	5
41	Snowshoes	6	0
44	Rubbing alchohol (in bottle)	0	2
44	Footpowder	0	3
46	Moleskins	0	1
46	Scissors	0	½

Walls

Page		lbs.	oz.
55	Pack	4	0

Kitchen

Page		lbs.	oz.
68	Food (see table, pages 68–9)	15	3
79	Booze bottle	0	3
94	Water purification tablets	0	½
96	Canteen(s) (empty)	0	14
100	Frying pan	0	15
100	Cooking pots	1	4

Kitchen (*cont.*)

Page		lbs.	oz.
100	Cup	0	3
101	Spoon	0	2
101	Sheath knife	0	6
102	Carborundum stone	0	1
102	Salt-pepper shaker	0	1
102	Sugar container	0	2
102	Detergent container (full)	0	5
102	Margarine container	0	1
103	Milk squirter	0	1
103	Bookmatches (7)	0	1
103	Matchsafe	0	1
104	Magnifying glass	0	2
104	Can opener	0	1/8
104	Flint stick	0	3/4
106	Stove (full)	1	7
110	White gas bottle(s) (full)	1	3
110	Funnel for stove	0	1/4
113	Stove windscreen	0	3

Bedroom

Page		lbs.	oz.
143	Tent	2	14
153	Fly sheet	1	10
155	Polyethylene sheet	1	5
156	Visklamps (5)	0	4
159	Tube tent	1	8
169	Groundsheet	0	12
171	Air mattress patch kit	0	4
173	Air mattress	1	14
174	Ensolite pad	1	2
186	Sleeping bag	3	1

Clothes Closet

Page		lbs.	oz.
199	String vest	0	7

Page		lbs.	oz.
200	String longs	0	7
200	Long johns	0	9
201	Undershorts (and ? spares)	0	2
201	Shirt (and ? spare)	0	9
201	Sweater	2	2
202	Short pants	1	9
203	Long pants	1	10
203	Belt	0	4
204	Gaiters	0	3½
204	Down jacket (light)	1	1
205	Down jacket (heavy)	2	0
205	Down pants	1	0
206	Down booties	0	4
206	Parka	1	4
208	Poncho	0	14
209	Cagoule	0	11
210	Cagoule footsack	0	6
210	Gloves	0	5
211	Inner gloves (and ? spares)	0	¼
211	Scarf	0	1
212	Balaclava	0	4
212	Swimsuit	0	2½
212	Bandanna	0	1¼
213	Hat	0	4
218	Bucket and bowl set	0	8

Furniture and Appliances

Page		lbs.	oz.
221	Flashlight, with batteries	0	3
223	Spare batteries	0	3
225	Spare bulb(s)	0	0
225	Sunglasses (and ? spares)	0	1
226	Goggles	0	2½
226	Anti-fog preparation	0	½

Retailers of Backpack Equipment and Foods Who Operate Mail-Order Services

This list is as complete and current as I can make it. But please remember (from page 16) to treat it as a guide, not a gospel.

The *star grading* is an attempt, inevitably fallible, to indicate the *range* of equipment that each firm offers. For example, ******** means "just about everything a backpacker could want, and a wide choice." The stars do not necessarily reflect quality of stock.

Additional symbols:

† Firms that specialize in a certain branch or branches of equipment
    —usually, though not always, of high quality.

‡ Firms that operate a general-merchandise mail-order service, of
    which backpacking equipment typically forms only a minor part.

UNITED STATES

Coast-to-Coast
‡ Abercrombie and Fitch: See New York.
‡ Montgomery Ward.
‡ Sears, Roebuck.

Arizona
† Camp Trails, 3920 West Clarendon Ave., Phoenix, 85019.
    (Packs and tents.)

California
† Antelope Camping Equipment, 10268 Imperial Ave., Cupertino,
    95014.
    (Packframes and bags.)

*** Gerry Mountain Sports, 228 Grant Ave., San Francisco, 94108.

*** Highland Outfitters, 3579 University Ave. (8th St.), P.O. Box 121, Riverside, 92502.

†* Himalayan Industries, 807 Cannery Row, P.O. Box 950, Monterey, 93940.

(Primarily, though not exclusively, packframes and bags.)

† Kelty Pack Inc., P.O. Box 3453, 1807 Victory Blvd., Glendale, 91201.

(High quality packframes and bags.)

** The North Face, 308 Columbus Ave., San Francisco, 94133.

(Branch stores: Palo Alto, Orinda, and Berkeley.)

(Specializes in mountaineering equipment.)

*† Sierra Designs (late of Point Richmond), 4th and Addison Sts., Berkeley, 94710. (Maker of high quality tents, clothing, sleeping bags, and, increasingly, other equipment.)

** Sierra Mountain Equipment, P.O. Box 15251, 2211 California St., Apt. 10, San Francisco, 94115.

(A small, "backroom," family operation.)

**** The Ski Hut, 1615 University Ave., Berkeley, 94703.

(Makers of Trailwise equipment.)

*** The Smilie Company, 575 Howard St., San Francisco, 94105.

(Catalogue costs 10 cents; tends to specialize in economically priced equipment; also mulepacking gear.)

*** Sport Chalet, 951 Foothill Blvd., P.O. Box 626, La Canada, 91011.

(Branch: Mammoth Lakes.)

** Swiss Ski Sports, 559 Clay St., San Franscisco, 94111.

**** Trailwise: See Ski Hut, above.

Colorado

†* Alp Sport, 3245 Prairie Ave., P.O. Box 1081, Boulder, 80302.

(Makers of high quality packs, clothes, tents, and sleeping bags.)

*** Colorado Outdoor Sports Corporation (Gerry Division), P.O. Box 5544, Denver, 80217.

(Makers of Gerry equipment.)

(Retail stores: Denver and Boulder. See also California.)

*** Gerry: See Colorado Outdoor Sports Corporation, above.

† Frostline Outdoor Equipment, P.O. Box 1378, Boulder, 80302.

(Do-it-yourself kits of lightweight equipment: tents, sleeping bags, down and other clothing.)

*** Holubar Mountaineering, P.O. Box 7, Boulder, 80302.
  (Retail stores: Boulder and Denver.)
  † Sportsmen Products, P.O. Box 1082, Boulder, 80302.
  ("Snowtreads" plastic snowshoes.)
  † Survival Research Laboratories, 17 Marland Road, Colorado Springs, 80906.
  (Survival equipment. Primarily for aircraft, but some for backpackers.)

Illinois
† Todd's, 5 South Wabash Ave., Chicago, 60603.
  (Boots and shoes.)

Maine
* L. L. Bean, Freeport, 04032.
  (Specialty: Maine Hunting Boots.)

Maryland
† Bishop's Ultimate Outdoor Equipment, 6804 Millwood Road, Bethesda, 20034.
  (Tents.)
* H & H Surplus Center and Camper's Haven, 1028 W. Baltimore St., Baltimore, 21223.
  (Catalogue costs 25 cents; emphasis on car-camping rather than backpacking gear.)

Massachusetts
* Corcoran Inc., Stoughton, 02072.
  (Emphasis on clothing and heavy hunting gear.)
† Fabiano Shoe Company, South Station, Boston, 02110.
  (Italian boots.)
* Don Gleason's Camper's Supply, 9 Pearl St., Northampton, 01060.
  (Catalogue costs 25 cents; emphasis on car-camping rather than backpacking gear.)
** Moor and Mountain, 14 Main St., Concord, 01742.
*** Eastern Mountain Sports, Inc. (formerly Mountaineering Supply), 1041 Commonwealth Ave., Boston, 02215.
  (Additional retail outlets: Wellesley and Springfield, Mass., and New Paltz, N.Y.)

Minnesota
‡ Gokey Company, 21 W. Fifth St., Saint Paul, 55102.
‡ Herter's Inc., Rural Route 1, Waseca, 56093.
  (570-page catalogue costs 50 cents.)

Missouri
‡ Gateway Sporting Goods Company, 3177 Mercier, Kansas City, 64111.
  (A very few items of interest to backpackers.)

New Hampshire
Peter Limmer and Sons, Intervale, 03845.
(Ski boots, mountaineering equipment.)

New Jersey
‡** Morsan, 810 Route 17, Paramus, 07652.
  (Also in Farmingdale, L.I., N.Y.)

New York
‡ Abercrombie and Fitch, Madison Ave. at 45th, New York, 10017.
  (Branches in Chicago, San Francisco, Colorado Springs, Short Hills [New Jersey], and Florida.)
  (Catalogue situation presently unsatisfactory. Backpacking stock varies store to store.)
** Thomas Black and Sons, 930 Ford St., Ogdensburg, 13669.
  (See also Ontario, Canada.)
** Camp and Trail Outfitters, 112 Chambers St., New York, 10007.
* Gloy's, 11 Addison St., Larchmont, 10538.
  (Mostly boating and heavy camp equipment, but some for backpackers.)
‡** Morsan: See New Jersey.
* Walter E. Stern, 254 Nagle Ave., New York, 10034.
† Woods Bag and Canvas Company, 16 Lake St., Ogdensburg, 13669.
  (Sleeping bags and down clothing.)

Oklahoma
‡ P & S Sales, P.O. Box 155, Tulsa, 74102.

Oregon

† Alaska Sleeping Bag Company, 334 N.W. 11th Ave., Portland, 97209.
(Clothing, sleeping bags.)

*** Alpine Hut: See Washington.

† Norm Thomson, 1805 N.W. Thurman, Portland, 97209.
(Clothing, including a few items for backpackers.)

Pennsylvania

‡ I. Goldberg, 429 Market St., Philadelphia, 19106.

Vermont

† Tubbs Products, Wallingford, 05113.
(Snowshoes.)

Washington

*** Alpine Hut, 4725-30th Ave. N.E., Seattle, 98105.
(Retail stores: Seattle, Tacoma, and Renton; Portland, Oregon.)

†* Eddie Bauer, 417 East Pine, Seattle, 98122.
(Best known for high quality down bags and clothing.)

**** Recreational Equipment Inc., 1525-11th Ave., Seattle, 98122.
(Additional retail store: 523 Pike St., Seattle; a cooperative.)

† Rainier Equipment: Seattle Tent and Fabric Products Company,
900 N. 137th St., Seattle, 98133.
Yakima Tent and Awning Company,
1316 S. First St., Yakima, 98901.

Wisconsin

‡ Laacke and Joys, 1433 N. Water St., Milwaukee, 53202.

CANADA

Coast-to-Coast

‡ The T. Eaton Company, Ltd. (head office: 190 Yonge St., Toronto 1, Ontario).

‡ Simpsons-Sears Ltd. (head office: 108 Mutual St., Toronto 2, Ontario).

Alberta

* Premier Cycle and Sports, 319 Seventh Ave., S.W., Calgary.
(Emphasis is on mountaineering.)
‡ Woodwards: See British Columbia.

British Columbia

** Arlberg Sport Haus, 816 W. Pender St., Vancouver 1.
(Good selection of food; retailers of Thomas Black's equipment
—see Ontario.)
‡ Woodwards (head office: Hastings and Abbot Sts., Vancouver 3).
(Branches in Alberta and British Columbia.)

Ontario

** Thomas Black and Sons, 225 Strathcona Ave., Ottawa.
(See also United States: New York.)

LIGHTWEIGHT FOODS

The following firms specialize in lightweight food for backpackers.
But many of the listed outdoor equipment retailers (and especially those
marked **** or ***) offer a wide range of such foods—including those
made by firms on this list.

California

Bernard Food Industries, Box 487, St. James Park Station, 222 S.
24th St., San Jose, 95103.
(Makers of Kamp Pack foods.)
Dri Lite Foods, 11333 Atlantic, Lynwood, 90262.
Richmoor Corporation, 616 N. Robertson Blvd., Los Angeles, 90069.

Massachusetts

Chuck Wagon Foods, 176 Oak St., Newton, 02164.
(Offer discounts for Scouts.)
Stow-A-Way Products, 103 Ripley Road, Cohasset, 02025.
(Very complete food selection; some equipment.)

Organizations That Promote Walking

Although the groups I've listed vary in size from a handful to the 63,000 of the Sierra Club, all of them, as far as I can confirm, include communal hikes among their activities—even when their names suggest otherwise. And you may, in spite of pages 6 and 310, sensibly prefer to walk in company. In any case, communal hikes are a safe way of getting to know the ropes—for an afternoon nature stroll or a month's wilderness backpacking.

No amount of research is going to drag up the name of every walking group in the country; and secretaries, not to mention entire organizations, come and go. So any list like this is sure to be incomplete; and it begins to die before it is born. But it should at worst offer leads for earnest seekers.

UNITED STATES

Coast-to-Coast

The National Audubon Society.

> Headquarters: 1130 Fifth Ave., New York, N.Y. 10028.
>
> Western regional office: Now building in Sacramento, Calif.
>
> Nationwide: 375 branches and affiliates.
>
> The society's walks are always nature walks; but do not forget that they are walks.

The Sierra Club.

> Headquarters: 1050 Mills Tower, 270 Bush St., San Francisco, Calif. 94104. Offices in New York and Washington, D.C.
>
> Chapters in the following (see listings under each): Arizona, California (11 chapters), Colorado, Illinois, Michigan, Nevada, New Mexico, New York, Oregon, Texas, Washington, D.C., and Wisconsin.

Regional

The Appalachian Trail Conference, 1718 N St. N.W., Washington, D.C. 20036.

This conference of trail clubs, which manages the 2000-mile, Maine-to-Georgia Appalachian Trail, is the surest source of up-to-date information on eastern seaboard walking activities. Listed clubs affiliated to the conference are marked ■.

Two allied organizations embrace more than a single state:

The New England Trail Conference (Secretary: Miss Edith N. Libby, 26 Bedford Terrace, Northampton, Mass.). Member clubs are marked ●.

The New York and New Jersey Trail Conference: See New York.

The Federation of Western Outdoor Clubs. Secretary: Mrs. Betty Hughes, Route 3, P.O. Box 172, Carmel, Calif. 93921.

The secretary will supply up-to-date information on walking organizations in all areas west of the Mississippi. Membership is open to individuals as well as clubs. Affiliated clubs are marked ♦.

Alaska

♦ South Eastern Alaska Mountaineering Association, P.O. Box 1314, Ketchikan, 99901.

Arizona

♦ Sierra Club: Grand Canyon chapter. Chairman: Dr. John H. Ricker, 555 W. Catalina, Phoenix, 85013.
Southern Arizona Hiking Club, P.O. Box 12122, Tucson, 85711.

California

♦ Berkeley Hiking Club, P.O. Box 147, Berkeley, 94701.
♦ California Alpine Club, 244 Pacific Bldg., San Francisco, 94103.
♦ Contra Costa Hills Club, 306-40th St., Room 3, Oakland, 94609.
♦ Federation of Western Outdoor Clubs: see Regional, above.
♦ Desomount Club, 30711 S. Ganado Drive, Palos Verdes Peninsula, 90274.
♦ Roamer Hiking Club, 3533 W. 74th Place, Inglewood, 90305.
♦ San Antonio Club, 750 S. Chapel Ave., Alhambra, 91801.

♦ Sierra Club.
  Headquarters: 1050 Mills Tower, 270 Bush St., San Francisco, 94104.
    Chapters (with chairmen):
    Angeles. Bob Van Allen, 4641 Newman Ave., Cypress, 90630.
    Kern-Kaweah. James W. Clark, 631 N. G St., Porterville, 93257.
    Loma Prieta. Walt Hays, 1711 Harte Drive, San Jose, 95124.
    Los Padres. Anne Van Tyne, 1319 Panchita Place, Santa Barbara, 93103.
    Mother Lode. Mrs. LaVerne Ireland, 734 Placer Drive, Woodland, 95695.
    Redwood. Maurice Wood, 1029 Johnston St., Napa, 94558.
    Riverside. George Shipway, 1327 Toledo Way, Upland, 91786.
    San Diego. William Phillips, 9463 Mesa Vista Drive, La Mesa, 92011.
    San Francisco Bay. Maynard Munger Jr., 7 Fleetwood Court, Orinda, 94563.
    Tehipite. Dr. Ed H. Daubs, 2711 E. Simpson, Fresno, 93703.
    Ventana. Rudd A. Crawford, 2884 Galleon Road, Pebble Beach, 93953.
♦ Tamalpais Conservation Club, 735 Pacific Bldg., San Francisco, 94103.

Colorado
♦ Colorado Mountain Club, 1400 Josephine St., Denver, 80206.
♦ Sierra Club: Rocky Mountain chapter. Chairman: James E. Byrant, 839 Mapleton, Boulder, 80302.
  The Wilderness Society, Western Office: 2422 S. Downing St., Denver, 80209.

Connecticut
■ ● Connecticut chapter, Appalachian Mountain Club. Secretary: Mrs. Charles H. Alexander, Bethmour Road, Bethany, New Haven, 06525.
■ ● Connecticut Forest and Parks Association. Secretary: John E. Hibbard, 15 Lewis St., Hartford, 06103.

Delaware
■ Brandywine Valley Outing Club, P.O. Box 7033, Wilmington, 19803. (Attention: M. J. Brinton.)
■ Wilmington Trail Club, P.O. Box 1184, Wilmington, 19899.

District of Columbia

- ■ The Appalachian Trail Conference, 1718 N St. N.W., Washington, 20036.
- ■ Potomac Appalachian Trail Club, 1718 N St. N.W., Washington, 20036.
- ◆ Sierra Club. Washington Office: 235 Massachusetts Ave. N.E., Washington, 20002; Southeastern chapter: Chairman, George Alderson, 323 Maryland Ave. N.E., Washington, 20002.
- ■ Wanderbird Hiking Club. Secretary: Rose Marie Walker, 6604 Wells Parkway, University Park, Maryland, 20782.
  The Wilderness Society, 729-15th St. N.W., Washington, 20005. (For western office, see Colorado.)

Georgia

- ■ Georgia Appalachian Trail Club. President: Dr. Edwin J. Seiferle, 4850 Northland Drive N.E., Atlanta, 30305.

Hawaii

- ◆ Hawaiian Trail and Mountain Club, P.O. Box 2238, Honolulu, 96804.

Idaho

- ◆ Idaho Alpine Club, P.O. Box 2885, Idaho Falls, 83401.

Illinois

- ■ The Prairie Club, Room 1010, 38 S. Dearborn St., Chicago, 60603.
- ◆ Sierra Club: Great Lakes chapter. Chairman: Mrs. Jean Leever, 10240 Huntington Court, Orlando Park, 60462.

Indiana

Alpine Club of Canada, Midwest USA section: See Canada.

Iowa

- ■ Iowa Mountaineers, P.O. Box 163, Iowa City.

Kentucky

■ Louisville Hiking Club. Secretary: Carlyle Chamberlain, 2112 East-view Ave., Louisville.

Maine

■● Maine Appalachian Trail Club. Secretary: James L. Faulkner, Kents Hill, 04349.

Maryland

■ Maryland Appalachian Trail Club. President: Dick Mowen, 945 West Washington St., Hagerstown.

■Mountain Club of Maryland, Inc. President: Dr. J. L. Colburn, 280 Roundhill Road, Ellicot City, 21043.

Massachusetts

■● Appalachian Mountain Club. Secretary: Robert H. Boehme, 5 Joy St., Boston, 02108.

■● Appalachian Mountain Club: Berkshire chapter. Secretary: Mrs. Ralph B. Rice, 221 Chalmers St., Springfield, 01118.

Michigan

♦ Sierra Club: Mackinac chapter. Chairman: Virginia L. Prentice, 507 Walnut, Ann Arbor, 48104.

Missouri

● Missouri Walk-Ways Association, 613 Locust St., St. Louis.

Montana

♦ Montana Wilderness Association, P.O. Box 548, Bozeman, 59715.

♦ Rocky Mountaineers, 2100 South Ave. W., Missoula, 59801.

Nebraska

Omaha Walking Club, 5238 S. 22nd St., Omaha, 68107.

Nevada

♦ Sierra Club: Toiyabe chapter. Chairman: Thomas E. Hoffer, 4095 Warren Way, Reno, 89502.

New Hampshire
■ ● Appalachian Mountain Club: See Massachusetts.
■ ● Wonalancet Outdoor Club, c/o Mrs. Elizabeth McKey, Wonalancet.

New Jersey
See New York: New York and New Jersey Trail Conference.

New Mexico
♦ Sierra Club: Rio Grande chapter. Chairman: Brant Calkin, Route 1,
P.O. Box 267, Santa Fé, 87501.

New York
Alpine Club of Canada, Eastern USA section. See Canada.
American Youth Hostels, 14 W. 8th St., New York, 10011.
♦ Sierra Club. New York office: 15 E. 53rd St., New York, 10022;
Atlantic chapter: Chairman, David Sive, Winer, Neuberger and
Sive, 445 Park Ave., New York, 10022.
■ The Finger Lakes Trail Conference. Secretary: Mrs. L. K. Wade,
2783 Brighton-Henrietta Town Road, Rochester.
(This group was formed in 1961 to put a foot trail across southern
New York State.) Constituent clubs (with chairmen):
■ Buffalo Hiking Club, Conservation Forum, Buffalo Museum of
Science, Buffalo.
■ Cayuga Trails Club. G. Frederick Mohn, 133 Fayette St., Ithaca.
■ Foothills Trail Club. Arthur Rosche, R.D. 1, Fish Hill Road,
South Wales.
■ Genesee Valley Hiking Club, Rochester Museum of Arts and
Sciences, Rochester.
■ Triple Cities Hiking Club. Miss Paula Strain, 95 Lisle Road,
Owego.
■ The New York and New Jersey Trail Conference, P.O. Box 2250,
New York, 10001. (This organization embraces the following clubs
and chairmen. Should their addresses become obsolete, they may be
contacted at the above permanent address.)
■ Adirondack Mountain Club, Gabriels, N.Y.
■ National Campers and Hikers Association, 7172 Transit Road,
Buffalo, N.Y.

■ New York Hiking Club. Harold Diamond, 7825 Fourth Ave., Brooklyn, N.Y.

■ New York Ramblers. Morris Oberband, 97–37 63rd Road, Rego Park, N.Y. 11374.

■ Taconic Hiking Club. Miss Anita M. Rioux, 30 Continental Ave., Cohoes, N.Y.

■ Torrey Botanical Club. Dr. John A. Small, Douglass College, New Brunswick, N.J.

■ Tramp and Trail Club. Miss Ellen H. Knox, 63 E. 9th St., New York, N.Y. 10003.

■ Union County Hiking Club. George Holding, 508 Lincoln Ave., Cranford, N.J.

■ Wanderbirds. William Hoeferlin, 556 Fairview Ave., Brooklyn, N.Y.

■ Westchester Trails Association. Miss Frances Brewer, 135 St. Pauls Place, New Rochelle, N.Y.

■ Woodland Trail Walkers. Miss Catherine Servas, 142 Lake Ave., Clifton, N.J.

North Carolina
■ Carolina Mountain Club, P.O. Box 68, Asheville.

■ Piedmont Appalachian Trail Club. Secretary: Miss Patricia Glidewell, 3513 D Parkwood Drive, Greensboro, 27403.

Ohio
■ American Walkers Association, 6221 Robinson Road, Cincinnati.

■ Central Ohio Hiking Club, YMCA, 40 Long St., Columbus.

■ Cleveland Hiking Club. Patric Simone, 3400 Archwood Ave., Cleveland.

Oregon
Alpine Club of Canada, Western USA section: See Canada.

♦ Angoras, P.O. Box 12, Astoria, 97103.

♦ Chemeketans, 360½ State St., Salem.

♦ Mazamas, 909 N.W. 19th, Portland.

♦ Obsidians Inc., P.O. Box 322, Eugene.

♦ Sierra Club: Pacific Northwest chapter. Chairman: Carleton Whitehead, 3035 S.E. Martins St., Portland, 97202.

♦ Trails Club of Oregon, P.O. Box 1243, Portland, 97207.

Pennsylvania

Keystone Trails Association, P.O. Box 144, Concordville. Constituent clubs interested in promoting the use of Pennsylvania foot trails:

■ Allentown Hiking Club. President: Eugene Schneck, 722½ N. 12th St., Allentown, 18102.
■ Blue Mountain Eagle Climbing Club. President: Richard C. Kimmel, 1020 Martin St., Lebanon, 17042.
■ Hiking Club of Lancaster. President: Jack Chambers, 601 South West End Ave., Lancaster, 17603.
■ Horse-Shoe Trail Club. William Nelson West, 1600 Three Penn Center Plaza, Philadelphia.
■ Nature Hiking Club of Philadelphia (Batona). Secretary: Miss Norma Geder, 144 Duffield St., Willow Grove, 19090.
■ Philadelphia Trail Club. Secretary: Mrs. Alberta M. Sargent, 205 S. Marion Ave., Wenonah, N.J. 08090.
■ Susquehanna Appalachian Trail Club. President: George Sleesman, 1412 Market St., Harrisburg, 17103.
■ Williamsport Alpine Club. Secretary: Samuel Harris, 1506 Almond St., Williamsport.
■ York Hiking Club. President: Frank Senft, 1957 Woodstream Drive, York.

Tennessee

■ Cumberlands Hiking Club. Mrs. H. T. Larkin, 302 Old Mountain Road, Chattanooga.
■ Smoky Mountains Hiking Club. President: Mr. O. K. Sergeant, 201 South Purdue, Oak Ridge, 37830.
■ Tennessee Eastman Hiking Club, Secretary. c/o Tennessee Eastman Recreation Club, Building 54D, Tennessee Eastman Company, Kingsport, 37662.
■ Tri-State Hiking Club. T. William Stutz, 1701 McCallie Ave., Chattanooga.

Texas

♦ Sierra Club: Lone Star chapter. Chairman: Orrin Bonney, 1204 Sterling Bldg., Houston, 77002.

Utah

♦ Wasatch Mountain Club, 425 S. 8th W., Salt Lake City, 84106.

Vermont

■● The Green Mountain Club Inc. Miss Minerva Hinchey, 108 Merchants Row, Rutland, 05701.

Virginia

■ Mount Rogers Appalachian Trail Club. President: Mr. Lee Garrett, R.F.D. # 1, Abingdon, 24210.

■ Natural Bridge Appalachian Trail Club. President: Mary Guenther, 1608 Belfield Place, Lynchburg.

■ Roanoke Appalachian Trail Club. President: Raymond E. Levesque, 2527 Churchill Drive N.W., Roanoke, 24012.

■ Shenandoah-Rockfish Appalachian Trail Club, Box 344, Scottsville, 24590.

Washington

♦ Alpine Roamers, Wenatchee, 98801.

♦ Hobnailers, P. O. Box 1074, Spokane, 97210.

♦ Klahhane Club, P.O. Box 494, Port Angeles.

♦ Mt. Baker Club, P.O. Box 73, Bellingham.

♦ Mt. St. Helens Club, P.O. Box 843, Longview, 98632.

♦ The Mountaineers, P.O. Box 122, Seattle, 98111.

♦ Olympians Inc., P.O. Box 401, Hoquiam.

♦ The Ptarmigans, P.O. Box 1821, Vancouver, 98663.

The Signpost: A Newsletter for Hikers and Backpackers. Editor: Louise B. Marshall, 16812 36th Ave. W., Lynwood, 98036. (Especially but not exclusively for "individuals, unassociated with any club, who walk for fun." Trips, equipment, techniques, conservation, personal ads. Annual subscription: $3.)

♦ Skagit Alpine Club, P.O. Box 513, Mt. Vernon, 98273.

♦ Spokane Mountaineers Inc., P.O. Box 1013, Spokane, 99210.

♦ Wanderers, 515 Floravista, Olympia, 98501.

♦ Washington Alpine Club, P.O. Box 352, Seattle, 98111.

Wisconsin

♦ Sierra Club: John Muir chapter. Chairman: Philip J. Wipperman, 6414 Lakeview Blvd., Middleton, 53562.

■ Wisconsin Go-Hiking Club. Membership Secretary: Gertrude Kantzer, 3863 N. 37th St., Milwaukee, 53216.
Wisconsin Hoofers. Dick Gerber, The Wisconsin Union, 770 Langdon St., Madison.

CANADA

Coast-to-Coast
The Alpine Club of Canada. Club Manager: W. C. Ledingham, 2974 West 28th Ave., Vancouver 8, B.C.
(The club is the Canadian equivalent of the Sierra Club rather than the American Alpine Club.)
Local sections: Calgary, Edmonton, Kootenay, Montreal, Ottawa, Toronto, Vancouver, Winnipeg, Eastern USA (New York), Midwest USA (Indiana), Western USA (Oregon).
Section secretaries change yearly. Enquiries addressed to the club manager will be passed along.

Canadian Youth Hostels Association. National Office: 1406 West Broadway, Vancouver 9, B.C.
Regional offices in Calgary, Edmonton, Halifax, Montreal, Toronto, Vancouver. See provincial listings.

Alberta
Alpine Club of Canada: Sections in Calgary and Edmonton. See above.
Canadian Youth Hostels Association: Mountain Region, 455-12th St. N.W., Calgary; North West Region, 10922-88th Ave., Edmonton.
Skyline Trail Hikers of the Canadian Rockies, 622 Madison Ave. S.W., Calgary.

British Columbia
Alpine Club of Canada: Sections in Kootenay district and in Vancouver and Victoria. See above.
B.C. Mountaineering Club, P.O. Box 2674, Vancouver.
Canadian Youth Hostels Association: Pacific Region, 1406 W. Broadway, Vancouver 9.
Island Mountain Ramblers. Secretary: Ron Facer, 440 Chestnut St., Nanaimo.

District Representatives:
   Courtenay: Don Apps, P.O. Box 19, Lazo.
   Duncan: Syd Watts, Bell-McKinnon Road, R.R. #4.
   Kelsey Bay: Pat Guilbride.
   Ladysmith: Jack Ware, Hambrook Road, P.O. Box 403.
   Port Alberni: Winnie Helem, 815 North Forth Ave.
   Victoria: John Cowlin, 3951 Margot Place.
North Shore Hikers, c/o 1192 W. 26th Ave., Vancouver 9.
Simon Fraser University Outdoor Club, Burnaby.
Varsity Outdoor Club, University of British Columbia, Vancouver 8.

Manitoba
Alpine Club of Canada: Section in Winnipeg. See above.

Nova Scotia
Canadian Youth Hostels Association: Maritime Region, P.O. Box 2332,
Halifax.

Ontario
Alpine Club of Canada: Sections in Ottawa and Toronto. See above.
The Bruce Trail Association. Secretary: Mr. Ray Lowes, 33 Hardale Cres,
Hamilton.
(The 450-mile Bruce Trail runs from Niagara to Tobermory.)
Canadian Youth Hostels Association: Great Lakes Region, 86 Scollard
St., Toronto 5.
National Campers and Hikers Association. Provincial Director: Bill
Robb, 8 Thorpe Road, Weston.
Niagara Escarpment Trail Council, P.O. Box 1, St. Catharines.
Toronto Hiking and Conservation Club, P.O. Box 121, Postal Station F,
Toronto 5.
Walker Mineralogical Club of Toronto. Bill Ince, 12 Redwing Place,
Don Mills. (Do a lot of hiking, mostly in search of minerals.)

Quebec
Alpine Club of Canada: Section in Montreal. See above.
Canadian Youth Hostels Association: St. Lawrence Region, 754 Sher-
brooke St. W., Montreal 2.

Pleasant Quotes for Contemplative Walkers

I nauseate walking.

WILLIAM CONGREVE

Today I have grown taller from walking with the trees.

KARLE WILSON
(Mrs. Thomas Ellis Baker)

The longing to be primitive is a disease of culture.

GEORGE SANTAYANA

I like to walk about amidst the beautiful things that adorn the world.

GEORGE SANTAYANA

Our mental make-up is suited to a life of very severe physical labor. I used, when I was younger, to take my holidays walking. I would cover 25 miles a day, and when the evening came I had no need of anything to keep me from boredom, since the delight of sitting amply sufficed. . . .

When crowds assemble in Trafalgar Square to cheer to the echo an announcement that the government has decided to have them killed, they would not do so if they had all walked 25 miles that day.

BERTRAND RUSSELL
Nobel Prize Acceptance Speech

I drew my bride, beneath the moon,
Across my threshold; happy hour!
But, ah, the walk that afternoon
We saw the water-flags in flower!

COVENTRY PATMORE

The civilized man has built a coach, but he has lost the use of his feet.

EMERSON

Hmph, your feet must be stronger than your head!

STRANGER
To Colin Fletcher, during thousand-mile walk

For my part, I travel not to go anywhere, but to go.

STEVENSON
Travels with a Donkey . . .

There is more to life than increasing its speed.

GANDHI

The swiftest traveler is he that goes afoot.

THOREAU

He that riseth late must trot all day.

BEN FRANKLIN

Walk while ye have the light,
lest darkness come upon you.

ST. JOHN, XII, 35

He travels the fastest who travels alone.

KIPLING

Can two walk together, except they be agreed?

AMOS III, 3.

I was never less alone than when by myself.

EDWARD GIBBON

In solitude
What happiness? Who can enjoy alone,
Or all enjoying, what contentment find?

MILTON
Paradise Lost

That inward eye which is the bliss of solitude.

WORDSWORTH

Solitude is as needful to the imagination as society is wholesome for
the character.

JAMES RUSSELL LOWELL

O Solitude! where are the charms
That sages have seen in thy face?

COWPER
Verses supposed to be written
by Alexander Selkirk

He went back through the Wet Wild Woods, waving his wild tail, and walking by his wild lone. But he never told anybody.

> KIPLING
> *The Cat That Walked by Himself*

O why do you walk through the fields in gloves,
Missing so much and so much?

> FRANCES CORNFORD
> *To a Fat Lady Seen from the Train*

Oh, he's a genuine backpacker all right. He's got a filed-down toothbrush.

> Overheard by Colin Fletcher

Who walks with beauty has no need of fear;
The sun and moon and stars keep pace with him;
Invisible hands restore the ruined year,
And time, itself, grows beautifully dim.

> DAVID MORTON

Mountains are earth's undying monuments.

> HAWTHORNE

"I'm sure nobody walks much faster than I do."
"He can't do that," said the King, "or else he'd have
been here first."

> LEWIS CARROLL
> *Through the Looking-Glass*

The Promised Land always lies on the other side of a wilderness.

> HAVELOCK ELLIS

The walking stick serves the purpose of an advertisement that the bearer's hands are employed otherwise than in useful effort, and it therefore has utility as an evidence of leisure.

THORSTEIN VEBLEN
The Theory of the Leisure Class

We Americans are sitting pretty—too pretty. The heart's a muscle and needs exercise. Try a walk this evening . . . every evening.

California Heart Association radio
plug

. . . the brisk exercise imparts elasticity to the muscles, fresh and healthy blood circulates through the brain, the mind works well, the eye is clear, the step is firm, and the day's exertion always makes the evening's repose thoroughly enjoyable.

DR. DAVID LIVINGSTONE

All men who explore
Deplore
That frustrating hurdle,
The girdle.

COLIN FLETCHER
(Unpublished)

I find that the three truly great times for thinking thoughts are when I am standing in the shower, sitting on the john, or walking. And the greatest of these, by far, is walking.

COLIN FLETCHER
(Unpublished)

When I am not walking, I am reading; I cannot sit and think, [but] books think for me.

CHARLES LAMB

To a person uninstructed in natural history, his country or sea-side stroll is a walk through a gallery filled with wonderful works of art, nine-tenths of which have their faces turned to the wall.

THOMAS HUXLEY

Solvency is entirely a matter of temperament and not of income.

LOGAN PEARSALL SMITH

He likes the country, but in truth must own,
Most likes it when he studies it in town.

WILLIAM COWPER

The book of nature is that which the physician must read; and to do so he must walk over the leaves.

PARACELSUS

Man is an animal, and his happiness depends on his physiology more than he likes to think. . . . Unhappy businessmen, I am convinced, would increase their happiness more by walking six miles every day than by any conceivable change of philosophy.

BERTRAND RUSSELL

Man . . . walks up the stairs of his concepts, [and] emerges ahead of his accomplishments.

JOHN STEINBECK

There is no cure for birth and death save to enjoy the interval.

GEORGE SANTAYANA

And the Lord said unto Satan, Whence comest thou? Then Satan answered the Lord, and said, From going to and fro in the earth, and from walking up and down in it.

JOB I, 7

I went to the woods because I wished to live deliberately, to front only the essential facts of life, and see if I could not learn what it had to teach, and not, when I came to die, discover that I had not lived.

THOREAU

Early and provident fear is the mother of safety.

EDMUND BURKE

Two roads diverged in a wood, and I—
I took the one less traveled by,
And that has made all the difference.

ROBERT FROST

If one advances confidently in the direction of his dreams, and endeavors to live the life which he has imagined, he will meet with a success unexpected in common hours.

THOREAU

We will go no more to the woods, the laurel-trees are cut.

THÉODORE DE BANVILLE

And as I turn me home,
My shadow walks before.

ROBERT BRIDGES

Index

A NOTE ABOUT THE AUTHOR

Colin Fletcher is widely known to hikers and readers alike. His articles on walking in *Field & Stream, Reader's Digest,* and *Sports Afield* have established him as the country's leading authority on walking. His two previous books, *The Thousand-Mile Summer* (1964)—about his summer-long walk through the desert and Sierra country of California—and *The Man Who Walked Through Time* (1968)—an account of his solitary journey through the depths of the Grand Canyon—have delighted thousands of readers. Mr. Fletcher was born in Wales and educated in England. He served with the Royal Marine Commandos in World War II. After the war he farmed and built roads in Kenya and Southern Rhodesia, and later prospected and laid out roads in Canada. Mr. Fletcher now lives in California.

A NOTE ON THE TYPE

The text of this book was set on the Linotype in Garamond (No. 3), a modern rendering of the type first cut in the sixteenth century by Claude Garamond (1510–1561). He was a pupil of Geoffroy Troy and is believed to have based his letters on the Venetian models, although he introduced a number of important differences, and it is to him we owe the letter which we know as Old Style. He gave to his letters a certain elegance and a feeling of movement which won for their creator an immediate reputation and the patronage of the French King Francis I.

Composed, printed, and bound by
The Book Press, Brattleboro, Vermont

Typography and binding design
by Winston Potter